UNAFRAID OF THE DARK

UNAFRAID OF THE DARK

A Memoir

Rosemary L. Bray

RANDOM HOUSE  NEW YORK

 Published in the United States by Random House, Inc., New York, and simultaniously in Canada by Random House of Canada Limited, Toronto.

Library of Congress Cataloging-in-Publication Data
Bray, Rosemary L.
Unafraid of the dark: a memoir / Rosemary L. Bray.
p. cm.
ISBN 0-679-42555-1 (acid-free paper)
1. Bray, Rosemary L.—Childhood and youth. 2. Afro-American women—Illinois—Chicago—Biography. 3. Afro-Americans—Illinois—Chicago—Biography. 4. Chicago (Ill.)—Biography. I. Title.
F548.9.N4B73 1998
977.3′11043′092—dc21
[b] 97-17499

Random House website address: www.randomhouse.com

Printed in the United States of America on acid-free paper

2 4 6 8 9 7 5 3

First Edition

Book design by Victoria Wong

To Mama, with all my love;
now I understand.

Preface

In 1960, and in the years that followed, America found itself on a particular path, committed to changing the lives of the poor. The country found itself challenged by its African-American population to live up to its promises of liberty and equality, and joined by whites who found that challenge worthy of their attention. America also found itself confronted with the growing awareness among its women that the freedom they seemed to enjoy was illusory.

None of these things was on my mother's mind as she signed the necessary papers that guided us into the hands of the Cook County Department of Public Aid. Her concerns were more mundane: food and clothes and a place to sleep for herself and for her family. But all those disparate circumstances would find their meeting place in me.

I was shaped by the welfare system and by the Roman Catholic Church, as well as by the fiery debate on civil rights and black self-determination that raged in the news and in my living room. I was molded by the feminism I learned about not just in books, but through the lessons I absorbed each time my father beat and terrorized my mother, each time he turned on me for my futile efforts to protect her. I was educated in the heart of the African-American community as well as the halls of white, Ivy League privilege. I was grounded in a sense of clarity about my history—and my destiny—as an African-American woman, and about the responsibilities that fell to me because of my origins. In the very best sense, I am a child of the 1960s—not a direct participant in the maelstrom of events, but a human being whose life and culture, politics and identity were formed in this crucible of American change.

Welfare—growing up on it, being in the system, leaving it to live my adult life—was for me part of that crucible of change. My mistake, and the mistake many of us made, was in believing that we might best repay the system that saved our lives by just getting on with life. We thought it would be enough to get an education and a job, to marry and start a family, to pay our taxes and vote, be ordinary and unexceptional citizens. It now appears that we were wrong. In attempting to downplay the circumstances of our early lives, we left others—mothers and children such as we once were—at the mercy of ignorant and vicious ideologues who have never regarded the poor with anything but contempt. Changes in the welfare system since the late 1980s have made it nearly impossible for this story to happen today. I have written this book, in part, to show the good that could happen—that did happen—under the welfare system of the 1960s.

Chicago in 1960, like much of America, was poised on the cusp of tremendous changes. Signs of these changes had been appearing for years, certainly since the end of the Second World War. Some changes were good ones: the median income for white families, for example, had risen to $8,758, from just under $6,000 after the war. For African Americans, the economic improvement was muted. Median income for Negroes and others in

1960 was $4,848, a little over half that of whites. Thanks to the intransigence of segregation, access to jobs that might have further lifted the black standard of living was extremely limited. This lack of access left African Americans stranded in the most vulnerable sectors of the economy, at a time when only a few scholars and researchers recognized just how vulnerable those sectors were. In 1954, the year before I was born, there were 13,346 manufacturing companies operating in the Chicago area, providing 890,000 workers with a living wage. Four years later, by 1958, there were almost two hundred more—the number of manufacturers had gone up to 13,521—but the number of workers had fallen to 857,000. It was only the beginning. As steel plants were automated and stockyards were closed, a changing economy would narrow the scope of a lot of dreams.

Such changes would have an extraordinary impact on the lives of African Americans in all the cities of the North. Migrants from the agricultural South, these black men and women moved by the hundreds of thousands from Alabama and Mississippi, from Georgia and Arkansas. They came in the years after the war to escape the heavy hand of Jim Crow and the pointless work of sharecropping; they dreamed of city streets rather than the endless fields. Mostly, they dreamed of a little more freedom. They were not stupid; they knew that white people hadn't yet changed. But they imagined the Northern cities as places with more room to maneuver, and they thought ahead to their children, many of them still unborn, who might know a world of more possibility than theirs. From the ranks of these hopeful migrants came Nehemiah Bray and Mary Love, the two people who would become my parents.

Mercurial and independent, with a sixth-grade education, my father came to Chicago from Pine Bluff, Arkansas, sometime in the 1940s. From all the stories I heard growing up, his mother was a wiry and punitive woman with a talent for beating her children into line and punishing them in cruel ways. Annoyed with my father for some infraction, my paternal grandmother sold his beloved used bicycle one day while he was at school. Years later he would inflict the same wound on us, probably without a conscious thought. Daddy grew up to be a hustler, a gambler with entrepreneurial hungers. When he wasn't gambling, he worked at starting businesses—which never quite worked out. For a long time, before I was born, he was a skilled butcher, plying his trade at a local Swift & Company plant in the stockyards.

My mother, Mary Love, came to Chicago in 1947 with a third-grade education, her schooling cut short by work in the Mississippi fields. Her own mother—my grandmother—was as much a mystery to her as my mother is to me. When Mama was two, a fire began in the fields near their house. Still weak from childbirth, my grandmother went out with rags to beat back the flames as they approached the house. The fire was extinguished, but the smoke she inhaled inflamed her lungs and killed her.

My mother grew up stubborn and angry, resentful that she did not have a mother as other girls did. When a neighborhood boy teased her about it after school, she beat him so thoroughly that the boy's father called on her father to complain. Mama would not attend school for very long. The combined strain of sharecropping and single parenting compelled her father to bring her home for good. She had dreamed of becoming a schoolteacher and one day getting out of Mississippi. Instead she was pregnant by the age of eighteen, married to a man she did not love, and eventually she became the mother of a son, J.D.

But her drive to leave Mississippi persisted. She left her first husband and, entrusting her son to her father until she could send for him, took the train up to Chicago. She lived with an aunt, Big Mama, in a room on East Fifty-sixth Street. For a while she worked in a laundry, pressing shirts. Then she got a job in a restaurant on Garfield Boulevard, the heart of Chicago's Black Belt, waiting on tables and cleaning up. That was how she met Daddy. He used to come into the restaurant just to see her, dressed in his sharpest clothes to impress her. He would buy a cup of coffee for a nickel and leave a fifty-cent tip to get her attention.

"He kept trying to get me to smile at him," my mother recalled. "I wouldn't pay him no mind for the longest time."

She was about twenty years old when they met—twelve years younger than my father. And though she tried to ignore him for a long time, eventually she married him. Seven years after they married, I was born at Cook County Hospital in May of 1955.

The early promise of my parents' marriage soon gave way to a difficult reality: a hot-tempered husband with an inability to keep an ordinary job and a pathological need to control, and an easygoing wife who realized too late that she had married the wrong man. Before I was born, Mama continued to work, this time in a laundry ironing shirts again. She was aware of his gambling habits, but they were not that consequential at the time—particularly since he was fairly good at it. One evening Mama arrived home from work to find the apartment filled with Daddy's cronies from the meatpacking house. Daddy was in the back room with a pair of dice, relieving his coworkers of their paychecks. A lot of people went home broke that night, she remembered: he was that good.

Once I was born, however, things changed. His gambling became secretive, more sporadic and less flashy. He became more traditional in other ways, too. Daddy refused to allow Mama to work. Her job was to raise me, he said, and he was willing to back up that opinion with force. He took on more tasks, some successful, some disastrous, and in spite of everything else I feel about him, I retain a fixed image of Daddy as a relentless worker who gambled, not a gambler who occasionally worked.

Sometimes Daddy hauled junk, and sold it in the open-air markets of Maxwell Street on Sunday mornings. For a time, he owned a store near the old Chicago Stadium, where he had all kinds of things no one would buy. Dubbed C & B Salvage, the store boasted cases of cast-iron pots and crystal vases, Confederate money, showcases filled with 1940s Bakelite jewelry—all beautiful antiques that in the early '60s was simply stuff too old for anyone to want. He made a living at whatever came to hand—he owned a lunch wagon for a time, and would prepare food for hours in the kitchen of his small apartment on a Saturday night before he took the wagon out (a practice he continued throughout my childhood). Sometimes he did construction, working with wire lath and plaster in the older homes of Chicagoans.

But in spite of his endless hustles, money was scarce for our family. It wasn't just the lure of the horses or the sporadic nature of his work. What may have overridden everything was his intense jealousy of my mother and his obsessive desire to track her every move. My mother had become disillusioned with her handsome gambler and his explosive temper several years earlier. She was on the verge of leaving him when she discovered she was pregnant with me—a fact that filled me with guilt throughout my adolescence.

Trapped by my birth, she could not leave me to seek freedom for herself. In truth, she would not leave me, or the brothers and sister that followed. She remembered what it was like to grow up motherless, and though she couldn't change what had happened to her, she was determined that it wouldn't happen to us. So she stayed with my father, as his fear and anger grew, as she bore the brunt of his unpredictable rages, endured the beatings that seemed inspired by everything and nothing. She started sleeping on the living room couch after my youngest brother was born. In those days, birth control was a haphazard undertaking, and she preferred risking my father's wrath to having any more children.

The times that Daddy gambled away the rent money grew more and more frequent. By the time we moved to the apartment on Berkeley Avenue that I always considered home, there were four children: myself, a sister, a brother, and another brother on the way. I was a sickly girl who didn't want to eat, and who possessed a host of allergies and bronchitis so severe I nearly died on one occasion. My brother showed signs of having some of the same problems. And Daddy's iron control of my mother's finances and life was tightening. "There were times when we hardly had a loaf of bread," my mother remembered. It was the prospect of not feeding us, of not being able to take us to the doctor, that helped her make the decision to sign up for Aid to Dependent Children.

Mama knew that the state of Illinois frowned on the presence of men in recipients' homes, so she simply told the caseworkers what they wanted to hear: Daddy wasn't around much, and he didn't have any money, even when he was around. It wasn't a lie: he spent long hours away, arriving only after he had exhausted all his options and his cash for the day. The state approved her, and before long, our five names had been added to the list of ADC (later AFDC) recipients in the state of Illinois. Our status yielded an even more precious commodity in Mama's eyes—a green card. This was not the green card associated with immigration, but a long green data-processing card that promised us access to medical care.

My father was noncommittal at first; it didn't bother him to pretend nonexistence, especially for a good cause—and extra money was always a good cause. That was before he realized that my mother had every intention of keeping that monthly check for us. Daddy despised what he could not control, and this show of defiance on her part enraged him. Her refusal to grant him even casual access to that pittance was the infuriating last straw. With rare exceptions, the two of them would remain forever at war.

The Aid to Dependent Children program, or ADC, had its origins in the Federal Social Security Act of 1935. Its purpose was to provide a minimal level of economic protection for children growing up without fathers—about 10 percent of all children during the disruptive period of the Great Depression. The historian Linda Gordon has written that what came to be known (from 1962 on) as AFDC, or Aid to Families with Dependent Children, was destined from its inception to stigmatize those most in need of its assistance. This was not intentional, Gordon says, so much as it was the inevitable consequence of a program designed as "small and temporary, because its framers believed that the model of the family in which the male was the breadwinner and the female was the housewife would be the standard."

Thus it was that the most pernicious requirements of ADC were institutionalized, in marked contrast to the requirements of other social insurance programs created at the same time, such as old-age or unemployment insurance. To receive ADC, you had to prove you were destitute and go on proving it at regular intervals. To get unemployment insurance or Social Security, you only had to apply for it. Once you were approved for it, particularly Social Security, it was yours indefinitely. Who you lived with or slept with, what you did with the money after you got it—these were no one's business but your own. To receive ADC, you had to relinquish any hope of privacy in your personal or social life. Who lived with you, or slept with you, or spent your money was now the business of the state.

The most significant decision in designing ADC came in how it was funded. Financed by general revenues alone, the program almost immediately became vulnerable to the charge that it was taking money from the pockets of "decent" people who paid income and property taxes. Old-age insurance was designed as a contributory program, funded in part through a separate payroll tax. Workers who ultimately received benefits were thus always viewed as "entitled" to the money, since it was supposedly theirs to begin with. In fact, Social Security has always used both contributions and general revenues to fund itself. Recipients always get back much more than they ever put in.

Even more harmful, Gordon writes, is the disregard built into the system for the invisible work that women do in caring for children and other dependents, such as aging parents. "This stratification," she writes, "created the meaning of welfare today. . . . Originally intended to serve what . . . seemed to be the most deserving of all needy groups—helpless mothers left alone with children by heartless men—AFDC became shameful, making its recipients undeserving by the very fact of providing for them."

Gordon puts her finger on an underlying premise that has helped to make the welfare system the scapegoat it has become. The dependence of women and children was assumed in the formation of the system; the dependence of men on old-age or unemployment insurance was not. However, the dependence and vulnerability of women and children has a basis in reality. A woman responsible for a child or children is more vulnerable than one without children. Her needs for shelter and food, medical care and other things to ensure her children's safety are more urgent, and certainly more intensely felt, than the needs of those women and men who find themselves on their own.

That reality has come head-to-head with new realities having to do with economic instability, with the disappearance of certain types of work, and with the rapid and permanent infusion of women into the workforce. In addition, the deep-seated need in many parts of our culture to control women's behavior—particularly their sexual and reproductive behavior—has shaped the welfare debate in recent years. The ugly specter of race has reasserted itself as well, bringing to bear on the welfare debate all the stereotypes of women of color as profligate and uncontrollable sexual beings producing illegitimate children to be supported by the state.

Now that debate has ended. The AFDC program, part of welfare as I knew it, is dead—and the guilty parties are legion. The federal guarantee of support to poor children was killed by political opportunism and misguided attempts to "help" poor kids. It was murdered by upper-middle-class pundits and working-class bigots and Christian moralists, abandoned by disappointed liberals, ignored by privileged and childless feminists. And it was killed by silence from those of us who knew better—and that includes me.

The year my family entered the welfare system, 1960, marked the thirty-fifth anniversary of the creation of the Cook County Department of Public Aid. In the introduction to its annual report, the department remarked that in the year of its founding, "102 staff members did the Department's work on an annual budget of $658,360. Today, a staff of 3,150 administers an average monthly . . . expenditure in excess of $13,000,000.

"There are those—uninformed on the details of government and critical of it in any case—who hold that this rise . . . is the mark of public sentimentalism, or incompetence, or both," the report continued. "It is not sentimentalism, but rather a realization on the part of an entire, wealthy, privileged community, that all its members must pull together in a hitherto unknown kind of public brotherhood, a conviction that the least lucky individuals should be helped—in some degree—by the charity of the lucky."

I stand now at midlife—writer, wife, mother—witness to a host of efforts that would make of my life and the lives of others an unfortunate aberration, a misguided attempt at social engineering, a lie. But I am not confused by these efforts, or by a shift in public sentiment. I know who I am. More important, I know who I was and I know who I became; I understand the journey from there to here. I am the great-great-granddaughter of slaves and the granddaughter of sharecroppers and the daughter of poor, proud, angry people determined to make more of me than they could of themselves.

I understand that there is a world of people determined to make me ashamed, make me embarrassed, make me forget what I know to be true. I understand that such people never go away.

But I have been given priceless gifts I have no right to squander: a family, a once-committed nation, the luxuries of education and political awareness, opportunity and time. Most of all, I understand that these things were mine for a reason: to secure for others what was once secured for me.

I had always imagined the path I traveled would remain there for others. I had always imagined that hands would guide the others who would follow me. But now the path itself is being overgrown by cynicism and greed and carelessness. The hands of those who once bolstered children traveling this road have pulled away, weakened by narrow minds and personal pain. The path itself has grown a thousand times more treacherous. And now there are those in our nation who ask us all to be practical, who insist that the journey cannot even be made. They are wrong; I know it can be done. But the secret in traveling the path is that it is impossible to travel alone.

It may be too late to undo the damage done to our characters as Americans by the erosion of our faith in the possibility of change. We have been poisoned by the idea that nothing we do matters, that nothing the government does will matter. This is a lie, and my whole life is evidence of that fact. I have been lifted up by hands both seen and unseen, both individual and governmental. People, institutions, governments—all of them have something to offer people, something particularly important to the least among us. They are all avenues of justice and hope. Each, in its own way, matters immeasurably. If anyone knows the truth of that, I know. It has been the story of my life.

UNAFRAID
OF
THE DARK

Chapter 1

Certain things shape you, change you forever. Years later, long after you think you've escaped, some ordinary experience flings you backward into memory, transports you to a frozen moment, and you freeze. Being poor is like that. Living surrounded by fear and rage is like that. I grew up hating the cold, dreading the approach of night. Thirty years later, a too-cold room at night can trigger a flash of terror, or a wash of ineffable sadness. Voices raised in anger can still make me shrink. Every now and then, a sudden, innocent move by my husband makes me duck to protect myself. It took many years for me to think of night as a time of rest.

I can't remember what awakened me first—my mother's urgent voice, the thick, sooty smoke, or the blasts of icy air through our bedrooms.

"Get up, Ro, go sit in the kitchen while I air out this room." I had bronchitis, and the smoke was already starting to bother me. I stumbled through the dark into the dim kitchen, lit only by the burners on the gas stove and the faint flicker from the broiler. The oven door was open, and though the rest of the room was still cold, the space near the stove was almost toasty. I coughed a little as my mother brought my brothers and sister into the kitchen, then disappeared downstairs.

The house's boiler was out again. An ancient coal contraption, it always seemed to go on the blink in the dead of winter, pumping thick black smoke through the house. Whenever this happened, only turning the boiler off until the morning would alleviate the problem. There was a janitor for our building, but Mama often knew more about the boiler than he did.

Mama came back upstairs and led us back to bed in the now-frigid room. We climbed into our beds as she went through the rooms closing the windows again. It was four A.M. or so; in a couple of hours it would be time to get up. But Mama wouldn't sleep anymore that night. Already I could hear her putting one of two big buckets into the kitchen sink. She would fill them with water and place them on the back burners of the stove so we'd have hot water for washing up. By morning, the water in the house would be ice-cold. As long as the stove was on, someone had to stay awake. That someone was always Mama.

Poor, afraid—these were not the only things I was. There were long stretches of time when I gave no thought to my condition. I was black, I was a girl, I was smart, I was the oldest of four: these were the things I knew about myself; this was the knowledge I held on to in my own little universe. My world was an area of twenty square blocks on the South Side of Chicago, bounded by Forty-third Street to the north and Forty-seventh Street to the south, and by Drexel Boulevard to the west and Woodlawn Avenue to the east. The neighborhood was called Kenwood-Oakland in better times, but those times had come and gone.

That cold room, that ancient boiler, that shabby kitchen—they are gone, too. A vacant lot dotted with old trucks and cars is all that remains of the building I grew up in—4466 South Berkeley Avenue. Ours was the corner building; a once-grand limestone mansion with a stone porch and beveled-glass windows, it had been hastily converted into several overpriced apartments. Berkeley Avenue was the kind of street where folks sat on their porches and played cards and drank wine. Neighbors fixed their cars in the street and changed their own oil, watching it run down into the sewer grates. Women waited on the watermelon man and the vegetable man, with their green, horse-pulled wagons, to shop for staples on Saturday. Our street was the kind of place where everyone knew each other by sight, and most likely by name: Miss Elizabeth and Mr. Jones; Yvonne and Jessie; Mr. Bob and Mr. Brown; Mama Woodward and Miss Kathy and Stafford, Clorine, and Rowena; Mr. Davis and Mrs. Davis and Diane and Deborah. And then there was us: Mrs. Bray and her four children. People rarely spoke of our father, except in rueful, hesitant tones. They knew enough about him to know they wanted no part of him.

The block itself was unremarkable, typical of the transitional neighborhoods in ghettos throughout Chicago. The buildings were mostly low-rise limestones and brick townhouses, interspersed with large apartment buildings. Directly across the street from us were the two biggest apartment buildings on the block. I always wondered what they were like on the inside, but we never even walked on that side of the street. The residents were the folks you heard at night—fighting, drinking, yelling at each other—when you were trying to sleep. The tenants regarded our family with great curiosity, but let us be.

If you walked two blocks to Forty-third Street, the limestones and apartment buildings gave way to once well-kept stores with prices too steep for us. The local department store, Alden's, sold a little bit of everything. Shoes and dresses, coats and hats. We looked a great deal, but we didn't touch. Our regular stops were the Walgreen's on the corner, the newsstand, the A & P and the

High-Low Foods, and, every now and then, the bakery in mid-block. It was a memorable place, not only for its pastry, but for its decorative blue mirrors, which lent the place a serene charm. I used to like to go in there just to see them. What most of the stores had in common was that white people ran them. Occasionally, someone black worked in them, but if there was ever a question, someone had to find a white man or woman with the answer. Yet I had never seen any white people living near us.

I didn't know it, but all of us were part of a great urban transition taking place in the Black Belt, a stretch of Chicago that extended roughly from Thirty-ninth Street to Sixty-third Street, from Lake Michigan on the east to as far west as Western Avenue, though we never considered such far-flung streets as "our neighborhood." The neighborhood we lived in was once an exclusive area occupied by white Anglo-Saxon Protestants, a situation that changed in the 1920s when German Jews began to arrive. The trickle became a wave in the years during and after World War II, and by 1950, 85 percent of Kenwood was populated by German Jews. In just ten years it would become 85 percent Negro. It was the same all along the Black Belt: between 1940 and 1960, the population of black Chicago would grow from 278,000 to 813,000. Ours was the kind of neighborhood that urban pioneers would, thirty years later, fight to resettle, to turn into a showcase of gentrification. (On Oakenwald—once a street so thick with gang members that Mama forbade us to walk there—one of the renovated limestones recently sold for $200,000.) Landlords took advantage of a combination of factors, including the profound residential segregation still common in Chicago and the dearth of housing for black families in these last days before the advent of public housing. Thus the six of us came to be wedged into a first-floor apartment originally designed as the public space of an impressive home.

Our front door opened from the hallway into the living room. The room was furnished with a couch covered in a green-blue, faintly iridescent fabric, where Mama slept each night, and a stuffed chair, a bookcase I pretended was mahogany, and a gigantic console radio. To the left, through a set of curtains, was the children's bedroom. To the right was an enormous room with built-in cabinets. This clearly used to be the dining room; for us, it was both dining room and kitchen. Next to that was a kind of alcove, complete with a little closet where Mama stored the old wringer washer she sometimes used. Across from the alcove was the one bathroom in the apartment, painted a succession of ghastly colors—except for a memorable coat of emerald green enamel, which I loved because I was a May baby, and emerald was my birthstone.

At the other end of the apartment were a back door and two rooms. One room, which was unheated, was used as a storage room. Mama kept the rollaway bed in there, and an old desk, and a big orange freezer that Daddy had hustled for her somewhere. Mama kept a clothesline hanging in that room, for drying clothes we were in no hurry to wear.

The other room was Daddy's room. It contained a dresser, a chifforobe where he kept his clothes from a past, flashy life, a double bed with a patterned headboard, and a night table adorned with pill bottles, a lamp, and a radio. There were also two ice-cream-parlor chairs—the kind with bentwood backs. The pair had been painted every conceivable color; you could see the layers that had chipped away from long abuse.

I knew a lot about those chairs. Sometimes we sat in them—gathered around my father's bed like soldiers at the campfire, listening to grandly told stories of adventure. Sometimes they fell victim to my father's rage, tipping over as Daddy lunged forward to beat one or more of us for some infraction. Sometimes they were used for the interrogation of my mother. Daddy would scream at her to sit her big ass down, and he'd close the door to berate her away from our terrified eyes. Sometimes I glimpsed her through a crack in the door; she'd be sitting in one of those chairs, wearing a flowered housedress, my father looming over her, screaming, cursing.

"You lying, no-good whore!"

I lay in my bed in the front room, crying in the dark. Two rooms away, my father continued his tirade against my mostly silent mother. I could tell from the air on my face that the room was ice-cold; the boiler was out again and the whole building most likely was freezing.

"You think I don't know about all your men, you stinking bitch? You think I'm some kind of damn fool?"

I heard my mother murmuring what might have been an answer. Then I heard the slapping sound of flesh against flesh, and the thump of my mother's body against a wall. I knew they struggled, because I could hear the grunts they made as Mama tried to defend herself and Daddy continued to attack her. The floor vibrated with the blows from their wrestling bodies. It felt as though they were fighting right up under my bed.

"You think I don't see all these men after your ass, you no-good whore? They used you up, bitch!" Daddy was screaming, growing hoarse with the effort, but the more hoarse he became, the louder he got. I could tell from the sniffles in the room that I wasn't the only one awake. My brothers and sister could hear them fighting, too. But I didn't say anything out loud. I was too busy monitoring the dreadful silences between his tirades, wondering whether he had killed Mama, straining to hear the murmur of her voice that would tell me she was abused, but still alive.

He started in again, with more blows, the sharp slap of his hand against my mother carrying clear through the house. I jumped up from my bed and ran through the cold rooms to where they were. "Leave her alone," I screamed. "Get away from her!"

Both of them turned toward me, standing in the doorway.

"Get your little ass back in that bed," my father snarled.

"I'm all right, Ro. Go on to bed, baby," my mother said, in the same moment. "He's not hurting me." Her voice was warm, but anxious; she didn't move from the chair.

"Stop hitting her! Why do you have to hit her?" I didn't understand what he was so angry about. Why couldn't they smile at each other, hug and kiss the way folks did on television?

Daddy ignored me, turning his attention to Mama. I wanted to go to Mama, protect her, make Daddy stop. But I knew if I stayed, he would turn on me, cut my skin with the leather belt he wielded, sometimes without regard to where its buckle was. I was too afraid to stay, ashamed of being so young, so small that I couldn't defend her. All I could do was go back to bed and lie there, listening to the ebb and flow of my father's rage, waiting for it to subside enough for me to sleep a little, crying and asking God to make it stop, hating the night and longing for morning.

In the morning, I woke up before my brothers and sister to the sound of the back door slamming and the distant roar of a starting car. My mother was in the kitchen, singing some spiritual under her breath. I was filled with an aching relief. He was gone for the day; Mama was all right. I went into the kitchen to see for myself, and she was there, in her flowered duster, getting ready to fry bacon, the dull silver of the coffeepot winking from the back burner of the stove. Mama had already poured herself a cup of coffee, which she sipped as she worked. When she saw me at the doorway, she smiled a little and reached over for a purple cup and saucer made of melamine. The cup was cracked and stained from too much use, but it was beautiful to me, a symbol of quiet time with her. She poured in a little coffee and a lot of milk, stirred in some sugar, and presented it to me at the kitchen table. All the while she worked, Mama talked.

"We have to wash clothes today, and go to the store. I need some neck bones. I'm going to boil them down with potatoes and onions, and make us up some corn bread. That ought to be a good dinner. I need soap powder too, but I got enough bleach. . . ."

I sat next to her, safe for the moment, listening to her make the list of things to do that day. It felt good when Mama confided in me about the work of the household, and I tried to be a help to her in every way I knew how. But the thing I wanted to do most, I couldn't do. I couldn't make Daddy leave her alone. I couldn't make them stop screaming, or make them act like the mothers and fathers on television. I couldn't make peace.

For all her passivity about my father, Mama was unbending in her insistence on a set of standards for herself and for us. We represented her, and she refused to tolerate anything that smacked of rude or thoughtless behavior. She was much kinder in her strictures than Daddy, but no less firm: there were kids we could play with and kids we couldn't, folks we could associate with and others to whom we were permitted to exhibit only a perfunctory politeness. "I hate a bum," she used to say as we followed her from chore to chore, and much of her time was spent distinguishing herself from the people she thought were bums.

My mother's endurance was a mystery to me. I understood why she said she could not leave us. I was grateful that she refused to disappear. But what I never understood was how she was able to do what she did for as long as she did it. It was my mother's genius at making do, combined with a vivid imagination and a surprising sense of humor, that made our lives work as well as they did. Yet there were no kind words for her, no respite, nothing to look forward to—except, perhaps, the dream, a conviction that our lives somehow would be different. There was only the relentless quest for survival.

She shopped ruthlessly, bargained, cajoled, charmed storekeepers and managers of all the little stores along Forty-third Street, where we shopped. She brought us with her everywhere she went, so there could be no denying that she had several mouths to feed. The butcher shop, redolent with the smells of sawdust and uncooked meat, was a place where she bargained for an extra piece of meat or a spare neck bone. She knew people sometimes felt sorry for her, and she didn't care, if it meant more food for her kids. Contrary to my father's opinion, she was not running around on him. There was no time or opportunity to cheat on your husband with four kids in tow. But she could have if she'd wanted to, because my mother was a big, pretty woman with sparkling eyes, and the men in the neighborhood noticed her. Even as a little girl, I came to recognize the slow drawl and insinuation in the voices of men who offered to help my mother with all those packages and all those kids. My mother always declined any offers, except for those from a couple of very familiar neighbors. I suspect that Daddy had taught my mother everything about men that she ever wanted to know. The result was the suppression—if not the end—of her desires. We became, and remained, her primary passion.

Mama's food store of choice was High-Low Foods on Forty-third Street near Drexel. Part of a small local chain that no longer exists, it offered sometimes slightly spoiled, always overpriced food that was nonetheless cheaper than the food at more prominent chains, such as A & P. For Mama, the most important aisle was the one with canned goods—rows and rows of them in bins stacked three high. There were pork and beans, creamed corn, mixed vegetables, sardines, Vienna sausages, and potted meat, all at ten cents a can. If she had the cart with her, she could roll home dozens of cans of everything it took to make a meal to stretch for six. Jack salmon was twenty-five cents a can. Jiffy corn bread mix was a dime a box; so was piecrust mix. We helped out of necessity, scurrying around the store like couriers, searching for forgotten items. If bacon was on sale, that meant baked beans with strips of bacon on top. If potted meat was plentiful that week, it meant lunches of potted meat sandwiches and mayonnaise with sweet pickle. If Mama found salmon, she could mix it with eggs and flour to make salmon croquettes.

Later, we would go to the A & P for frozen orange juice, milk and sugar, and Cheerios or cornflakes for breakfast. It was Mama's chance to say hello to Miss Mildred, who worked at the checkout counter. And it was a chance to earn Plaid stamps, which Mama kept in a drawer. Every few weeks, we'd all get redemption books and sit around on Saturday night, pasting in the stamps, talking about what we could get. Mama once used them to buy clippers to cut my brothers' hair; she still has those clippers. She got a really nice set of drinking glasses, too, that we could use for the holidays; they had white flowers etched on them. Most days, we used old jelly jars and some aluminum cups we had.

Food stamps made things easier. The formal Food Stamp program began in selected areas of the United States in 1961. I cannot remember a time when we did not have those slender coupon books, put aside in an old purse my mother kept in a dresser drawer. For a certain amount of money each month, say fifty dollars, you could buy sixty-five dollars' worth of food stamps. There was a host of rules about their use; no toilet paper or diapers were permitted, but milk and bread and other food staples were allowed. Stamps had to be in their books. You weren't allowed to tear out a five-dollar coupon and run to the store for some basics. And in the early days of the program, even your change at the checkout came to you in food-stamp coins: plastic disks of burgundy or gray.

Mama bought food stamps at the same place she conducted all of her AFDC-related business: at the currency exchange—the closest thing to a bank in the ghettos of Chicago. In other cities, these are known as check-cashing places. Whatever they're called, they are the financial institutions of the poor. Mama cashed her check there and bought food stamps, got money orders to pay the phone company and the gas company, even bought stamps to mail her bills. The charge for their services: as much as 1 percent of the total amount cashed. Not terrible, but enough for us to notice.

The endless counting of change, the rush to search out dropped pennies, the constant monitoring of the curbs and vacant lots for empty pop bottles—these are the memories that exhaust me. I am profligate with money in response to all those years of relentless scrimping. I flail against them by going into grocery stores and buying what I like. I never look at prices; I don't want to know. I simply shop until the money runs out, determined in this one thing at least to have what I want: not the things that are cheaper, not the things on sale, definitely not the generic, no-frills food that reminds me of the packages of government food we sometimes got from church. I had no shame about eating it; it didn't taste worse than the other food we ate. But to see those packages now, to actually buy them and keep them in my house, would mean I had gone backward, and one of the few things my mother and father agreed on was the importance of never going backward. Whenever you move, they always said, go forward.

One of the truths that seem to elude most welfare reformers is the pervasive sense of fear and tension that accompanies that monthly check. I learned to decipher that look of tension in my mother's eyes: it's the fear of knowing that the best you can do is to give a little something to everyone you owe. Not enough to pay them, sometimes not enough to placate them, but just enough to remind them—and you—that you can never really catch up.

When I listen to one of the periodic television spectacles on reform—in which people who have enough money to pay their bills, but not enough to get a new car, take out after welfare recipients for buying steaks—I have to laugh. Not one of them could survive for a week on what my mother raised four children on every month for more than twenty years. And steak was not part of that equation. Even if it were, is that what welfare reform is after—keeping cheap, tough steaks out of the mouths of the unworthy? Not one of these bitter people understands how hard it is simply to live with the money any state provides. There is no money to plan ahead, to shop cheaply, to prepare for an emergency. There is no ability to set aside a bit for the future; the present occupies all the attention of anyone on welfare. Our contingency fund was the streets and alleys, where we searched for bottles we could turn in for the deposits. Sometimes we used the money to buy candy; other times we used it to buy bread or milk, or whatever small staple we were running out of before the check arrived.

Once, Mama sent me to the store to buy a loaf of bread. Heedless of the surroundings, happy to be out walking on my own, I stumbled and fell, dropping the carefully hoarded change. I found all of it but a nickel, and the feeling of terror nearly consumed me. It was not just the fear of getting a beating for losing the money. It was the anticipation of my mother's disappointment in me. I knew better; I was the oldest. How could I have lost that precious money? Crying in the street, looking for the lost coin, I met an elderly man who gave me a nickel out of his own pocket. I hesitated about taking money from a stranger, but I got over it when I realized I couldn't go home without that bread. I ran to make up for lost time, and if my mother noticed that my eyes were red, she didn't say anything.

That was the difference a nickel could make. Sometimes there were pennies for candy: Mary Janes and Squirrel Nut-Zippers, candy buttons on wide strips of paper and candy shoelaces we tried to use as whips. But each of us came to understand just how little there was for anything that wasn't absolutely necessary, as we learned to recognize the anger in our mother's voice that was rarely there unless we asked for things she couldn't afford to buy.

Sometimes the fear is a matter of timing. Late mail, a bureaucratic mix-up, and a carefully planned method of survival lies in tatters. One month, in the dead of winter, the check was late and every bill in the house was due; some were overdue. When the gas man came to turn off the gas, my mother went outside to meet him, but for once her considerable charm failed her. In spite of her pleas that the check was on its way, he turned the gas off anyway.

I can only imagine what went through my mother's mind as

the man left. Surrounded by four hungry children under the age of seven, living in an apartment without cooking gas. What was memorable for me, however, was my mother's response to the crisis. As she surveyed the room for her pots and utensils, Mama announced that she had a surprise for us. For all her worries, Mama loved to play, and she had a better sense of humor than any mother I knew in the neighborhood.

"We're going to have a picnic," she declared. When one of us said it was too cold for a picnic, she said we were going to have it in the back room. If having the gas shut off was a tragedy, you wouldn't have known it from Mama's explanation. She told us to go and get our coats, then she opened all the windows in the unheated back room. With the help of a huge old paint bucket, some leftover charcoal, and one of the racks from the useless oven, Mama improvised a grill. While we looked on in childish delight, Mama made hamburgers and cooked them over the bucket, while the smoke wafted out the windows. We thought it was the coolest thing in the world.

Daddy was not nearly so sanguine about this event, or any other. As usual, he blamed my mother for everything: the late check, the gas turnoff, the whole idea that we were living in this apartment like bums. Their fights were long, loud, and frequent, and even though the neighborhood could hear him every evening, no one ever said a word. He was simply more regular about his explosions than other men in the neighborhood, men who saved their outbursts for weekends, or a night of heavy drinking. My father needed no such impetus. It was the kind of man he was.

One of his great talents was understanding and using the power of fear, a skill I suspect he learned from his own mother. It is possible that he was simply at the mercy of his own uncontrollable demons. But it is just as possible that he understood the importance of surprise, of a feigned irrationality. What better way to keep your wife and children in line than to keep them guessing—regaling them with stories of your life as a hobo before bedtime, then waking everybody in the house a few hours later, a .38 in hand, threatening to kill them all? Daddy had always liked guns, always kept them around—a rifle in the closet, a .38 under the mattress or in the drawer by the bedside. It was the sense of complete randomness that led to much of my early terror of him. It was a terror which, by adolescence, had given way to a hatred for him that defined me and my responses to everything in my world.

It took many years for me to understand some of what drove him. Part of his problem stemmed from his own frustrations and bitterness about the hand life had dealt him. Daddy was a man who was born to lead—a company, an organization, at the very least, a family. He was intrinsically a patriarch, hungry for control in a world where black men controlled nothing, not even themselves. I didn't know it then, but it was like being on the set of *A Raisin in the Sun,* witness to Walter Lee Younger's evil twin. Manhood for my father, as for Walter Lee, meant providing for his family. Like Walter Lee, Daddy was haunted by the vision of white male affluence he saw only from the periphery. For Walter Lee, it was the life of a chauffeur that brought him face-to-face with temptation; for Daddy, it was his own entrepreneurial bent that led to a hyperawareness. Daddy's quest for manhood spilled over into a lust for domination. White folks aren't shit, he reasoned, but they have everything I want: money, power, the deference of women and children. Day by day, year by year, my father's hunger for white male privilege would be weakened and ultimately denied.

Part of his rage, too, was rooted in my mother's behavior. He was possessed by a weird, obsessive jealousy toward her. It was stoked, not by any unfaithfulness of hers, but by her complete devotion to us, at Daddy's expense. For her part, I suspect that she had made her choice long before, in keeping with a certain ethos among African-American women of nearly every generation: my life is not important; it's the children I have to worry about. All the devotion that, in a different world and a different, happier marriage, Mama might have lavished on my father, she spread freely among us, leaving my father outside an ever-tightening circle. The more he pushed to enter, the tighter the circle closed.

It did not help that my father hated women, held them in vitriolic scorn—a legacy of his mother's fierce brutality—and despised any woman who exhibited anything akin to an independent spirit. Black women in particular, he believed, had no idea of how to be real women; white women were real women. White women didn't make decisions without asking their husbands; white women spoke softly and catered to their men. Black women were hardheaded, spoke for themselves, had their own opinions, listened to no one. "The only free people in the world," he used to say bitterly, "are white men and black women." Even a woman as relatively powerless as my mother was too much for him, and though I was tolerable enough as a little girl, as I grew older it was clear that I was already beginning to exhibit some of the same stubborn resolve that my father possessed. In either of my brothers, he would have found this development charming. In me, it would eventually prove to be anathema.

But I was still a girl far from womanhood, and most of my suffering came from the fear that he would one day really hurt my mother, even kill her. I dreaded the idea that one day I might be left alone with this angry man, might find myself responsible for raising my brothers and sister. Once, I came inside and found Mama in bed, clutching her side in pain. Mama *never* went to bed in the daytime. My father had kicked her in the side when they'd fought the night before. I kept asking her if she was sick. She kept trying to soothe me, encouraged me to go in the other room to play. But I couldn't leave her alone; she might die without me. I hovered close by and read to myself, stories about happy girls from large families with no troubles to keep them up at night.

My deep protectiveness of Mama grew from moments like this. It was my job to stick up for her, even when I couldn't stick up for myself. But perhaps it was my way of looking out for me. Unlike my father, who was always looking for things about me to fix or to change, she always let me be. She was not indulgent in any sense of the word; she had no patience for foolishness or disobedience. But she talked and listened to us, paid attention to and understood us.

My two brothers and my sister were as adoring of Mama as they were fearful of my father. Each of them, though, had such different ways of coping. My brother Hiawatha found refuge in retreat. In spite of the scorn with which my father consistently treated him, Hiawatha loved him, and felt powerless to choose between him and Mama. He hated arguing and any kind of confrontation, and hid whenever it arose. I can remember, somewhere in the middle of every argument, the sound of a door closing—my brother turning away. I hated his cowardice; it made me angry and left me even more alone and powerless than I already felt. Brother, as we called him, was a scant fifteen months apart from me in age. In everything else, we were friends and allies. But when it came to the specter of our parents and their fierce arguments, Brother quietly withdrew.

My sister, Linda, was the most obviously ambivalent. Three years younger than I, she was my father's favorite child. Sensitive, with a gentle disposition similar to Brother's, she had all the girlish charms I lacked, and all the traditional trappings of girlhood I resolutely shunned. I think these traits made her more comprehensible to my father. He was a lot clearer about what to do with a daughter who played with dolls than with one who wanted cars and a chemistry set. Thus, the rage he exhibited toward my mother and me rarely found their way to her. If I was jealous of anything, it was the relative ease with which she dealt with Daddy; unlike me, she pleased him in nearly everything she did.

Lost amid all these family dynamics was my baby brother, Terry. Five years younger than I, he arrived at a time when I imagine Daddy was still attempting to instill in me some sense of maternal feeling, a backward way of helping me help my mother. I resented having to pay so much attention to Terry, who had the biggest head I'd ever seen on a living baby, and apparently had the lungs to match.

To Brother and me, it seemed crying was his only function. I had once read that singing in the ears of infants helped them to keep quiet. So for days after Mama brought Terry home, my brother and I took turns trying to shut him up with our childish voices. Years later, Mama told us that of all her children, Terry was the one who finally wore her out. One evening, she said, she handed him to Daddy, announcing that if he didn't take this crying child, she was going to throw him out of the window. How I wish I could remember that scene! The idea that my father would pick up the slack sounds like the stuff of fantasy.

Even more unbelievable is the notion that my mother would lose her patience in any significant way. Of course we got on her nerves, and she was the kind of woman who was quick to say so. But I always envision her as someone with a bountiful understanding. She was the same with others as she was with us. Mama was the neighbor who knew nearly everyone and helped nearly everyone. We never had a lot, but whatever we had, Mama was willing to share, especially when children were involved. One of our neighbors across the street sometimes spent all her money on liquor, then did without food for herself and her daughters. It was my mother whose bell she rang in the hours after school to ask for slices of bread and some peanut butter. Sometimes Mama would give her the bread, sometimes she would give her pop bottles she had been saving for us to turn in.

Mostly people knew Mama because her life revolved around us. Whenever anyone saw her, she was on her way to take us to school or pick us up from school, or she was going to the store for our dinner or coming back from the store with groceries. She sat on the porch and watched us play with the two Davis children, Diane and Deborah—the Davises were the only family on the block whose company Mama and Daddy approved of. We drew awkward hopscotch patterns with old chalk, tossed pebbles for our turn instead of pennies, jumped rope if we could con Mama out of her clothesline, played Mother-may-I on the front porch steps—all under my mother's ever-present eye.

She was more her real self when Daddy wasn't home. She spoke freely to the neighbors, traded stories about children, mentioned sales at the High-Low and the A & P. She felt especially drawn to the older people in the neighborhood, men and women whose families had gone away, or had died out, and who had no one. The local handyman, Mr. Bob, was like that. Thin and dark, he wore a greasy baseball hat and overalls no matter what the weather. Like my father, and so many other men on our street, he smelled of sweat and dirt, cigarettes and coffee and work. Mr. Bob talked slowly, in an effort to contain his profound stutter. He lived in a room some blocks from us, supported himself doing odd jobs in the neighborhood. On weekends, though, when Daddy was most often gone, Mr. Bob came by to visit with Mama and play with us kids.

Another neighbor, Mr. Brown, was the same way. Big, coarse-looking and loud, he was possessed of a sweet nature, and always had, I think, a secret crush on my mother. Mr. Brown did have family—a daughter who hated him on sight, if the stories I pieced together from eavesdropping were accurate. She rarely came to see him, and called only occasionally, usually when she wanted something. Mr. Brown came to my mother for her sympathetic ear. She listened to his heartbreak, and relied on him a bit to help get her to the store or carry bags. He was constantly telling us what a good woman my mother was. I wondered why his daughter didn't like him; I would have traded fathers with her in a heartbeat.

We became most attached, though, to a woman who lived across the alley from us, in a basement apartment near Ellis. Flora Woodward was from Alabama, and according to my mother her story was a sad one—married to a man who died young, leaving her to raise their only child, a daughter. That daughter died in her twenties, poisoned by a jealous woman over the man they had in common. Now Mama Woodward was all alone, and for months we watched her ascend and descend the small concrete steps to her apartment, with the help of her thick brown cane. When she was outside, she often watched Mama walk with us to Drexel Park, or to the candy store. Mama always talked to her, and as the older woman revealed more of her story, Mama found in her the mother she had lost so early in life. We gradually began to call her Mama Woodward, and she would come to be the only grandmother I ever knew.

My siblings, these few neighbors—they, along with my parents, constituted a large part of my world. What was most real to me, even as a child, was the sense of a double life, a sense that would repeat itself, with several variations, for many years. There was the normal life of my childhood. We were silly and happy together. We laughed a lot, and trailed along with Mama everywhere in the neighborhood. Our neighbors knew us and we knew them; we were bound by the common rules of respect for grownups. We spent a host of unremarkable days together, with only the typical family squabbles to interrupt our peace.

But sometime in the late afternoon or early evening, the dreaded sound would pierce the apartment—the succession of heavy kicks at the back door. That was Daddy's signal. Sometimes his hands were full of things, sometimes he was simply too lazy to fish for his keys; sometimes I think he just wanted to make everybody jump. For whatever reason, the sound was our warning. Our laughter became muted, even hushed. A book we might have been glancing through gained our total attention. All our games would end, as Mama walked to the back door to flip the latch that would admit him to our former sanctuary.

Day by day, Daddy became more of an outsider. It would be easy to say that my mother's decision to enroll us in ADC was the catalyst for the change in him, but that can only account for part of it. Even if he had held down a nine-to-five job in the stockyards, or in a factory, there was something about my father that had been fundamentally damaged long before he was embittered by the circumstances of his life, by the pact he tacitly made with a faceless bureaucracy. His paranoia grew as we did; he always suspected that we were keeping things from him, and in many ways we were. We denied him knowledge of the people we were becoming; we had convinced ourselves he would never understand.

On welfare, my mother joined the ranks of unskilled women who found the state more reliable than their husbands. Daddy joined the ranks of shadow men who walked out back doors as caseworkers came in front doors, who for a slew of reasons lost their last, tenuous grip on the hallowed patriarchal family that was never truly real for African Americans. Barred from the opportunities white men typically had to create their lives from scratch, shut out of every avenue of male dominance that white men routinely enjoyed, black men like my father found themselves without identity as men at all.

Daddy became the secret member of our household, the person we were instructed to lie about—and we lied about him often, unblinkingly. I never understood, though, how anyone in his or her right mind would have believed the lie. It was one thing to hear our childish protestations in daylight, another to hang around at night and listen to the changed sounds of our household. There was just as likely to be screaming as laughter, just as likely to be slammed doors as music.

Yet there were glimpses of an opposing vision of my father, one I could never reconcile with the man I grew to loathe. This specter was one of a mysterious man: conspiratorially tender, attentive, even sentimental. Once, when I was a little girl, I awoke to the sounds of bare feet against the linoleum in the kitchen. When I padded through the living room and stood by the pantry door, I could see Daddy, lit by the light of the open refrigerator, rummaging for breakfast in what must have been the middle of the night. He asked me if I was hungry; I wasn't, but nothing could have made me say anything but yes.

Daddy made bacon and eggs, and fixed me a little plate, and we ate quietly in the dark, our meeting punctuated only by the smacking of our lips, and by my promise that we would keep our breakfast a secret. When we were done, and Daddy had gathered the plates and put them together in the sink, he hoisted me up onto his back. I clutched him tight as he rode me through the living room and into the bedroom where my siblings slept. He tucked me in and kissed me good-night. In those days, my sleep was still peaceful.

This rare vision of my father grew rarer still. In its place, there appeared over the years a grasping, driven stranger with big plans for his oldest child. In this ambition for me, my mother and father found an otherwise elusive common ground. As children of sharecroppers, both my parents had forgone a formal education to work in the fields. My father had always wanted to work for himself; my mother had harbored since girlhood the doomed dream of becoming a schoolteacher. They came to the North to leave their poverty and ignorance behind, and though poverty had followed them—and their children—they were both determined to beat back ignorance.

This was their inspiration, I think, for beginning to teach me how to read right after I turned three years old. I remember them sitting with me in a kitchen; my father had lost his temper because I didn't seem to be catching on. My mother told him that I would never learn anything if he kept yelling at me. Exasperated, he dared my mother to teach me herself. She said she would, and in fact she did. What I find most amazing is that neither one of them thought three was too early for me to start reading. And when I consider that Mama had only a fundamental knowledge of reading herself, I know teaching me was no small task.

For help, she relied on a friend, Rosalie Holmes, a nurse who lived near us. Miss Holmes was one of the few friends my mother had that my father did not object to, so it was easy for Mama to call on her for assistance. Mama printed the letters of the alphabet on notebook paper, then tacked the sheet to the wall near the pantry door with a tiny nail. She would go over and over it with me. Then she would choose words that she liked, and ask Miss Holmes what they meant, and how to spell them. She would write everything down, then teach me what Miss Holmes had taught her. This way, Mama and I learned together.

The first word we learned was *opportunity;* I spelled it out loud in a singsong voice as often as anyone would allow me. It looked like such a big word on paper. I loved the way I felt when I could say it and spell it; I loved the look of amazement on the faces of adults when I could do something they were sure I could not do. In a few months, I could spell words out when I saw them on signs, or labels, or posters. Mama and I were on a bus one afternoon, and I began to point out letters and words that I knew. There were only a few passengers on the bus, and one of them was a very old woman who, after asking my mother how old I was, gravely pronounced that I wasn't long for this world. It was my high forehead, she said, and the way I could already read. Clearly, I had been here before, and didn't have long to stay. Mama was polite at the time, but made fun of it later when we got home. For years, though, I was scared; I wondered if the lady meant I was going to die soon.

But I never wondered about whether I should read. When my parents spoke quietly together about how smart I was, they sounded almost like a regular father and mother. Even better, I had become fascinated with knowing things. I liked reading stories and seeing the people and places show up in my head as though there were a television in my brain. I liked reading the comics and trying to figure out all the jokes in them. I liked reading the rest of the newspaper, too. I didn't understand everything I read, but I could recognize names. They were the same names that Daddy was always talking about with Mama as he lay in his bed in the evenings, smoking Chesterfields and scattering pages everywhere.

If I learned reading and writing at my mother's knee, I learned politics from my father's passion for current events. Daddy brought home all the papers most of the time—the *Daily News* and the *Sun-Times* and the *American* and the *Defender,* the daily black newspaper. Daddy read the *Tribune,* too, though he didn't trust it. It was a common understanding among black people of my parents' generation that the *Chicago Tribune* was a racist newspaper. That, combined with the *Tribune*'s typical support of Chicago's mayor, Richard J. Daley—a man my father loathed—resulted in a news outlet that folks in the know read only as a formality. I liked the *Sun-Times* as a child, because its tabloid size made it easier for me to hold. I paid attention to it because Daddy did, and because it seemed to me that everything in the world was happening all at once.

Daddy talked a lot about the state of the nation, and he liked watching and listening to other people talk about it, too. He watched the Sunday opinion shows as much as he was able. I grew up with the sound of Lawrence Spivak filling my house on Sundays; *Meet the Press* was Daddy's favorite show. The first big political discussions I recall—monologues delivered by my father as my mother listened with varying levels of interest—were all about the presidency of the United States. He had disliked Eisenhower's slow movement to protect black children in Little Rock, and he thought Nixon was a snake. (Even Daddy couldn't have guessed that later events would encourage him to revise his opinion of Nixon downward.) A Democrat to the core ever since the New Deal, he had admired FDR and felt even more strongly about Eleanor Roosevelt, especially her up-front support of Negroes, as in her response when Marian Anderson was denied permission to sing at Constitution Hall in Washington, D.C.

He liked John F. Kennedy, and thought it was significant that Kennedy was a Roman Catholic. That had a lot to do with why

Daddy announced to Mama one day that we were all going to be raised Catholic. For him, it was a strategic decision with great implications for our future—Daddy believed strongly in strategy. From where he sat, it seemed clear that if a Catholic could be elected president, Catholics would become very powerful and influential people. He had flirted with the idea of our becoming Jewish, since he regarded Jews as the other religious group with influential members—and also viewed them as the only group of white people he could be bothered with. You could talk to Jews and reach an understanding, Daddy always said, because they were the only white people who had been through anything like what colored people were going through.

Still, Kennedy's rise was persuasive, and so was the financial incentive of being Catholic when your children were going to be sent to Catholic school. Both my parents believed that nuns would really teach us, and tuition at Catholic schools was lower for Catholics than for non-Catholics.

That's how my mother came to sign up for catechism lessons at St. Ambrose Church at Forty-seventh and Ellis. I was old enough to sit quietly with her in class, and to study the green booklet I came to know as the Baltimore Catechism. All of us were eventually baptized on the same quiet afternoon in a room of the church equipped with a marble baptismal font. Each of us had to pick a "baptismal" name. If we had been infants, our given names would have been chosen with an eye toward the saints of the Catholic Church. I chose the name Barbara, because I liked the way it sounded. I also liked the ritual of acceptance into the Church. I loved the quiet and the peace there, the smell of incense and the glow of candles and the giant echo my little footsteps made. It all seemed very godly, and I was a little girl who did a lot of praying. Part of that came from my mother, who said her prayers in front of us nearly every night. She sang spirituals all the time, especially in the morning, as she worked by herself in the kitchen before any of us were up.

Mama was raised in the Pentecostal faith, but she had no special reservations about praying in a Catholic church; for her, it was all the same God. Still, the staid Latin hymns were not the songs she sang throughout the day. On Sunday, she tuned the television to *Jubilee Showcase* on Channel Seven. A white man named Sid Ordower was the host, and the show featured gospel singers from Chicago as well as parts of the South, including the show's "house" quartet, the Norfleet Brothers. Mama watched *Jubilee Showcase* for the same reasons many of our neighbors did: it felt familiar and personal, and it was a rare chance to see black people on television.

I learned to listen to both kinds of religious music. The Catholic hymns sounded angelic and otherworldly, a kind of visitation from on high. They were unfamiliar at first, but still incredibly beautiful. The gospel songs sounded in my head like the voices of old friends. They were vital and intense, the way people around me always seemed, and they had the added attraction of telling stories and issuing ultimatums: "Go tell that long-tongued liar, go tell that midnight rider, tell the gambler, rambler, backstabber—tell 'em: God almighty's gonna cut you down." They all seemed to offer immediate, melodic promises of justice.

But the Pentecostals had no schools to speak of, and as I turned six, in the spring of 1961, it was my parents' intention that I get a real education—something my father was convinced could never happen in the segregated Chicago public schools. He had spent hours listening to the news, mumbling under his breath about the superintendent of schools, and talking about the men in Chicago government he called "no-good sumbitches." That he would place me in the hands of such people was unthinkable. Instead, we were all placed—one by one—at the St. Ambrose School, in the firm grasp of the School Sisters of Notre Dame.

Chapter 2

In 1961, John Kennedy started the Peace Corps, a handful of African nations declared their independence, and the Freedom Riders began their mission to desegregate the cities of the South. None of these things was as noticeable to me as the change that came over our household that year. We still laughed, still played with each other and went to Drexel Park every afternoon with Mama, reaching for branches of what we called the thorn tree and tearing loose a few thorns with which to tease and terrorize each other. Mama still turned rope for me to jump in short spurts—my breathing was too labored for me to continue very long. I still watched *Here's Geraldine,* a local children's TV show with a foolish giraffe, and *Garfield Goose and Friends,* a cartoon show hosted by Frazier Thomas and featuring Garfield Goose, King of the United States.

What was different that summer was the sense of expectation: my brother and I were set to begin school in the fall. I was six, my brother barely five. But both of us could read, and after approaching the nuns about us, my mother was told to bring us in for registration in August. It was Daddy who took it upon himself to prepare us for our new lives as students. It was all well and good to play, he said, but soon playtime would be over.

"An education is the only thing that the white man can't take from you," he used to tell us. Daddy had always talked about white people, but this conversation was different. It was the first of a thousand such cautionary moments, in which he tried to make it clear that the stakes for my life were higher than I knew. I didn't know any white people then, except the few I would see in the stores on Forty-third Street. But even at six, I knew they ran the world. They were the people you saw doing everything interesting and important. They sang the songs (except for an occasional song by Nat King Cole) on WIND, the popular music station that my father listened to religiously. They read the news on television, they wrote the stories in the papers (if you didn't count the *Defender*). White people counted, and colored people didn't.

Daddy had other ideas. The white man was slick, he told us, always trying to put you in what he called "the trick bag," that dreaded place of low expectations and limited options. It didn't matter how hard you worked, or how well you did your job, my father believed. White people were determined to do wrong, could never be trusted, and, when push came to shove, would turn their backs on you in a heartbeat for someone white.

This was why, Daddy said with manic fervor, education was the most important thing in the world for a Negro to have. "You have to be able to outthink them. They can hate you all they want, but they can't dig in your head and take your brains." It was my father's burning desire that we learn enough to work with our heads, to do a white man's job one day. That's why things were going to be different for us. The most important difference was an end to television.

Daddy hated television, except for the news and a few select shows. More specifically, he hated the idea of children watching television. I doubt that he paid much attention to Newton Minow's famous speech earlier that year, castigating television as a "vast wasteland" before the National Association of Broadcasters. But if Daddy had heard it, he would have concurred. "You can't learn a damn thing from television," he raved. "That's what's wrong with all these niggers out here now, sitting on their asses in front of a TV instead of picking up a damn book." On school nights, Daddy decreed, television was off-limits. We were welcome to watch TV when we came home from school on Friday night, during the day on Saturday, and Sunday, too. But on Sunday at ten-fifteen P.M., when the local newscast was done, so was the television for another week. The only exception was the news, which Daddy always watched and which we were permitted to see as well, if anyone was interested. I was.

It wasn't the news I craved at age six or seven, or even a chance to watch TV or see the commercials. What drew me to the television set in the living room was the presence of my father, at home and without rage—or at least without rage directed at us. When he hunched over to watch Chet Huntley and David Brinkley talk about the growing tensions between Kennedy and Khrushchev, I saw a middle-aged man in his undershirt and boxer shorts making declarations about Russia—and not making them about my mother. I didn't really get why the United States and the Soviet Union were mad at each other. All I could tell was that Khrushchev was bad, and had threatened to bury us. I was a lot clearer about the sit-ins at lunch counters, about the beginning of the Freedom Rides through the South that year. Daddy raved loud and long about "those cracker bastards" who refused to let colored people vote or go to school. As he talked, angry at strangers instead of us, I felt a curious relief. But I felt scared and sad, too. As I looked at the pictures in *Jet* magazine of neatly dressed colored people being dragged along the ground, or having food dumped on them, just because they wanted to be in the same places as white people and do the same things, I had to wonder whether, in this thing, Daddy was right. Something *was* wrong with white people. Why were they like that?

On a hazy morning in September 1961, I walked with my mother and brother to the courtyard of 1014 East Forty-seventh Street—St. Ambrose School. As we arrived, boys and girls were already lining up for the morning procession into church for eight o'clock Mass. I was dressed in the blue-and-gray jumper and white blouse that were my uniform; a white lace scarf had already been carefully fastened to my head. A scarf was a requirement for girls. If you didn't have one, the nuns would help you make do with a Kleenex tissue, but the effort would earn you a disapproving look. I lined up with the first grade and went in to Mass; it was the first time I'd been in the church on a day other than Sunday.

I loved church from the start. St. Ambrose felt beautiful to me, reverent and quiet. The floor was red-and-white linoleum tile, shining as though water were continually poured over it. In two alcoves, one on either side of the sanctuary, small altars held rows of votive candles, which flickered in white and red glass holders. Perpendicular to the altars were the confessionals, each with two small doors of carved wood on either side of a larger door, where the priests heard neighborhood sins each Saturday afternoon.

Living as we did in the waning days before Vatican II, we attended the Latin Mass each morning. The Masses were all the same: the priest in glowing vestments in the color of the liturgical season, his back turned to those of us standing in the pews. The consecration was my favorite part. I knew from the catechism that this was the magic part, where bread and wine were turned into the body and blood of Christ. A lucky altar boy rang a cluster of bells to signal the moment of transubstantiation.

Church was everything my house was not: quiet, polished, respectful, and orderly. And school, it turned out, was much the same. After Mass, we all filed into our classrooms and stood by our desks. We opened the day with prayer and the Pledge of Allegiance; religion was the first class of the day. Both my brother and I were placed in the first grade with Sister Bernice, a solemn older nun who made it clear that she expected order. She produced workbooks and proceeded to pass them out. I had a big, thick pencil to print with, and the pulpy, newsprint-like paper that was so popular in elementary schools of the 1960s. Sister asked us to do the first page of exercises in the workbook—quietly, of course.

I looked at the first page with disbelief and disappointment. These were *baby* words! *Cat, dog, hat*—I already knew those little words. I thought school meant I was going to learn big words. I looked around to catch my brother's eye, but he wasn't looking in my direction. I filled in the blanks and looked up, expecting that I would get to move on to something else. But Sister was patrolling the classroom, and my new classmates were hard at work, their heads bowed.

It didn't take long for my restlessness and disappointment to start feeding on each other. I kept scanning the classroom for something to do. Finally, I saw a copy of the *Sun-Times* on Sister's desk. Reading the paper would give me something to do while I was waiting for everybody else. So—to the horror of Sister Bernice—I got up from my seat, took the newspaper off her desk to look through, and went right back to my desk. I was reprimanded, of course, though not severely. I think she was too shocked to really punish me. It was only a few weeks after that incident when the principal, Sister Panis, entered my first-grade classroom in the middle of the day and asked for me. Some of the other children giggled, but I was scared. I couldn't think of anything I could have done that would get me in trouble with the principal.

I was told to collect my coat and my lunch box from what we called the cloakroom, though not a one of us had ever seen a cloak. I followed Sister Panis to the classroom next door, Sister

Marcille's second-grade class. Sister Marcille was young—perhaps in her early twenties—and even prettier than Sister Panis. I put my things away as directed and took my newly assigned seat. It turned out that I wasn't in trouble at all. I was being promoted to the second grade.

The children in the second grade didn't look too happy to see me. They thought I was a big baby. Worse, through the grapevine I had already been labeled as the worst thing a little girl could be: I was "smart." I didn't know how difficult that would be; I was too happy about being in a different grade than my brother. Mama and Daddy would be proud. Best of all, I'd finally get to read real stories in real books, not those dumb baby words. But it wasn't that simple. When it came to reading, I was still bored. To help me adjust, the nuns placed me in reading classes with the fifth grade. Later, Mrs. Goldschmidt, who worked as an aide in the principal's office, was my private reading teacher. We sat and read together every afternoon for a while.

I think they feared that school would become dull for me. The danger, however, was not that I would become bored with school, but afraid of it. I was never frightened inside the classroom. Always, I was happiest with books and my teachers, learning things I wanted to know. But on the playground, in the lunchroom, at recess, I was a pariah. I was younger, smarter, and much more awkward than the other second-grade girls. Worst of all, I was a good girl who liked being good. Amid the serene structures of St. Ambrose, where no one yelled and the rules were always the same, doing the right thing was easy. My classmates chafed against rules they viewed as mean and strict. But life with my father had already given me a different perspective; these kids didn't know what mean was.

So I always did my homework, and answered the extra-credit questions, and read the optional books. My desire to earn the praise of the nuns brought added benefits at home: nothing shielded me more effectively from my father's tantrums than the presence of homework. It wasn't that he didn't continue to curse and threaten, only that he did less of it. When he stalked into the kitchen and found me doing homework at the kitchen table, my workbooks stacked around me like a paper fortress, he let me be. Those few hours of homework provided the lion's share of whatever peace I had at home.

But what saved me at home put me in jeopardy at school. Even at seven, girls have cliques, and I wasn't in any of them. The girls in the in-groups had nothing but contempt for me. To them, I was a nauseating little Goody Two-shoes. To me, they were wild girls who cursed and talked back to teachers—two practices that would have earned me the beating of my life, and not just from my father. My mother, whose dreams of schoolteaching had faded but never died, made it clear that teachers were always right. She visited our teachers often, and advised them—should we do something they didn't approve of—to "beat their behinds, then send them to me." For my mother to hit us meant we had crossed a line into the unforgivable, and any spanking from her was more psychically than physically painful.

Thus I was completely unable to join with this small group of junior anarchists, even if I'd wanted to. That made me a marked woman. The final straw came after the annual standardized tests given to all the students at St. Ambrose. When the results were posted, I was number one in my class in every subject except math, and even there I was in the top five. That's when girls started telling me they were going to "meet me outside."

Two or three of the girls ganged up on me, out of sight of the nuns, and hit and scratched me and ripped my uniform. I went home disheveled and crying, and my mother was furious. She asked me why I didn't fight back; I told her there were too many of them. There were, too, but I also didn't want to fight them; I didn't want to fight anybody. I'd seen enough fighting already to last for years. The next day, my mother was waiting at the gate for me after school; it was a ritual she continued for years afterward in an effort to keep me safe.

Part of me was terribly lonely; I wondered what it would be like to be popular. But part of me realized popularity would be pointless. Even if I were the most popular girl at St. Ambrose, my father wouldn't allow me to go anywhere or do anything with anybody. The one girl at school I could talk to was Barbara, who lived about five blocks away from us in a townhouse development. Her parents had scraped together enough money to buy a unit in a low-rise community constructed of cinder block, but still with a little front yard and backyard. Barbara and I shared a great passion for all things religious. We sat next to each other at morning Mass and wrote nearly invisible notes to each other with our fingers on the polished pews.

I could talk to Barbara, but I was told by my father to stay away from the rest of the kids. He was right about some of the girls, and I didn't want to be anywhere near them. But I could tell that there were a couple of girls who would have been my friends if I could have spent any time with them. One of the girls, Denise Young, was tall and light-skinned; she had a younger brother about the same age as my brother, and a mother who was almost as nice as mine. They lived only a half block away, on Ellis Avenue, in a great Victorian rooming house with a massive staircase I had seen one afternoon, on a surreptitious visit there.

One Saturday afternoon in spring, when Mama said we could go outside, I led a secret excursion to Denise's house with my brother and sister; my baby brother was too young to come with us. We spent the afternoon running around in the wilderness of the building's backyard. The old fencing behind the house had fallen apart, but even my inexperienced eye could see that there had been a garden there. Weeds and flowers bloomed together in profusion, and what once had been an arbor held the remains of old grapevines. There was even an old blackberry bush that in a few months would be thick with fruit. I recognized it because there was one just like it in their front yard. On Sundays during the summer and fall on the way to church, we used to shake that bush and eat the berries that fell from it.

We returned home a few hours later, sure that we had managed to sneak in a couple of hours of fun. But my heart dropped when I saw my father's old car parked on Forty-fifth Street. He wasn't supposed to be home yet, not for hours. Suddenly the glow of the afternoon was gone, replaced by the sick dread I had known most of my life.

"Where have you little niggers been?" He was standing in his room, just inside the back door, a leather belt already in his hand. If I'd been alone, I would have lied and said I was just out, walking around. But my brother was an inveterate truth-teller, and he confessed at once that we had been at Denise's house.

"What did I tell you about running around with these niggers out here? None of them are no damn good!"

All of us had started to cry, mostly out of fear of the beating that was coming. But I was angry, too. There was nothing wrong with Denise and her mother and brother. They were nice. And we hadn't done anything wrong. My mother came in from the kitchen, attempting for a moment to intercede.

"They wasn't doing nothin' but playing, Daddy," she said. "They just kids; kids are gonna play." Not for the first time, I wondered why she called him Daddy, when he wasn't her daddy.

"You don't know shit about raising kids, you ignorant bitch! You ain't got time to take care of these children. You too busy loping the streets and running after your men! You ain't shit, either!"

By now his voice was loud, the spittle flying from his mouth as his tirade continued. He reached for me and I screamed as the doubled-up belt fell across the backs of my legs, leaving a band of raised skin.

It was a weird dance we did as he beat me, his calloused hand grasping one of my wrists to keep me in place, my wild flailing movements to get away from him, the welts that formed across my other arm as I sought to block the blows that couldn't be stopped. Above my tears I could hear Brother and Linda crying, the anticipation of pain even worse than the actual beating. Abruptly, he let me go.

"Now get your little ass out of here," he said, and reached for my brother. Incredibly, Hiawatha stopped him and asked if he could pray first. I was unbelievably angry, not at my father, but at Brother. What was there to pray about? As he sank to his knees, amid my father's scorn at his "little sissy ass," I felt my disgust begin to rise. It was bad enough to get beaten, humiliating enough to cry. But to voluntarily get on your knees in front of this man—it was just too much. Each night, we had to do it, when we said our formal prayers before bed: "Oh, my God, I am heartily sorry for having offended Thee, and I detest all my sins, because I dread the loss of heaven and the pains of hell, but most of all because they offended Thee, my God, who art all good and deserving of all my love. . . ."

I never thought of them as real prayers. I saved my real prayers for late at night, when I lay in bed trying to sleep, and trying to figure out why my life was the way it was, why, if God loved me, he let Daddy hurt us and scare us all the time. I would never have anything real to say to God in front of Daddy. As he began beating Brother, I went into the bathroom to put cold water on the welts that covered me. When I saw Denise at school the following week, she wanted to know when we were going to come over again. I said I didn't know. We passed her house every day, but we never went there again.

I didn't know much about the South, except that it was where both Mama and Daddy were born. I also knew both of them had sworn never to return. Daddy had always said he'd rather be dead and in hell than live in Arkansas again. His grandfather, he said, was full-blooded Cherokee, and was made to leave his home and walk to Arkansas. He used to visit his grandfather in the little house he lived in on a small parcel of land. Daddy's face would light up with remembered glee as he described his grandfather's insistence that no white person would ever come near him again. He kept a rifle with him to back up that promise, and Daddy used to tell us how his grandfather would start shooting just as soon as anybody white appeared.

I knew Daddy shared his grandfather's sentiments. Each night, we watched the news from the Southern battlegrounds, and Daddy cursed white people. He believed there were exceptions, and was willing to admit all white people weren't alike. But he continued to believe the biggest proportion of them were "no damn good," and he pointed to the television pictures for evidence to reinforce his own experience.

It was pretty hard to refute my father; as far as I could tell, white people surely hated us. One day I was sitting with my mother as we watched a group of white police set dogs and hoses on a group of marchers. I remember watching the water blow one man down the street like a pile of old rags. Finally I asked Mama, "Why do the white people hate us?" She didn't have an answer for me, and said so. I couldn't figure out what it was we could have done to make them so angry with us.

For all his anger and his cynicism about white people, Daddy believed in America—at least on paper. He talked about the Declaration of Independence and the Constitution at every opportunity, if only to point out the error of white folks' ways. White people wrote the rules, then changed them when they realized those rules might have to apply to us. I looked up the Declaration of Independence so that I could read it. I didn't understand all the ornate language, but I did understand the beautiful, heroic part: "We hold these truths to be self-evident, that all men are created equal . . ."

I already knew that all white people weren't the same. There were still a few white families living in Kenwood, though by that time, the neighborhood was 85 percent Negro. St. Ambrose was nearly 100 percent black. Only the priests, the nuns, and a few straggling neighbors from the old days remained in the parish.

For a while, there were a couple of white girls in school with us. One older girl, named Cynthia, was big in every conceivable way, and she delighted in picking on other children. Once, during recess, she got into an argument with several of us that culminated in her admonition that we should "act our age, not our color." I wasn't completely sure where she got that from, but I knew from the way she said it that it didn't sound good. I went to Sister Panis to complain about it, and Cynthia was called into her office shortly thereafter. She never spoke to me again, only glared. And soon she was simply gone.

There was an elderly white couple, the Fitzgeralds, who went to the nine o'clock Mass each Sunday, just as we did. We looked for them each week after church was over. I sought them out because they were friendly, and because I could tell they admired us and my mother's way of raising us. And with the mercenary heart of a child, I especially loved that they often had a shiny quarter for each of us, or a dollar bill that they gave to my mother so that we could have ice cream or some other treat. The first few times the Fitzgeralds made this gesture, my mother tried to refuse the money. But they wouldn't hear of it; they seemed either to like us, or to be amazed by us. They always had something nice to say about how we looked, how well-dressed and well-behaved we were, how smart we seemed. Theirs were the kinds of comments that would make me initially suspicious now. At the time, I thought they were just friendly, decent people—they seemed to go out of their way to be kind.

Daddy, however, insisted that white people were faking. They were always polite to your face, especially up North. But they were sure to be calling you a nigger when they got home. "White people aren't your friends," he would preach. "The only friend you've got is a dollar."

As much as I loved school, I loved it more as the holidays approached. The weather got crisper, the air and the light seemed altered. It felt good being dressed warmly in the cool Chicago air. I looked forward to the approach of snow, and wondered if we'd get a white Thanksgiving. Even the art classes changed. Mimeographed drawings of broomsticks and witches' hats and jack-o'-lanterns evolved into turkeys and Pilgrims and the harvest cornucopia. These were the weeks I most wished for the biggest box of Crayola crayons—sixty-four different colors and a sharpener, too.

It was a kind of suspended time: the newness of the school year had worn off, the major holidays of church and state were approaching, but not yet begun. Halloween was only marginally important to me, since we were not allowed to trick-or-treat in any but the most limited way. And because my father's sister Nancy had been horribly poisoned years earlier, Daddy had a phobia about our eating food that came from other people. So Halloween was more a formality than anything else. Besides, the church captured all our attention during the last days of October. My favorite celebration was the Feast of Christ the King. The church had a solemn afternoon ceremony, in which the girls all dressed in white and walked in a great processional around the church, behind the priests and the acolytes, the censer filling the room with the smoke of incense. The entire ceremony was in Latin, and though I understood very little of it, I understood its ritual beauty and felt intoxicated by the hymn we sang, over and over: "Pange lingua, gloriosi. . . ."

It was the fall of 1963. I was in Mrs. Howard's third-grade class that year. Mrs. Howard, an elderly white woman with a benign manner, was one of the few lay teachers in the school. For weeks, we had been preoccupied by preparations for the Feast of Christ the King and, a few weeks after that, the school's Thanksgiving play, in which each grade would have a part. We were all in the school auditorium one afternoon, rehearsing the Thanksgiving play, when Mrs. Howard was summoned from the room. When she came back, she had a peculiar look on her face, and asked us to return to our classroom seats at once.

A few minutes later, the announcement was made: President Kennedy was dead. We were sent home early, but there was none of the sneaky happiness of a surprise day off. People who were on the street were crying, or looked stunned. More often, the steps and doorways of the houses and apartment buildings seemed deserted; everyone who was at home was glued to the television set.

Our whole family sat in miserable silence in front of the television all weekend long. Mama didn't say much, and even Daddy was speechless by comparison with his usual bluster and outrage. I was terrified. Everybody knew that John Kennedy was a great man, I thought, but they shot him anyway, for no good reason. How did we know whether we were safe? If somebody that important could get killed, I wondered, couldn't we get killed, too? I asked Mama and Daddy if we were going to get shot. They both said no, nobody wanted to shoot us.

"You know Hoover had it done," my father said grimly to the television. J. Edgar Hoover, the head of the FBI since there'd been an FBI, was my father's number one suspect. Daddy said Hoover didn't know us, so there was nothing to worry about.

We all watched as Kennedy's coffin was rolled through the streets of Washington, and as he lay in state in the Capitol rotunda. So many people crying, just the way I was crying, I thought. Lots of black people coming to see him lie there, standing in line for hours. I wished I could go, wished I could see him and say good-bye; it seemed so important. The saddest part of all was watching the funeral, looking at Jackie Kennedy standing there with her children. Caroline was only a little bit younger than I was, and I felt bad for her. Her daddy seemed like a nice man; whenever I saw pictures of him with his children, they were always laughing. What an awful thing to have someone kill your father when he was nice, I thought. When her little brother gave a salute on the steps of St. Matthew's Cathedral, following the funeral mass, it seemed like the saddest thing in the world.

In school later that year, we had to try to write a poem about anything we wanted, and so I wrote a poem about President

Kennedy dying. It was the first thing I ever wrote to show anybody else. I remember the first of the three verses.

When President Kennedy passed away,
The world was very sad that day.
The United States was wrapped up in grief,
At the death of their commander in chief.

There was more, about how young he was and how nice he seemed, and how he had to be in heaven. I sat at the kitchen table for hours working on it, looking up words that would say what I meant, then trying to find a way to make them rhyme. My habit of reading reference books for fun was paying off; I had a dictionary and an old paperback thesaurus to find the words I wanted.

When I turned in the poem, my teacher asked me who had helped me with the words. I told her I had done it myself. "Where did you learn a word like *span*?" she asked me, quoting from another of the verses. "It was in the dictionary," I said. I'd picked it because it let me talk about the fact that the president didn't live a very long time, and because it rhymed with *man*. But I didn't tell her all that, in case she thought I was trying to get smart with her. She just looked at me a little strangely, and told me to sit down.

I asked Mama if I could send the poem to Mrs. Kennedy so she would know how sorry I was about her husband. She said yes, and bought me a stamp. I printed the poem over again on a clean piece of notebook paper so it wouldn't have any mistakes in it, folded it up to fit one of the small envelopes Mama had from Woolworth's, and put the stamp on the envelope and mailed it to the White House, because I didn't know where else to send it.

A few weeks later, Mama met me after school. She was very excited. "You got a letter back from the White House," she said. I couldn't believe it; I thought she was kidding until she handed me the large, flat package. When I opened it, there was a letter from Mrs. Kennedy, thanking me for my poem and telling me that it would be saved and placed one day in the John F. Kennedy Library that the family planned to build in Boston. There was also a black-and-white picture of the Kennedy family, taken before the president was killed.

Even Daddy was excited about my news. He told all his friends, and Mama told all the neighbors and showed them the picture. I walked around with the letter all that day, reading it over and over again. It's long gone now, and I realize in retrospect that it probably wasn't from Mrs. Kennedy, but from a member of her staff. But none of that mattered then. What mattered was that I had written something to express the way I felt about something that was important to me. I had sent it to someone I'd never met. That person had read it and liked it and wanted to keep it, even though she had never met me. It was a good feeling, to think of her reading my words.

Now that I'd had a taste of writing and being read, I wanted more. But my desire for total immersion was met with exasperation by my parents. No matter who had read my poem, no matter how many more poems I wrote, I still had a life that had nothing to do with rhymes or words looked up in a battered dictionary.

If my weekday life was filled with study and concentration, it was the weekend that contained the elements of the real world. But in the summer of 1964, and for many summers after that, there were precious moments of freedom amid the work of the household.

My mother, the quintessential child of Southern sharecroppers, believed that though you might not have much, what you did have should be clean. She allowed us the luxury of sleeping late on Saturday morning—and late to my mother meant eight-thirty or so. By that time, she'd already been up for hours, washed one load of clothes and hung them out in the backyard, or draped them over the clothesline in the back room. By the time we got up, bacon was frying, grits were cooking, and she had put toast under the broiler, or fried it in one of the big cast-iron skillets. The jelly jars we used for glasses were already on the table, filled with Ann Page orange juice and a healthy dose of cod-liver oil. And as we stumbled to the table, still half asleep, she was already parceling out work assignments.

There were four of us, and each child was responsible for one room. If you were too young to clean, you still had to help. Absolutely everyone had something to do, and nothing else could happen that day until you had done your job. The bedroom and living room smelled like Old English lemon oil or red oil (depending on which was most recently on sale). The kitchen and bathroom smelled like Pine Sol and Clorox. From the youngest to the oldest, we wielded dust rags and mops and brooms until the dirt was gone. Mama insisted that we all—including the boys—learn to do everything.

I was never in love with housework, and had declared to my mother sometime earlier that there was no reason for me to learn how to do all this because when I grew up, I was going to hire a maid. Mama was unimpressed, and suggested that since the maid had not yet arrived, I would still have to do my share. In summer, though, I raced through my work rather than complain, and urged my siblings to do the same. The sooner we were finished, after all, the sooner we could go.

We all knew that when we finished doing what we had to do, we could cajole my mother into taking us to the library, with a trip to the playground afterward. The library was the part I was most interested in. As soon as we were through cleaning—which often involved a frantic hunt for library books that had fallen under our beds or behind the bathtub—Mama would tell us to wash up and put on decent clothes. While we did that, she would go to the second drawer of the dresser that sat in our kitchen, beneath a mirror. The dresser had long been painted over to conceal the worn and peeling veneer, but we had already dusted it and put a clean dresser scarf on top. In the drawer was the old black felt pocketbook, the kind of purse I used to envision my mother carrying when she was out on a date, when she was free, when both she and the purse were new.

The pocketbook was only serviceable now, a repository for the really important records of our household. Mama kept our birth certificates there, and vaccination cards from the Chicago Board of Health. She kept the books of food stamps there, extracting a book each week before she shopped for food, and the green cards for medical care when she needed to take us to the doctor. But the pieces of paper she stored there that were most important to me were five buff cards she kept in a zippered pocket near the clasp. Each of them had one of our names on it, typewritten, and a red expiration date in one corner, and at the bottom were the words CHICAGO PUBLIC LIBRARY.

A trip to the library was like a great excursion to a different country. To get there, we had to walk a mile. But the distance between where we lived and where we were going was much greater. To get there we traveled beyond the usual parameters of school and church and the shopping strip we frequented, into the manicured lawns and gardens of Hyde Park. I loved the walk as much as the destination itself. In the middle of the anger that was my home, and the upheaval of a changing world in which it seemed I had no place, our semimonthly excursions to the library were a piece of perfection. I had around me at one time all the people I loved best—my mother and brothers and sister—and all the things I loved best—quiet, space, and books.

We went to the T. B. Blackstone Library, on Forty-ninth Street and Blackstone Avenue, not far from Lake Michigan and the former home of the Oriental Institute of the University of Chicago. The library is nestled in a far corner; you could easily miss the building if you didn't know what you were looking for. But once you were inside, you could never mistake it for anything else. We passed through two sets of heavy brass doors to the lobby of the library, a great domed entrance with a floor of mosaic tile and a ceiling adorned with what I used to imagine were the angels of books. They were great gilded figures armed with harps and with scrolls and other instruments of learning. All we could hear was the steady hum of an electric fan—a big rotating floor model that swept the hallway and fluttered the papers on the bulletin board near the door—and the industrial clunk-thud of the machine at the checkout desk that recorded the date each book was due.

If we turned right, we could see an alcove with tables; this led, in turn, to a spacious reading room, filled with shelves of periodicals and adorned with a gigantic and ancient globe that sat in front of the largest windows. At some point during every visit, I found my way into that room to touch the globe, to finger the ridges and the painted canvas already frayed and separating from its sphere. I liked to look at Africa, with the coded colors of the different countries like the Belgian Congo and Rhodesia, and try to remember which countries were fighting to be free like we were. I had heard Daddy talking about it, arguing with the television as someone discussed it on a news show. And I had seen pictures on the news of people with no shirts on, gathered together marching. But I didn't really know anything about Africa except what I saw in the Tarzan movies, which I watched a lot, but thought were really strange. (Why did that white man live in a tree?)

More often, though, we turned left, toward the card catalog and the librarians' desk, and a long corridor that led to the children's room of the library. The adult sections were suspended above the corridor on the library's second level, but Mama never went up there. Reading was as hard for my mother as it was easy for me and my brother. She used her card mostly to take out books for me that the librarian wouldn't let me have because she said they were for adults. I wanted to argue, but Mama wouldn't let me. She simply checked out the books and gave them to me when we got home.

Mostly, though, I found stacks of books to read in the young adult section. While Mama sat with my little brother and sister, Hiawatha and I roamed the children's room at will. He gravitated to the space and missile books, which I thought were boring and stupid. I loved the storybooks—all the fairy tales—and later I began to read books of mythology, working my way from the Greek and Roman myths, which I didn't really like all that much, to the Norse and Egyptian myths, which completely captured my imagination. I spent weeks reading and rereading the stories of Thor and Loki, then switched to reading about Isis and Osiris and Ra and the great architects of the pyramids, who were buried to keep them from revealing the location of the tombs they had designed.

When I wasn't reading about myths, I was reading about science: not the missiles and spaceships Brother preferred, but the birds and the bees—literally. I brought home a giant book of birds and searched the skies and trees for anything other than robins and pigeons. And I read about bees because I liked the idea that all of them listened to the queen, and couldn't go on without her. I went through a phase of loving books with practical science experiments, and used up a whole bottle of white vinegar by pouring it on the sides of our apartment building to prove that it was constructed of limestone. It seems that vinegar bubbles when it comes in contact with limestone, so I spent an afternoon making little dribbling, fizzy sections all over one side of the house.

One Saturday, as I wandered through the young adult section, I saw a title: *Little Women,* by Louisa May Alcott. I could tell from looking at the shelf that she'd written a lot of books, but I didn't know anything about her. I had learned from experience that titles weren't everything. A book that sounded great on the shelf could be dull once you got it home, and every bad book I brought home meant one less book to read until we went back in two weeks. So I sat in a chair near the shelves to skim the first paragraphs.

"Christmas won't be Christmas without any presents," grumbled Jo, lying on the rug.

"It's so dreadful to be poor!" sighed Meg, looking down at her old dress.

"I don't think it's fair for some girls to have plenty of pretty things, and other girls nothing at all," added little Amy, with an injured sniff.

"We've got Father and Mother and each other," said Beth contentedly from her corner.

It was a good thing I'd already decided on some other books to take home, because I didn't look through the rest of the section that day. I read and read and read *Little Women* until it was time to walk home, and, except for a few essential interruptions like sleeping and eating (Mama had long ago banned books from the dinner table), I would not put it down until the end. Even the freedom to watch weekend television held no appeal for me in the wake of Alcott's story. It was about girls, for one thing, girls who could almost be like me, especially Jo. It seemed to me a shame that she wasn't black; then our similarity would be complete. She loved to read, she loved to make up plays, she hated acting ladylike, she had a dreadful temper. I had found a kindred spirit.

We would stop on the walk home to play in Farmer's Field, a big playground with sprinklers and swings and monkey bars and merry-go-rounds. I had never really been in the habit of playing much; any kind of exercise made it hard for me to breathe, and by this time, my sedentary habits were ingrained. So while Mama sat and watched my siblings, I sat absorbed in my treasures of the afternoon. The only sounds you could hear were the voices of other children, and the whispery rustle of the wind through the big trees all around, and the faint hiss of water from the children's sprinkler. Everything smelled warm and green, and I could be content to sit on the bench forever, if only I had enough to read.

But eventually, Mama would say it was time to go, and we would make our way back across Forty-seventh Street toward home. By the time we got back, it would be five or six in the afternoon, and Daddy might already be in the house, lying in bed, reading the paper or the racing form and listening to the news on the radio. If we were lucky, he was only interested in what kinds of books we'd gotten from the library. If he went back to reading the paper, chances were fair that the rest of the evening would proceed without incident. Every now and then, he would want a demonstration evening, with my brother or me reading out loud to him. Or he would decide it was time to find out whether we had memorized our multiplication tables. He'd had my mother print them out on the cardboard inserts from the stockings she bought. The cardboard held up better than notebook paper, and it was cheaper besides.

Sometimes we would have to recite our threes or our sevens. I used to wonder why he would never pick easy ones, like twos or fives, which I could figure out in my head even though I might not have memorized them. But Daddy rarely did that. I often thought he picked the ones we were unlikely to know so he'd have something to yell or beat us about. Sometimes he'd simply blurt one out: "What's nine times seven?" "Three times eight?" And if we were wrong, if we took longer than he liked, off went the television for the evening, away went the books we'd all picked out so carefully. Instead, we were seated at the kitchen table as though we were on the electric chair, our heads bent over cardboard. I was usually the one sniffling, trying not to cry. I hated math anyway, and my father's obsession with memorization wasn't helping me one bit. But if he caught me crying, I was likely to get a beating, presumably so Daddy could give me "something to cry about."

In an hour or so, as bedtime approached, Mama usually attempted to run interference on those evenings when we felt under house arrest. She used plausible reasons: I need to wash the girls' hair and press it for church; Ro needs to polish her shoes and wash out her slip. Eventually, after another pop quiz, I would be paroled into the mundane duties of preparing for Mass the next morning, tasks that felt like freedom to me. One reason my father was usually persuaded to back off was his own weariness, and the necessity of his getting up to go to Maxwell Street the next morning.

Sometimes nothing at all was wrong on a Saturday night, and we went through our preparations for church as a matter of course. Our hair was washed in the sink (we never did have a shower), usually with Prell, and towel dried. As my sister and I sat in front of the stove, Mama would do our hair, pressing the damp strands with hot combs and greasing our scalps with Dixie Peach pomade. Mama hardly ever burned us, and even then it was typically only with steam from the contact between the hot comb and our damp hair. We had to lay out our clothes for the next day, too; Mama wouldn't stand for goofing around on Sunday morning. And even though we took a bath every other day as long as the water was hot, we certainly had to take one on Saturday night before we went to bed. Nobody looking like a bum was going to church with Mama.

On Sundays, Daddy was gone long before we got up for nine o'clock Mass. He had risen at three A.M. in his work clothes and headed for a garage where he kept an old truck filled with odds and ends he tried to sell each Sunday in the open market of Maxwell Street. The earlier he arrived, the better the spot he'd get to sell his goods. Daddy and everybody else we knew called it "Jewtown," a reference to the now-dwindling numbers of Jewish merchants who had once sold their wares from the storefronts in the area. He would be home by noon, sometimes even earlier. Serious shoppers were out on Maxwell Street by seven A.M. and finished with their business by ten A.M. or so. By noon, only tourists and amateurs roamed the market area, and Daddy had even less patience with them than with dedicated customers.

His absence made the house peaceful on those mornings; we could dress and comb our hair and grease our legs without disturbance. Mama usually started dinner: she would place a pan of chicken and dressing in the stove on low heat as we were about to leave, so that dinner would be done by the time we got home. There was no time for breakfast, and no need, in any case; those of us able to receive communion were not allowed to eat before Mass anyway. So the morning was taken up with brushing our teeth and listening to *Jubilee Showcase* before we gathered up our prayer books and scarves and gloves at about eight-thirty to walk the three blocks to church.

I was conscious that many of our neighbors were on the lookout for us each Sunday morning. Even people who didn't really know us knew our little troupe by sight: a big pretty woman with carefully pressed hair, a simple dress and coat and stiletto-heeled shoes of patent leather, herding four young children down the street in front of her. Our four brown faces were shiny with Vaseline; it made us all look crisp and new. Mama's face never shone; it was covered instead with a thin layer of Overton's face powder, which she applied with a puff. Just before we left the house, she would add a single coat of bright red lipstick.

We were Mrs. Bray's children, and people said good morning to us and to our mother all along the way. Especially if the weather was nice, we saw several of our elderly neighbors, including Mr. Johnson, who sat on his stoop on Ellis a half-block or so from us. He was always friendly, with a big smile and a wave, especially to me. We passed St. James Methodist Church, where my brother went to his Cub Scout meetings, and walked up the stone steps of St. Ambrose to take our place in the pews. In the summer months, we sat with Mama; during the school year, we were expected to sit with our classmates. Each of us clutched a Sunday offering envelope, with the name of the church printed on it, each sealed tight with a single dime inside. Sunday Mass was as much a school requirement as daily Mass, and anyone who didn't attend got demerits—unless you "made up" your absence by attending another Mass that day and having the attending priest sign your church bulletin, to be presented to your teacher the next morning. For the most part, we did not miss.

Once Mass was over, we walked back home, to be met by the smell of cooking food and the sound of a Sunday news show. You would know whether someone black was a guest by the way my father sat up in bed, talking to the television more than he usually did, shouting out a "Ho, now!" when a guest got somebody particularly well-told-off. While Daddy watched, we changed our clothes and hung around, hoping to gauge his mood from the discussions on TV. If he was too tired, or too angry, we would spend the day reading and playing. But if the weather was sunny, or Daddy had a desire for company, it would be a day to go for a drive.

Going for a Sunday drive was the only thing we did that other families seemed to do, too. After Mama had fed us all and we had washed and dried the dishes, we piled into the car and Daddy headed for Forty-seventh Street and Lake Park toward the entrance to Lake Shore Drive. From where we lived, Lake Shore Drive was a major artery to the expressways to the West Side, where both my father and mother had sisters living.

Daddy's sister, my aunt Marie, lived in a tiny house that fronted the Congress Parkway near Presbyterian–St. Luke's Hospital and the Cook County Hospital. She and my uncle Barney had four children, all much older than we were, and their small home was decorated in a fussy, ornate style—from elaborate chandeliers and lamps with crystal teardrops to sectional sofas covered with clear, industrial-strength plastic that stuck to your thighs. Still, Aunt Marie and Uncle Barney were very proud of their little home, and were the soul of hospitality whenever we arrived.

By contrast, Mama's sister, Mattie (or Aunt Teddy, as we called her), lived in a series of apartment buildings. Eventually, she and her family moved to a gigantic, brand-new housing project on

Lake Street called the Henry Horner Homes. The big apartment seemed airy and clean, with three bedrooms for eight people, a kitchen with brand-new appliances, and sparkling linoleum on the floor. The only drawback I could ever see was the fact that their bedrooms all faced the El; every few minutes—night and day—you could hear the screech and rattle of the speeding Lake Street train. My cousins said it didn't bother them, and after a while, I scarcely noticed it when we would visit.

I was envious of both places—the way they looked in comparison to our shabby little apartment, the way Daddy constantly made reference to how something looked at Aunt Marie's or Aunt Teddy's house. All Daddy's comments were couched in his best company voice. I was always impressed by how ordinary Daddy seemed when we would go out to visit family. It was one of the most frightening things about him, almost as though someone else were inhabiting his body, waiting to change into this other man. I had learned to recognize the bitterness in his voice whenever he talked of what others had that he did not. I had learned to listen for it as a way of preparing myself for what might lie ahead. If anything he saw or heard or felt were to trigger his virulent ambitions, we might hear about his covetous disappointment all night long.

Sometimes it did not even take a visit to our relatives to set him off, only a seemingly innocuous drive through the parts of South Chicago into which we rarely ventured. One particular neighborhood, Pill Hill, always captured my father's attention. Perhaps he was so drawn to it because it was a black middle-class neighborhood. Daddy would ease his ancient Buick down the tree-lined streets of East End Avenue or Eberhart or Cornell Avenue and look at the neat little bungalows with flowers and awnings, the gleaming picture windows adorned with an elegant lamp or with tasteful, concealing draperies. Street after street, he would drive and talk about how good these people's lives must be, how close he had come to living just this way, how he had never made it because it was all my mother's fault, how she would never support him in anything he wanted to do. I couldn't decide if it was his gambling she wouldn't support, or his fragile entrepreneurial efforts. But whatever the idea, it was my mother's fault that he had failed.

"Your mother never wanted anything; she never wanted shit. She never tried to help me like a woman's supposed to do."

My mother always sat in the front seat, resigned to the escalating tirade of abuse. "What was I supposed to do?" she sometimes asked him.

Daddy never seemed to have an answer, only a steaming rage that grew with each mile he drove. Occasionally he would stop the car to survey a street, his big hands leaving the wheel in an encompassing sweep as he pointed to the rows of little homes and the neatly dressed children on skates or bicycles.

"You all should have had this. This is how you should have been living—not that shithole we're in. This is where you should be."

When I was smaller, I used to try to console him, to say to him that it didn't matter about not living there, that nobody really cared about that. But Daddy met my childish efforts with a fury I now recognize as pain and shame. "I care!" he would scream, his voice filling the interior of the car as he floored the gas pedal and drove toward the expressway in a rage. He would always begin by taking out his anger on the car, hurtling toward home at breakneck speed, frightening my mother as he wove in and out of traffic, cursing every car in his way.

I hid my face in fear of a dreadful accident. I clutched the armrest and darted looks at my equally frightened brothers and sister. I wanted to explain the rest of what I always tried to tell him; I wanted to say that I didn't care where we lived, if only he would stop fighting and yelling and being angry all the time. I didn't care how we lived, if only he would stop scaring me.

Sometimes the wild driving would calm him down; sometimes it wouldn't. Sometimes Daddy would continue the fight into the evening, sometimes he would take to his bed and stay away from the rest of us as the evening went on. We would enter the house in silence and take off our good Sunday clothes, sit down in the living room to watch the last of our rationed television shows. There were the automatic favorites: always *Lassie* and *My Favorite Martian*. Always *The Ed Sullivan Show*, because it was another chance to see colored people on TV.

Sunday night was cake and ice-cream night, too. Sometimes Mama would have made a cake from Betty Crocker mix she'd found on sale. Sometimes she would buy a pound cake. There were times when Daddy would bring home cake from Maxwell Street for us to have later. And the four shiny quarters we often got from the Fitzgeralds usually went toward four pints of Walgreens ice cream for a dollar, or a half-gallon for a bit more, when it went on sale.

We had an ice-cream scoop with a thick black handle, and Mama would use it to place a perfect sphere on top of our slice of cake. And one of us was always responsible for taking some in to Daddy if he was not at the kitchen table with us. As soon as the last drop was scraped up out of our bowls, it was time to get ready for bed and for school the next day. Books and clothes had to be laid out, teeth brushed, and hands washed. In our pajamas, we watched the news, then paraded into Daddy's room for prayers and a good-night kiss.

As I leaned over to kiss him each night, I could smell the sourness of Chesterfield cigarettes that clung to him, to his fingers and his sheets. It seemed that my head and stomach always ached in these moments before I was relatively safe in my own bed. If it had been a good day, a day when he had not been angry, I did my duty with a distant neutrality. If he had spent the day raving, I felt like a liar. Why wish this man a good night? I really wished that he were dead.

Chapter 3

Everyone on our street knew who was on welfare and who wasn't, who had a man in the house, who didn't. Everybody also tacitly agreed it wasn't anybody's business, least of all the state of Illinois. It never occurred to anyone to reveal the circumstances of another family; the household in jeopardy could just as well be your own. This collective silence was a practical one; no one could possibly raise children on the money provided by AFDC. There were nearly 25,000 AFDC cases on the books in Cook County in 1960, accounting for about $4.3 million distributed to 105,000 women and children. That worked out to an average of a little over forty dollars a month for each member of the family; about two hundred dollars a month for a family of five. If you were eligible for food stamps, you received an extra fifty dollars or so. By the time a woman paid rent, half that money was already gone.

Thus, nearly everyone in the system had some underground source of extra money. Some women actually had jobs, doing daywork off the books. Others held part-time jobs in local stores;

still others made extra cash by working policy—the Chicago numbers racket. And some women, like my mother, had surreptitious help from the men in their lives. A sporadic laborer could never be the sole support of a family. But, in combination with AFDC and food stamps, a man's paltry wage turned into enough money to move a family from desperation to subsistence.

This logic was unspoken among the women in the neighborhood, but by the time I was nine or ten, I pretty much had figured it out. The government kicked in money for the basics: rent, food, lights, gas. It was up to everybody to hustle the rest. At the time, I suspect, the government wasn't clear that it had entered into such a bargain, but we certainly were. I suspect my father felt both enraged and relieved at my mother's entry into the welfare system. It was her partial declaration of independence, and he resented it bitterly, yet we were a burden he couldn't carry along with the burden of his gambling affliction. Some part of him must have been glad to know we would not live utterly from hand to mouth.

What I'm sure he resented almost as much was my growing awareness of our situation. Even more than my smart-mouth questions, Daddy loathed my understanding of all the machinations of welfare. Once Mama and I sat at the kitchen table, fantasizing over a couch on sale at Nelson Brothers, a local furniture chain that specialized in low quality and high prices. I gazed at the price and intoned that it would cost too much—and besides, we were on welfare and the caseworker would wonder where we got it. Daddy was furious; I was confused. To keep ourselves together, we needed a common story, a common set of lies, to be told at appropriate times, a common understanding of what was at risk. There were things I had to know if I was to do my part.

Besides, I had become the mediating voice between my parents—especially my mother—and the outside world. There were always forms to fill out, or questionnaires to complete, or official-looking papers to read. Mama managed to do most of these things, but not very well. It fell to me, and sometimes to Hiawatha, to read the documents and explain what had to be done. I was the person who read the lease for our apartment before Mama signed it. I was the one who explained that the Department of Public Aid wanted verification of certain information by a certain date or our benefits would be altered, perhaps even discontinued. I did these things because I could. I did them because I was the oldest, and because it was my job to help my mother. But there was no way to do them and remain unconscious of the attitudes that surrounded welfare and the attitudes that prevailed in our household.

I was very aware, for example, of how important caseworkers were, and how important it was to give them the right impression. I didn't see them very often, usually during the summer months or during school vacations. But despite the parade of varying faces—some black, some white—over the course of my childhood, the central theme was one I copied from my mother: how to help this woman and her four children get by. My mother was easily a welfare poster child, and I knew that well enough to contribute to that image. I always made it a point to have a book in my hands when the worker came; whatever I was reading acted as a kind of cloaking device. I could be in the room, listen in, but be ignored, since I was just a little girl reading.

My mother's only bone of contention with the workers was in the matter of our schooling. More than once, a caseworker tried to impress upon my mother the inappropriateness of spending part of her monthly grant to send us all to St. Ambrose. Why couldn't she just send us to public school like everyone else? My mother was steely but gracious, as she reminded them that she wanted us to have the education she never got, an education we could not get in Chicago's segregated public schools. Only one caseworker said outright that the state of Illinois was not sending her money so that we could go to private school.

"Once you send it to me, it's not your business what I do with it," my mother answered, in a voice that brooked no further discussion. "I'm taking care of my kids."

I marveled at my mother's coolness under fire; this was nothing like the placating voice she used in Daddy's presence. Even as she spoke, Daddy's clothes were carefully hidden in a closet on the other side of what was really his bed, out of the traffic pattern of the house, so a caseworker would have to be really bold or nosy to go looking for evidence. Mama's demeanor, I think, always precluded that search. Though she obviously wouldn't hesitate to stop a worker who crossed her boundaries, it was mostly her easy charm that smoothed the way for us, her ability to enlist people in her cause: the well-being of her children. As the oldest, I played my part well. I was appropriately polite, thoughtful and studious-looking, not altogether unaware of the impression I made, always quiet, always reading, always located somewhere near my mother, monitoring the conversation for a clue of some unknown danger.

Threats of exposure to the authorities came only from the occasional outsider, like the precinct captain who canvassed for Mayor Daley door-to-door one year. He arrived at the front door one afternoon to recruit my mother's vote, issuing a barely concealed threat that a vote for the opposition, a Republican named Benjamin Adamowski, would cause her welfare benefits to mysteriously disappear. Mama, who'd been in the midst of making dinner when the bell rang, excused herself from the front door for a moment, then returned with the biggest butcher knife in the house. I only saw my mother from the back, but I saw the face of that unfortunate man, who began to back away from the door as my mother declared: "If you don't get your ass off this porch I'll cut you from asshole to elbow." The retreating precinct captain must have heard our shrieks of astonished laughter for blocks. We had never seen Mama do anything like that in our lives. Later, I asked her what we would do if he really meant it, if they'd really throw us off welfare. Mama soothed me with a combination of gentleness and scorn. "Don't even think about that ignorant old bastard," she told me, sounding almost like Daddy for a minute. "That nigger can't do nothin' but run around scaring people. He think everybody's a fool."

Mayor Daley's machine hacks did a great many things akin to threatening women and children. For nearly as long as I'd been alive, Richard J. Daley had been mayor. His was one of the last, certainly the greatest, of the old-style political machines, and in my childhood years, it was well-oiled indeed. Precinct captains like the one who threatened my mother were commonplace: this was one of the few positions of relative power reserved for blacks in the Daley organization. Of course there were a few other black people who had been rewarded for their faithful service to Daley, my father said, frequently referring to them as "those handkerchief-head Negroes" and "Uncle Tom sumbitches."

According to my father, our alderman was one such traitor. Claude W. B. Holman was the alderman of the fourth ward. To my father "a hand-picked stooge" of Daley, Holman was a prominent attorney in the Negro community and an associate of Congressman William Dawson. Daddy's contempt for Holman was exceeded only by his hatred of Dawson, whom he constantly referred to as "that Uncle Tom sumbitch" for his refusal to support school-desegregation efforts in the House and on the local level. But if Daddy hated Dawson for his backward positions on the grand stage of national politics, his invective against Holman was constant, vituperative, and locally based.

He raved constantly that Holman was incompetent, that Daley had bought him off, that he couldn't even get the garbage picked up. In Chicago, this was a serious matter; clean streets were a kind of permanent legacy of the machine. Our street was no dirtier than most, but it was afflicted with an enormous pothole near our front door; Daddy complained about it all the time. One night, after dinner, Daddy was listening to the radio. Usually, he kept it on WIND or WBBM, but this particular evening he had tuned into WGN Radio's *Extension 720,* a call-in interview program that preceded by a good many years what we call talk radio.

On this particular night, Alderman Holman was the guest. He was talking about the black community in Chicago in general and in his ward in particular, and Daddy cursed him with virtually every breath. At a commercial break, I told Daddy he ought to call in himself and tell Holman what he thought of him and about the hole in the street. Daddy decided that since it was my idea, I ought to call him and tell him off. My brother and I found the number and dialed, not really expecting anyone to answer. But sure enough, one of the producers picked up. I was instructed to turn my radio down, and in a few minutes I was on the phone with the alderman. I told him that it was terrible the way he didn't look after the people on Berkeley Avenue; I even brought up the hole in the street. I ended my little editorial with the words: "I'm really ashamed to have you as an alderman!"

My mother thought this exercise was an enormous waste of time, and in a lot of ways, she was right. As I talked, the alderman got increasingly huffy at my nine-year-old impudence, and when I concluded by saying I was ashamed, he responded: "Well, you go right on being ashamed, and I'll go right on being alderman." I was furious: he hadn't listened to a word I'd said. He thought I was just a kid who'd been coached as a joke. But Daddy was delighted; he reviewed the entire phone call for hours afterward, and he winked at me as I went to bed. I felt warm and happy from my father's praise, and just as disgruntled by Holman's dismissal. It wasn't my fault I was a little girl. Besides, I wasn't going to be little forever. I knew a lot more about politics than he thought I did—though a lot less than *I* thought I did.

Martin Luther King, Jr., and Malcolm X were heroes in our house. Of course, so were Ralph Bunche and Fannie Lou Hamer, and Edward Brooke and Nat King Cole, and Bill Cosby and Mahalia Jackson. If you were black and breathing and making a contribution of any kind to the race, you had a place of honor in the Bray family. If you had earned that place by agitating white Americans, so much the better; that was why Dr. King and Malcolm X were especially honored people. The news clips were thrilling and frightening all at once: amid the anger in the faces of white people, so calm, and with such quiet sad eyes, Dr. King walked and prayed and preached, to rapturous responses from my parents as they watched him on television.

I knew who Dr. King was, of course, from all the stories in the news. But I first read about him thanks to the Ebony Library of Black History, published by the Johnson Publishing Company. Daddy had brought three huge volumes home with him one day from a foray into Maxwell Street. One was about great escapes from slavery; one was about emerging African nations. But the third was the story of the Montgomery bus boycott and the young minister who organized and led it. In my corner of the kitchen, my feet on the radiator, I propped the wide volume on my lap and read the whole story without a break.

I still remember the part where, on the morning of the boycott's first day, Dr. King's wife, Coretta, called him onto the porch to see what he had been afraid to believe would happen: a succession of buses, passing his house, all absolutely empty. His happiness in those pages was mine; it was like a fairy tale in which the good guys were people just like you. Always a sucker for a good story, I found it doubly rewarding because it was true.

But it was frightening to think of men and women and children who were dying down South in the course of the work they did, or just because they happened to be there. When four little girls about my age were killed in the bombing of the Sixteenth Street Baptist Church in Birmingham, even my mother talked to the television. "It's a damn shame, killing those children. They were nothing but babies," she said. All I could think was: "They were almost the same age as me." I wondered whether they knew they were going to die, if they even expected it. It was just another reason for me to be afraid at night.

Every time I looked in the paper or at television, somebody was dying; even white people were dying. When Viola Liuzzo was killed in Selma, Alabama, and the reports showed the shocked faces of her grieving children, I felt afraid for them. I knew how I'd feel if something happened to my mother—I couldn't stand it. Was it hard for them to look black people in the face, I wondered, as if we were to blame for what had happened to their mother?

These women and children and men were the martyred dead, and I admired them. Martyrs were a hot topic for the devout Catholics among us. I knew all the people who died in the South were going to heaven, just as I was convinced that the people who killed them were going to hell. My father was anxious to send all the white people of the South to hell with them, along with as many Northern whites as he felt could be rounded up. Death, my father believed, was the only lasting cure for the racism of most white people. "Every one of them sumbitches needs to be dead," he would say, flinging down whatever he was reading that had outraged him, striding from his bedroom to hold forth to Mama about the latest Southern outrage.

There was no need to look to the South for trouble, though. At home, the newspapers regaled readers with accounts of the marches led by a man named Al Raby against the public school system and the police. Bastions of respectability that they were, the Chicago newspapers resented even the implication that the sentiments of white Chicagoans could be in any way equivalent to those of the whites in Southern states. There were outraged editorials and condescending news analyses that made my father sputter, that I read but understood only in the most literal way.

It was plain from all the news coverage on both fronts that Dr. King was deciding to bring the freedom movement to Chicago. The very air I breathed was filled with the notion of agitation.

Even the winos along Forty-third Street read the papers as they sat and drank on crates in the early-summer sun; they talked about Selma, and Birmingham, and the other towns of the South from which some of them were reluctant exiles.

As usual, we were transfixed by the nightly news reports. Folks sat on their stoops and argued about whether even Dr. King could move the hearts of Northern whites. Bull Conner was one thing. But this was *Chicago*—with Gage Park and Bridgeport and a dozen other neighborhoods that nobody black in his right mind would walk through, even in daylight. And this was Mayor Daley's town—how would Dr. King manage to outthink Daley?

The very idea of a confrontation between King and Daley made my father's mouth water. He had hated Mayor Daley for as long as he lived, it seemed; you could tell whenever Daley was on TV or radio from the way Daddy would start cursing. Nobody ever got called a bigger "sumbitch" than Daley did. One of the things about him my father hated most was his unwavering support of the school superintendent, Benjamin Willis. When he heard that Dr. King had planned a march against the city government in general and Willis in particular, my father prepared to be there before Dr. King got off the plane.

Willis had been a thorn in the side of thinking Negroes for years. Faced with a ballooning school enrollment, for example, he instituted double-shift class scheduling. Instead of a full day of school, students went either in the morning or in the afternoon. The fact that 90 percent of double-shift students were Negro endeared him to no one but the defenders of segregation. As early as 1962, in fact, the Chicago Board of Education and Willis himself had been censured by the U.S. Civil Rights Commission.

Still, the overarching excitement came from knowing that Dr. King was actually coming to Chicago. He spoke all over Chicago that week. I got to see him in a parking lot across from St. James Church on Forty-sixth Street and Ellis. As kids we were always in that lot, riding our bikes at breakneck speed until dusk. They built a platform for Dr. King to stand on while he addressed a crowd of hundreds of folks who lived nearby. My brother was a Cub Scout and part of the honor guard that welcomed him. I don't remember being jealous, just proud. We had come early because of my brother's duties, and so we were right up front; I was pressed against the platform. I wish I could remember the specifics of what Dr. King said, but I know he talked about freedom and that was what we wanted most to hear. And I know I touched his shoes, shiny black and plain, because I was at nose level with them and I wanted to be able to say I had touched him.

When the speech was over, he climbed into a black car. I was right next to the window as the door closed. I waved at him. And he smiled—a real smile that a little girl could feel—and waved back at me as the car drove away.

We marched with him that Sunday, my whole family and I. As hot as it was, we dressed as if for church. Daddy wore a suit, his good Florsheim shoes for all that walking, and a hat. We marched all day, through downtown Chicago, to protest against the policies of the board of education. Daddy had already lodged at least one protest with the public schools: he refused to let us go to them. But that didn't change his intent to protest on behalf of those children who did attend. "Willis must go," we shouted, over and over. On that hot summer day, no one could have told the thousands of us in the streets that the world would not soon be made new. But summer turned to fall, and Chicago's radically segregated world would remain intact for some time longer. It was my first lesson in how hard change really was to achieve.

I loved fall, and the three-block walk home from St. Ambrose was almost a big playground. The leaves were scattered on lawns in layers an inch deep; the sidewalks were a launching pad from which to dive into the piles of crunchy golds and oranges and reds. The sky grew strange and pale gray, the wind shifted gears in preparation for the coming winter. Fall made me feel a bit lonely, a bit sad, already a bit hungry for the eventual spring.

My head was always filled with thoughts like that, and I filed them away to pull out for myself at night, especially if it was a night free from my parents' arguments. In the drowsy aura that surrounded me just before sleep, I could retrieve memories of all the things that pleased me just to look at them. Walks home, kicking the golden leaves along Ellis Avenue, were one of my favorite things to remember.

I was ten years old, not very tall, a bit on the stocky, awkward side. All I really wanted, as I considered the question during my descent into sleep each night, was books, Mama, and a quiet place to read. Sometimes I would have more elaborate fantasies. Once I saw a commercial about an evening in New York City. The camera swept the skyline of a brightly lit Manhattan; deeply romantic piano music ambled in the background. Sometimes I dreamed of living in New York. I would be grown up—twenty-one, maybe even twenty-five years old—and whatever I did for a living, I would make ten thousand dollars a year. That would be enough to take care of Mama and myself. I would even take her to California, a place she often said she wanted to see.

At that moment, though, my life was fairly well defined, along the usual route of home and school and church. Confession shaped our Saturday afternoons, as all four of us trooped to church to report our sins, do our assigned penance, and collect holy water from the urn near one of the chapels. We took the holy water home for Mama in a carefully washed cough syrup bottle. She used to sprinkle it around the house—a kind of ritual she hoped would keep our home a peaceful one. It was yet another unworkable strategy, as futile as the votive candles she sometimes burned in hopes of a happy home. If all these things were meant to convey peace and tranquillity, no one had mentioned it to my father.

Still, I loved God. I can't say why, only that I did. I used to ask God why Daddy had to be that way, so mean to Mama, so scary. At times, I could console myself with the knowledge that I was earning stars in my heavenly crown for having endured so much discord. Other times, I kept wishing I could cut a deal with God:

more prayer and devotion, for example, in exchange for tranquillity. Mama tried often to console me in the face of my furious questioning about why she didn't leave, or make him stop. "Trouble don't last always," she would tell me. Well, you could have fooled me. It seemed to me that we had already spent eternity surrounded by difficulty. I concluded that all this unhappiness in our house was my martyrdom of sorts. I didn't like it at all, but the nuns had made me very familiar with suffering, and I had decided this was mine. This didn't interfere with my sense of devotion or my love of the sacraments. I still said the Rosary on the first Friday of each month. I still prayed quietly for my guardian angel to protect me: "Angel of God, my guardian dear, to whom God's love commits me here, ever this day, be at my side, to light and guard, to rule and guide. Amen."

Indeed, I had been given the privilege of laying out vestments for the priests each afternoon for their Masses the following day. It was a reverent pleasure to go from the schoolyard into the sacristy of the church, to the small room fragrant with incense and melting wax, and do my simple tasks, aware of the layers of clothing I must make available for the priests, remembering always the colors of the season—violet in the days of Advent and Lent, white for the holiest days of Christmas and Easter, and so on. Always, before I left the room, I looked inside the church vault at the chalice, set on a kind of pedestal, untouchable by anyone except the priest himself. It was a mortal sin, I had been told, for anyone other than a consecrated priest to be in physical contact with the vessels for the Eucharist. And so I prided myself on being exceedingly careful.

My brother Hiawatha, as devout in his way as I was in mine, was an altar boy of serious purpose. He talked often about becoming a priest, and was always the one the priests would call upon in the case of an emergency—an early-morning funeral, or some other occasion on which an assigned acolyte was unavailable. He even made a few dollars now and then. I'm sure that had something to do with my deciding to go to Father Walsh, the priest who coordinated the work of the altar boys, and tell him of my desire to serve Mass. But I also know I wanted a chance to stand in solemnity before the cross, to swing the aromatic censer, to get physically closer to God. And I wanted to see what happened at the altar when one of the altar boys rang the circular set of bells at the moment in the Mass where the bread and wine are transformed into the body and blood of Christ. Everything happened with the priest's back to the church. I wondered, as he lifted his hands in prayer above the cup, whether little sparks flew out, or perhaps a barely perceptible shimmer in the air around the miracle itself. I wanted to see for myself.

I went in search of Father Walsh one afternoon after completing my work in the sacristy. I was nervous, for I had enough awe of the priests never to speak to them unless spoken to first. But my desire had become urgent enough to carry me through my fears. I found him near the altar that afternoon, and told him that I was just as willing as my brother to serve Mass, and wanted to know what I should do to register.

"You cannot serve Mass, Rosemary," he said to me quietly. "You are a girl, and girls do not serve Mass."

I suddenly felt hot all over; the burning eventually concentrated in my head and face. I was too in awe of Father Walsh to say what I was thinking, too aware of my status as a little girl with an obligation to obey my elders, especially elders who were priests. I excused myself and walked deliberately back to the sacristy. I can remember thinking, with my every step, that God had made me a girl, that I hadn't asked to be one, that I loved God as much as my brother did. By the time I reached the room filled with vestments, I was in a rage with the God who had thrown my devotion back in my face. I made my way through the hushed room to the vault where the altar vessels were kept. As always, the door was open. The chalice, the platen—they were there. I took my brown fingers, as hot now as my face, and placed them on the chalice, gripping it hard, so God would know I meant every move, and I dared Him to send me to hell.

My heart left the church at that moment. I said nothing to my parents, because I knew there was no way I could get out of going to Mass. But only my body showed up from then on. And though I wasn't aware of it then, there were plans afoot that would take me away from St. Ambrose altogether.

One day when I came home from school, Mama and Daddy were talking in Daddy's room. For once they seemed more curious than antagonistic toward each other. Mama asked me how I felt about the idea of going to a new school. It would be far away from where we lived, and I would have to take a train to the North Side of Chicago by myself, she said. Right away, my ten-year-old's spirit of adventure was kindled. The idea of doing anything by myself was a small miracle.

It seemed that my mother had told our caseworker that we were all doing well in school, but that she was worried about me. The kids were still picking on me every day, and Mama still had to meet me after school. What's more, the nuns were just as concerned, but for different reasons. I needed a bigger challenge, according to my sixth-grade teacher, Sister Maria Sarto, one she felt I might get at another school with more money and resources. There were several such schools in Chicago, but the big requirement was a scholarship to pay for my going there. At least one of those places was a boarding school, which I was more than ready for. But neither of my parents was ready for that step. I was too young to be away from home, they said. My mother was especially appalled; in her mind, boarding school was where white people sent their children to get them out of the way.

So the caseworker had found out about this other school, the Francis W. Parker School, and had brought my mother the application form. She told Mama to fill out the application and send it back to the school. I looked at it and knew I would have to be the one to fill it out. It didn't take long to do, and a few weeks after we mailed it we were notified that I would have to take some kind of test before a decision could be made. I didn't mind that. Not long after, I found myself in a big room with a lot of kids, filling in those computer-scored blank ovals. I was too excited to pay real attention to how few black people were in the room. My mind was on getting to go to this school. It was something I could do without the constant presence of my siblings, without people making fun of me all the time, something that was mine alone.

On Holy Saturday, the day before Easter, a letter came in the mail from Parker. My mother let me open it; I had been accepted. I screamed and ran through the house. My brothers and sister gawked; my parents grinned at each other in a rare show of united pleasure. What I didn't know for many years was that Sister Maria Sarto had called the school and spoken to the principal and some of the teachers about me. One of the teachers she spoke to that day would make a terrific difference in my life a few years later. But all I knew at the time was that I had done something that was an honor for the family.

Not long after, they sent a list of the clothes I would need; though the school was nonsectarian, I would still be wearing uniforms. But these were not the ugly blue-and-green plaid of the parochial school. These were quieter colors, solid navy blue and white, with light-blue blouses or knee socks allowed. Mama and I scrounged through thrift shops all summer, looking for skirts to cut down for me. For the first day of school, however, we found something special. It was a light-blue dress—a woman's dress—lavishly embroidered with flowers of every imaginable color and intertwined with leaves and stems of forest green. I thought it was the most perfect, pretty thing I ever saw. It even had a big skirt to swish when I twirled around in it. Mama bought it and cut it down for me to wear, tucking in the sides and waist with her old Singer pedal sewing machine.

On the morning of the first day of school, Mama went with me, and cautioned me to pay close attention. She would go with me the whole way this first time; after that, I had to go each day alone. I was eleven; it was thrilling. We walked to Forty-seventh Street and took the bus to the El. That part was familiar; I had been this way on trips downtown. Then we gave the attendant our transfers so she could punch and return them and climbed the long stairs to the elevated platform. Mama reminded me to always say "Return, please," to hold on to my transfer until I was on the Clark Street or Broadway bus. Transfers were good for an hour in Chicago; you could ride buses and trains in any order as often as you wanted, until your time ran out. That's why it was important to look at the time punched on the little transfer clock. The trip to school would take just about an hour, and bus drivers routinely gave you a little more time.

On the train, I stood at the little window up front, just as I would have if I'd been going anywhere with Mama, and watched as the tracks descended into the caverns under downtown Chicago. I counted the stops as I always did: Roosevelt Road, Harrison, Jackson and State, Madison-Monroe and State, Randolph and State. That was as far as I'd ever gone on the El until recently. The train took an enormous screeching turn; the sparks flew from the wheels of the train and sputtered out. Then we were pulling into the stations new to me: Grand and State; Chicago and State. Finally, Mama tapped me on the shoulder and told me our stop was next. Clark and Division was painted red; that was how I would teach myself to remember where to get off the train until it became automatic. We went through the turnstiles, and walked up the stairs into the open fall air.

The sun was shining that day; the streets looked so clean you could eat from them. And in contrast to the handful of rugged, slightly rundown stores that occupied Forty-third and Forty-seventh Streets near our house, this intersection was overrun with stores: shoe shops and restaurants, a huge Woolworth's, a jewelry store. The street was full of people, not the slow procession of my neighbors headed for the store or the bus stop, but a steady, vigorous stream of people, going—it seemed—everywhere.

Mama directed me to walk across the street and stand at the bus stop. I could take a 22 or a 36 bus, and both of them would stop where I wanted to go. The school was at Clark and Webster, she said, and I could ask the driver to stop at Webster. Or I could get off at Belden, the next stop, and walk back a half-block. We rode past high-rise buildings in formation, and townhouses that looked like cleaned-up versions of our own building. Soon we rode past another private school, the Latin School, which I would learn later was Parker's archrival. The bus ride gave me my first glimpse of Lincoln Park, and I wondered where the famous zoo was to be found. It turned out to be in back of the school; the zoo's entrance was right across the street from the football field.

Soon my mother buzzed for the bus to stop, and we got off across the street from a low, sprawling brick structure, with lots of windows, a courtyard with trees, two playgrounds, and a huge playing field. The signs directed us to the front entrance, a set of stairs with a driveway in front and a low brick wall running the length of the property. As Mama and I came up the steps, I could hear the buzz of children's voices. When we reached the top and peered through the windows, I saw a huge space filled with children and teenagers. I was incredulous: there were hundreds of kids there, and every one of them, it seemed to me, was white.

No one had told me. They had talked about what a good school it was. They had talked about what a wonderful thing it would be for me to come here; they had talked about how many more interesting things I would be able to do here. Not one soul—not even my parents—had thought to mention a crucial detail. I would be going to school with white people, and anyone with an ounce of sense knew white people were dangerous.

I literally backed away from the door. "Mama, those people are white!" I couldn't believe she looked so unexcited. "They'll kill me!" She watched the same news I watched; she knew white people had thrown bricks at us in the demonstrations in Chicago years earlier. She knew as well as I did that white people sicced dogs on little boys in Selma and blew up churches in Birmingham while little girls were in Sunday school and shot people in the back in Mississippi and nearby Cicero and spit on them everywhere. Now she wanted me to go to school with them? What could she and Daddy have been thinking about?

Mama took my hand and pulled me through the door. "Girl, these kids ain't going to bother you. You're here to get an education." We walked inside to the near center of the hall. What looked like chaos had its own curious sense of order. What seemed to be a milling crowd was in fact a cluster of several grades, including my own. I was to be in Mrs. Reid's seventh-grade class. My mother found Mrs. Reid just in time; at eight A.M. the bell rang, and the crush of students began heading for stairs, some up, some down. I was headed down. I looked back helplessly at my mother. "I'll be up here," she said.

Inside the classroom, Mrs. Reid asked the new children to stand with her. The other new kids were boys; at least one of them was handsome; all of them looked as though they belonged there. The teacher asked for volunteers, seasoned students to act as guides for the newcomers. When my turn came, only one hand went up. It was attached to a thin girl with curly brown hair and braces; her name was Monica. I had no idea at the time that she was already as unpopular as I would become. When homeroom was dismissed, she came up to me and grabbed my hand, offering to show me around. By the time I located my mother, Monica already was leading me off to the library. "Look Mama, I have a friend," I said to her.

For a very long time, Monica was my only friend. I was fine in the classroom. The work was challenging, not hard, and there was always something interesting to do, a project you could make up for class. Monica and I both loved science, as it turned out. She and I both wanted to be doctors—not such a popular thing for eleven-year-old girls to want in the 1960s. But we were so weird, no one was surprised.

I was surprised at the number of kids in my class who were Jewish. It might never have come up if it hadn't been for the fact that several of them were being confirmed, or bar mitzvahed. I had heard of confirmation; I'd been confirmed the previous year. But the solemn ceremony of the bar mitzvah was new to me. Monica wasn't going to be bas mitzvahed, but she was Jewish, too. I learned a lot that year about the High Holy Days and Jewish food (which it turned out my father knew all about from his abortive attempts at restaurants). I learned about dreidels and Purim (which I loved because it involved one of my favorite characters from the Bible, Esther) and Yom Kippur. I could appreciate the idea of having one day a year to confess every bad thing you'd done, as opposed to doing it continually, every Saturday afternoon, as Catholic kids did.

I also learned Jesus was a Jew. I cannot account for how it was that I missed that minor detail, but I did. When Monica pointed out the logic of it—how he had to be a Jew or they would never have called him Rabbi in certain parts of the New Testament—I was stunned. Monica and I were constantly having great debates over religion. We were much more preoccupied with it than with race. For a while, I kept trying to baptize her; I would wet my hands in the water fountain and chase her around the playground, reciting the words from the Baltimore Catechism: "I baptize you in the name of the Father, and of the Son, and of the Holy Ghost."

But after going to my classmates' bar mitzvahs and seeing the solemnity and beauty of the ceremony (and looking at the astounding gifts they received afterward), and after long religious discussions with Monica, I decided that I should be Jewish too. My parents had a fit. My father said: "What, being black isn't trouble enough; you want to be a Jew too?" I realize now that my desire had more to do with wanting to be like my best friend, with wanting to belong, than it did with any kind of conversion experience. But it took a particular incident to make it clear to me just how much I didn't belong.

It was the afternoon I went to play with Susie Levitt after school. She had asked me over to play earlier in the week. Because I was under strict orders to come home directly from school, going to her house required special dispensation from my parents, since I'd get home after dark. But Mama and Daddy seemed glad for once that I was making friends, and they'd agreed to let me go.

I knew the way to her house from the address: I passed within a block of where she lived each morning. I got off the bus a bit earlier than I usually did, and walked around the corner onto a street of immaculate brownstones. When I reached her address, a narrow, five-story house, I climbed the stairs and was momentarily confused. I couldn't figure out which apartment was hers; there was only one bell, with no message about how many rings would signal her. I took a chance and rang the bell once, figuring someone would direct me to where she lived.

A white woman in a uniform answered the door. When I told her I had come to see Susie, she opened the door wider and let me inside. I looked around for the mailboxes in the vestibule; there were none. I walked into the front room as Susie came downstairs. Something astounding dawned on me as we said hello: there were no apartments. The whole house was hers to live in. Susie asked if I wanted to see the house. I did. She took me through the parlor to the formal dining room and into the kitchen, where a black woman about my mother's age had her back to us. Susie asked me if I wanted a snack; I said no. The woman turned and smiled slightly at me and said hello. I said hello softly, then followed Susie out and upstairs. On the next level, another woman in uniform was ironing clothes as we passed. We walked up and up the elegant winding staircase until we reached the top floor, and Susie opened a door into what looked to me like Paradise.

In the life of every young girl, there is one fantasy. Some girls want the most beautifully dressed life-size doll. Others dream of a shining prince to take them away one day to live as his wise and beautiful queen. My fantasy was small: one day, I would have my own room. I had never even given any thought to what would be in the room; I just knew that one day I would have a room that no one was in but me. Susie already had such a room, but she had more. The room contained the decor of a little girl's dreams. Everything in it was white and gold: the dresser, the mirror frame, the vanity and most of all, the four-poster canopy bed. White curtains floated across the top, sheltering the bed like clouds.

I wanted to know where her brothers and sister slept. She cheerfully showed me her siblings' rooms—none the room of my dreams, but each separate and apart. I don't remember what we did that afternoon. I only remember feeling numb and vague. All the way home I replayed the scenes at her house. By the time I got to Forty-seventh Street to take the bus home, the contrast was evident. The noise of the train, the smells of barbecue from the shack across the street, the sporadic blare of Motown in the record shop as customers checked to be sure the 45 they wanted to buy was the right one, the strolling people in late afternoon, all dark like me, all different from those who inhabited the world I'd left only forty-five minutes earlier. I was different, too.

I walked home from the bus stop, back down Ellis Avenue, past the tansy growing in the cat lady's yard, past the blackberry bush, past Denise Young's fence. I turned on Forty-fifth Street, past the wisps of morning glory vines and the pods filled with next spring's seeds, across the alley to knock on the back door. Mama let me in and asked me if I'd had a good time. I said I had. What else could I say, when anything else would have worried her? Daddy wasn't home yet. I walked through to the front room and put down my school things, hung up my coat. My sister and brothers were playing, Mama was cooking. I walked back to the bathroom, painted a year earlier a brilliant emerald-green enamel that I now saw emphasized the cracking walls. I shut the latch tight before I sat down on the toilet and started to cry.

Being black was not the worst of it; I realized that afternoon that I was poor, too. I would not have my own room, or a white-and-gold canopy bed. Suddenly it was clear—the way my blue skirts and white blouses looked and felt so different from the other girls'. The soft wool they wore did not come from Sears or Goldblatt's, but from Marshall Field or Saks Fifth Avenue. My blouses were not cotton, they were 100 percent drip-dry polyester. I didn't have penny loafers or Bass Weejuns. I had shoes from the 2-for-$5 store. I knew the facts of all these things long before; I had joined with my mother in planning around them. But this was the day I felt it—how different, how really different I was.

When I was cried out, I wiped my face over and over with cold water until I could pass for normal. Fortunately, no one had paid much attention to how long I'd been in the bathroom. They assumed I had started reading something and lost track of time, as I always did. They were wrong this time. Something in me had broken somehow, but I was determined that they wouldn't know. For them to know, it seemed to me, would mean they would feel bad. And I didn't want Mama or Daddy or anybody to feel bad. We couldn't help being poor. It wasn't anybody's fault. And if I hadn't started going to that school, I probably wouldn't even have known. But it was too late for me; I knew that now. And in the months that followed, except when I was with a couple of people like Monica, I grew more silent and unhappy in my awareness. Now I know the feeling for what it was. I was ashamed.

Chapter 4

I didn't plan to become a thief, but I became one just the same. One moment I was lingering in the girls' locker room, amazed at the way my classmates ran around naked, and embarrassed at the idea that anyone would see my pudgy body. The next moment everyone was gone and I had slipped into my gym suit without an audience. As I walked toward the stairway to join my class, I passed an open locker that held someone's Coach bag. I looked into the locker and reached in to touch the smooth leather. The bag was open, and I lifted the flap to look inside. There were two twenty-dollar bills there.

Just like that, I took one of the twenties, folded it carefully, then inserted it deep into my sock so that I could feel its sharp edges against my foot. I joined the others upstairs, running and jumping as awkwardly as ever, but with a cynical secret. I wondered with guilty pleasure whether the owner of the Coach bag would miss the money right away or whether she would only notice after school when she went shopping. Then I wondered what I would do with the money. Maybe I would buy lip gloss with it.

Or candy to pass around at school like the other kids. I had to decide what to buy and where to put it. There was no way to take the money home, because I would never be able to explain where it came from. I wished I could say I had won a contest, or found it on the street. But Mama wouldn't believe that for a second.

When gym class was over, I hid in a bathroom stall while removing the sock containing the stolen money. All around me I could hear the high-pitched chatter of girls, talking about their parents, about the coming weekend, about dances at the Fortnightly, about new shoes. I came out of the stall, still in my blue gym suit, while the other girls sat nonchalantly in their training bras and panties—or nothing at all. I opened my locker with my empty hand and eased my fist with the money into my own worn vinyl bag, an acquisition from Goodwill. Once I had placed it safely there, I proceeded to change my clothes, hiding as much as I could behind the locker door so that no one could see the girl's undershirt I still wore.

There was no immediate outcry from the victim of my folly; I don't know when she noticed the money was gone. I only know that the next day, the missing money was the talk of the lower school. I tried to act as though I had no interest in the news; in fact, I listened for every theory about the thief. It didn't take long for my name to come up. After all, who else would steal money? Who else would need to? The theorists were right about me, and it hurt to find myself living out a stereotype. I was doing just what white people always said black people do whenever we got the chance—steal, cheat, lie. I knew it, but I couldn't stop it. There was something about the feel of money in my pocket, a soothing sense of being protected I refused to give up. For a moment, I was like the rest of them.

There was a candy store on Belden where everyone bought treats. I'd been there before, with the fifty cents a day my mother put together for me so I could buy milk, or something else to drink for lunch. This time, I entered not with change, but with folding money. I bought candy enough to share, though I couldn't share any with my sister and brothers, for my mother would have wondered where all the candy came from, and lying to her would have made it worse. After school, I wandered down Clark Street toward the drugstores that sold cosmetics. I craved lip gloss, the Yardley Slickers that the other girls carried tucked in the pockets of their sweaters or in their small purses, clear gloss with a waxy perfume that I always associated with school itself. I paid for the white tube with red and blue bands, thinking to myself how wonderful and cool the tube felt, reveling in the smell.

It was the start of a pattern: I would steal money from carelessly left purses, hoard it for a time to buy small items for myself, then steal more when the money was gone. I felt guilty, angry, exhilarated, and placated all at once. My classmates, who had never exactly opened their arms to me, froze me out nearly completely. If Monica suspected me, she never said a word. But the school was onto me; I knew they were poised for me to make a mistake. One morning during recess, I was sitting inside the classroom. I almost always stayed inside reading; few people other than Monica talked to me anyway. When I looked up at some point, my eye fell on the slim, plain wallet on the top of a desk. There was no reason to suspect anything other than mere carelessness on my classmates' part. They were forever leaving things lying around, with the expectation they would still be there when they returned.

I walked over to the wallet and looked inside—a single dollar bill was there. As I prepared to put the money in my pocket, something made me glance up. As I did, I saw one of my classmates peering through the window of a side room, watching me while pretending not to. He ducked his head and feigned nonchalance, but I knew better. I walked out of the classroom with the wallet, and up the stairs. I turned the wallet in at the school's main office, telling one of the secretaries in my most sincere voice that I had found it, and had looked through its meager contents without success to see whether there was some way to identify the owner. I walked back to my classroom with a bitter smile. How dumb, I wondered, did they think I was?

On another occasion, the head of the lower school came into the girls' locker room after we had dressed and demanded to search my locker for some money that was missing. The request astonished me; I hadn't taken anything this particular time. So I opened my locker and let him look through it freely. He didn't find anything, and he looked frankly as surprised as I felt. The next day, he asked to see me. He was direct with me: he suspected I was responsible for the thefts, but he couldn't prove it. He wanted them to stop—at once. I said very little, out of shame, I think. But he frightened me when he said that if they continued, he would have to speak to my mother. The last thing I wanted was for anyone at home to know what was going on. Life already was bad enough.

At home, things were the same—and yet they were not the same, because for the first time in my life, I could feel the growing space between my days and the days of the rest of my family. I still had a host of regulations to follow. School let out at three-thirty P.M., for example, and shame on me if I wasn't walking in the door at four-thirty; unless I had special permission, I had to come home directly after school to arrive before dark, especially the early dark of a Chicago winter. But the rhythm of my days was irrevocably different from that of the rest of my family. In a strange way, I had begun to assume my father's habits: up before anyone else and gone all day, home long after everyone else had arrived. And like my father, I spoke very little about the things I'd seen. My focus was school and classes, books I might have to read. The loneliness and anger and shame—all things I could avoid as long as I was doing schoolwork—these things I kept hidden, sometimes even from myself.

Daddy had decided that Hiawatha and I needed to learn a trade, and he had settled on our learning to type. So at age eleven, when other junior high school girls were spending Saturday mornings watching *American Bandstand* or *Soul Train*, my brother and I were on the Cottage Grove bus to Seventy-ninth Street. With a transfer, we rode west on the Seventy-ninth Street bus to Cortez Peters Business College. Cortez Peters was a black-owned business school, run by a Mr. and Mrs. George Cabiness. On Saturday morning, they taught beginning typing for young people, and my father had enrolled us both, at the princely sum of a dollar fifty a week for each of us.

The building was located near the newly built Dan Ryan Expressway in a neighborhood known to Chicagoans as Chatham. It was a black middle-class neighborhood, with the neatly trimmed lawns and small bungalow houses common to the city's civil servants and professionals. But it was the first such neighborhood I had ever seen up close, except for our family's occasional Sunday drives. At Peters, my classmates had parents who worked as bus drivers or firemen, or secretaries or teachers or nurses. They wore cute clothes that looked mostly new. They were nothing at all like my brother and me.

Most of the time, we brought our own money to pay for class. But one Saturday morning, Daddy told us to wait for him so he could drive us home—because he had arrangements to make with the front office, I think. He was on his way to work at one of the odd jobs he always had, usually involving some kind of construction or plastering work.

When my brother and I came out of class, Daddy was at the front desk, preparing to pay tuition. On the low vinyl sofas around the area, several other parents and their children sat, chatting with one another, making out checks. One small group was discussing a fraternity dance they would attend later in the year. It was clear they were talking about some college fraternity; perhaps they were Alphas or Qs. The names meant nothing to me then, except that I knew them to be part of the black middle-class life I knew of only from *Jet* and *Ebony* magazines.

I didn't like these people, sitting in the hallway, glancing over at my brother and me as though they wanted to keep their children away from us. What made me angriest, though, was the way they all looked at my father. He stood in his dusty and battered work clothes, reaching into a stained pocket with his big hands and pulling out a handful of bills, crumpled in his fist. These nicely dressed fraternity-party people stared at him, as though he were a bug.

Daddy smoothed the old bills out into some kind of order and counted them out to the cashier, his neatly blocked hat pushed back a bit above his forehead. Still they stared, wondering what a man like that would be doing there among them. I wanted to hit them, and for the first time in my memory, something about my father tugged at my heart. Perhaps it was the way they looked at him. Perhaps it was the difference in him whenever he came into the building—his voice still strong, but tentative now, as though unsure of his reception. He was so much more polite, and as the prim receptionist took his money and gave him a receipt, he offered his thanks in such a formal way: "Thank you ever so much," like a butler in a bad British movie. I barely knew this man, so low-key, so deferential.

At home, he was himself again, and there was never any kindness or deference to us in the matter of typing practice. At a parent-teacher conference, Mrs. Cabiness reported to our father that we continued to make too many mistakes. This was a result, she said, of not knowing our home keys without looking at the keyboard. My father could not see spending those handfuls of bills on teaching children who were not typing perfectly. So he designed his own drill to train us.

That afternoon, Daddy sat each of us down, in turn, in the alcove outside the bathroom, where the typewriter, desk, and chair were placed. He tied scarves around our eyes like blindfolds. He would call out a letter and we were to type it. If we were right, he'd call out more letters; if we were wrong, he'd slap us across the head. This would go on for a half hour or so for each of us, every few days. It was terrifying to be hit when you didn't know when or where the next blow was coming from. It's not as though I typed the wrong letters deliberately, yet I always seemed to be making even more mistakes—a product of my increasingly shattered nerves. My brother was just as terrified as I was, but he seemed almost numb to the experience; while I cried, he rarely even made a sound.

My hatred for Daddy in those moments was fiery and pure. One afternoon, just as he had hit me for the third or fourth time, I jumped up and tore the blindfold from my eyes and screamed at him to leave me alone. In response, he got his belt and began to beat me; the welts rose and I screamed until I was hoarse. When he got tired of beating me, I shouted through my tears that one day I would grow up and tell the world about him, about the way he treated us. Daddy jeered at my rage, his anger mostly spent. "You little heifer, you ain't doing shit!" My mother coaxed me away from him, tried to soothe me, remind me that things wouldn't always be this way. All I knew was, this was the way things were now: he hated me, and, finally, I hated him back.

I was eventually caught at school with my hand in someone's coat pocket, preparing to extract some money that was put there to lure me. I have no memory of feeling anything at all except terror about my parents' reaction. The school called my mother, and for more than a moment, I considered not coming home at all. That night, as the three of us convened in my father's room, Mama was so amazed and disappointed, it was nearly impossible to look at her. Of all her children, I was the one who everyone imagined would cause the fewest problems.

My father's reaction was even more frightening. He said nearly nothing. He did not yell—at my mother, or at me. He did not beat either of us. He simply lay there in bed, quietly and sadly, while my mother explained to him what the school proposed. His silent sorrow nearly undid me. For the first time, I was sorry for every dime I had ever taken.

The school was not going to throw me out, it seemed. Instead, it was going to do something my parents could not do: give me an allowance. Every week the school would provide me with five dollars to supplement the carfare and fifty cents a day my mother scraped up each morning. It was not the same as shopping at Saks, but it would mitigate the enormous gap between the affluence of my classmates and my own comparative destitution.

Both the teachers and the principal were also concerned about my state of mind. They wanted me to see the school psychologist, Miss Cassidy, each week for counseling. This two-pronged approach, they hoped, might ease my pain enough for me to stay in school. Perhaps they could even get to the root of what might be bothering me.

If it hadn't been for the look on my parents' faces, I might have laughed. I couldn't begin to tell anyone what was bothering me. It was so much more than not having any money. I was so afraid all the time, so tired of the noise and the fights and the rage, the nightmares I had had for years and the blinding headaches I had since developed. But if I told anyone, people might start investigating—our family, my mother, even my father. Mama would get in trouble for keeping a roof over our heads the best way she knew how. They might take me away—even separate all of us from each other. My family wasn't even close to perfect, but it was all I had, and I was set on keeping it.

But I wanted to stay at Parker, and so I went to see Miss Cassidy every week. For the most part, we talked about school, about how different I felt from the other children, how much of an outsider I was. When it came to matters at my house, I was resolutely silent. I said no more and no less than I needed to say to assure people that I was cooperating. If the psychologist thought I was hiding anything, she kept it to herself.

I didn't think it would help to talk to her, but it did. Home was still the same terrifying place, but the new terrors that came with changing schools were much more manageable. In Miss Cassidy's office, I didn't have to pretend that everything was all right and that my life was just like everybody else's. We both knew what a lie that was, but talking to her made it seem a lot less like the end of the world.

The allowance that the school gave me made possible the pleasures of normalcy in small things. I could go with Monica after school to the Golden Cup for fries and a Coke, participating in this most popular of junior high rituals just like everyone else. I even had extra carfare to take the bus to Monica's house after school, something I'd been invited to do, but didn't feel I could, because I knew Mama didn't have the money to give me.

In this way, I met Monica's parents and her older sister, Beth. Her father was a psychiatrist and her mom was a teacher who had quit her job to stay home with the girls. We'd come in and Mrs. Rosenthal would greet us, make us sandwiches, and ask about our day. Monica and I would sit around and listen to music—everything from the Beatles to James Taylor—and talk about being doctors. I didn't know what kind of doctor I wanted to be, but Monica was clear: she wanted to be a surgeon. Of course, she'd had more years to think about it than I had. I had noticed that about the kids at Parker. They had ambitions that seemed set in stone, decided upon after what seemed years of thought and study. I had ambitions, too, but never with the same striking level of detail.

Monica and her family lived in an apartment, just as I did, but the resemblance ended there. Their place was enormous and filled with light, with lots of books and simple decorations and furnishings. I knew Monica was well-to-do, but I never felt the same sense of shame or embarrassment at her house that I'd felt that day with Susie Levitt. Her parents were gracious to me; they looked me in the eye when they talked to me, and I came to realize they were happy that Monica had a friend.

By the end of the year, Parker seemed less frightening to me. It still wasn't a second home; most of the girls still stayed in their cliques, and most of the boys still treated me as though I had a communicable disease. But some of the girls were actually pleasant to me, and Monica and I had come to count on each other and our common fascination with the science lab. By the end of seventh grade, I could almost imagine sticking around.

My eighth-grade teacher was a man named Delafield Griffith. He was tall, gaunt, with stringy hair and protruding teeth. The other kids thought of him as a hopelessly awkward, out-of-style instructor thrust upon us for the year. I learned to adore him. Unlike Mrs. Reid, whose demeanor toward me was one of benign friendliness, Mr. Griffith really liked me—and it showed.

I had always had teachers who were interested in my scholastic abilities, especially at St. Ambrose. But Mr. Griffith's attitude toward me was completely different. He was always mildly sarcastic when he talked to us, but he spoke to me with utter straightforwardness, and always with a warm look in his eyes. As he taught us about China, he answered my questions about the Ming dynasty with unfailing respect, even telling me about books I could read if I wanted to. Of course I read them, which only increased my classmates' exasperation, but I didn't care. It was enough to see the slight smile on his face when I wanted to talk about something I'd read, or the way he listened to my theory about something even if I was wrong. I was still pretty quiet with most other people at the school, but in class with Mr. Griffith, I was vocal, energized, animated. He was my first real crush.

It's not hard to understand why. Mr. Griffith was as different from my father as he could be. He was kind. He never once yelled at me. He always paid attention to me. And he was the first man I ever knew who praised me. I can remember it so clearly. I was talking to Mr. Griffith in the lunchroom; we were sitting by the windows facing the courtyard. The sun was everywhere, and even though it was early in the school year, it definitely felt like spring.

He asked me how I liked school, and which subjects I liked best. I confessed to loving reading, of course, and told him how whenever I read, all the people came to life inside my head. "It's like having a movie screen inside my forehead," I told him. And then he looked at me, straight into my eyes.

"Do you know you're the kind of student that a teacher waits his whole life to teach?" He said other things that were meant to encourage me; he knew what a struggle it was for me to fit in with most of the other kids. But I can't remember anything else he said, except those words and the look on his face as he said them. Nothing could have induced me to leave Parker after that; nothing my classmates could say would matter again. Mr. Griffith saw me, knew me for who I was and who I might be. It was enough.

Part of the eighth-grade curriculum at Parker was the study of slavery and the Civil War; part of that study was reading *The Adventures of Huckleberry Finn*. The entire class was sensitive to the references to "nigger" Jim, but as long as Mr. Griffith was there, I didn't feel particularly weird or self-conscious. I'm not sure that my classmates weren't uncomfortable, though. I could tell they were worried about me, what I would say or do. A couple of them would sneak little looks over at me, as though I were about to blow up. They could have saved their energy; I wasn't so angry about white people during slavery as I was angry about white people here and now.

At one point during our Civil War studies, we went to see *Gone With the Wind*. I cringed through nearly the entire movie. As we were walking out, one of the meaner boys in the class asked me if I'd imagined being a slave. I told him I had imagined I was Scarlett O'Hara. Whatever had made me say that? I wondered. When I watched cowboy movies, I rooted for the Indians—after all, they'd gotten here first. Yet I understood Scarlett O'Hara; a part of me knew and identified with her. When she pulled those green velvet drapes down from the window so that Mammy could make her a dress, she was no different from my mother. When she stood in that barren field and swore that she'd never be hungry again, I made that vow with her. Yet she enraged me throughout the rest of the movie. At the point when she slapped

Prissy, I wanted to reach through the screen and murder her.

I wasn't good at subtleties of feeling in those days, and I'm not sure where my conflicted imagination would have taken me if I had not read another of Mr. Griffith's suggestions: *Jubilee,* by Margaret Walker. I knew slavery was desperately unfair; I knew that it was the institution responsible for my being a little black girl in Chicago and not Lagos (or some other city, to be forever unknown to me). But it was from reading *Jubilee* that I learned exactly why black people like my father believed nothing white people said or did, no matter what they promised. In one of the book's most striking scenes, a character reveals a back so scarred it looks like the trunk of a tree. I knew the red, sore welts that leather belts made from all the times my father had hit me. So how could someone go on beating you that long?

I read that book and walked around with it, thinking to myself for a long time. One day, after class, I lingered to talk to Mr. Griffith. There wasn't a lot to say. I just wanted to ask him something.

"Was it really like this?" I asked him. "The way they treated black people?" I knew it was bad, but these were the first details I'd ever truly absorbed. Mr. Griffith said it was really like that for black people. That left me with a single question that made my throat ache with the asking.

"Why did white people do this?" I asked him. He knew what I meant; not the here and now, but the ugly start of it. Not the sociopolitical reasons, or the economic rationale that slaveowners had perfected to make it all right, but the thing in their hearts that made them link our common histories forever. Mr. Griffith was the first white person I knew to ask, and when I did, he looked so sad. He put one arm lightly across my shoulder and walked with me out of the classroom.

"I don't know why," he told me. "I don't know why anyone would do it."

By now, I had spent almost two years on the fringes of white America—at least this part of white America—and I was not impressed with what I saw. It was bad enough that my classmates were cliquish and often mean—not just to me, but to anyone who wasn't like them. I knew my being black didn't help me get along with them, but it wasn't the only source of their disdain for me; I was just too weird in other ways.

But what did amaze me was their near-complete indifference to what was going on between black people and white people in America. They were conversant with the growing opposition to U.S. involvement in Vietnam; in fact, that seemed to be the central theme of their political awareness. It wasn't that I was unaware of Vietnam; my father spent as much time watching *Meet the Press* as he always had, calling Robert McNamara a lying sumbitch. But there were so many things happening in this country that seemed so much more urgent. This became my first exposure to the hierarchy of racial concerns. What did integration matter to whites, who had already arrived, whose place was secure? The struggle for racial equality and opportunity was a noble but distant issue for them. My passion about the issue, scarcely concealed in class discussions, and supported only by Mr. Griffith's steady ability to listen, was just another reason for me to be set apart.

My time at Parker contributed to my reassessment of Martin Luther King—he was lame. He had not been able to convince Northern white people—not even children—that racism was a clear and present danger to American life. White people seemed bored, particularly Northern whites, who felt they were exempt from the discussion because they had never called anyone a nigger or stood guard at a schoolhouse door to prevent black children from entering.

I was old enough to understand some of the dangers of what Dr. King, for all his supposed failures, was attempting to do. I knew enough from listening to my father that Dr. King was in the midst of taking incredible risks, broadening his base to include poor and working-class white people in his programs, a decision

I judged as betrayal. At that point in my life, I had never seen a white person with problems, and I was possessive of Dr. King and his talents. White people wanted everything, it seemed, even our heroes.

People like Stokely Carmichael and H. Rap Brown made a lot more sense to me. White people were afraid of these men in a way that earned them my respect. These brothers were not hoping that someone would let them be free one day, maybe, please. They were the embodiment of the immediate human impulse to crush the people intent on crushing you. In short, they weren't begging.

Dr. King came far too close to begging to suit me. I didn't see the point anymore of trying to discuss civil rights with white people. We tried to be nice, it didn't work. So now it was time to kick somebody's behind, somewhere. I brought to this line of reasoning all of the experiences of my playground years. All through elementary school, I had tried to obey the nuns and their discouragement of fighting. I routinely watched enough fighting at home to loathe it. I was too afraid of being hurt by a bigger child to be any good at fighting to defend myself. And yet, in a situation in which it was necessary for me to defend someone else (my brother, my best friend), I found in myself the will to get past being afraid and fight for real, and win.

I learned to love the feeling that people who once thought of me as a target now thought of me as someone to leave alone. In one case, I had even become friends with a girl in the fifth grade who lived to pick on me—until my whole family helped me beat her up. So far as I could tell, the same principle applied. If white people thought they were about to get hurt, they might change their minds about black people because they would have no choice. Maybe we ought to smile and pray a little less, and demand a lot more.

It was spring break at my school in April 1968; it was a Friday night, and my father was in the hospital across town. My mother had gone to visit him, and I was in charge of making dinner and keeping an eye on my brothers and sister. I was shaping hamburger into patties and watching television when the newscasters interrupted the program to say that Dr. King had been shot.

I put down the hamburgers and cried. I looked out the window to assess the reaction of my neighbors, but the streets were eerily quiet. The phone rang; it was Mama calling from the hospital to find out how we were. I told her to turn on the news; it was clear she'd been in transit and didn't know.

There were riots in Chicago, but we only saw them on television. I found out later that angry mobs had roamed up and down Forty-seventh Street, burning a car dealership and breaking windows in several stores. A couple of classmates called, and at least one of them wanted to know whether we were safe—did we want to come and stay with them? I wanted very much to go; I wasn't the least bit afraid, but the idea of spending a couple of days in relative luxury was wonderful. My mother, with great anger, told me to say no thanks. "You don't need to be with white folks, you need to be at home." It was clear she wasn't in the mood to be bothered with white people, even white people we knew.

By the time I got back to school from spring break, the students and staff were saddened by Dr. King's murder, but not especially burdened by it, the way everyone was at home. My classmates were a lot more preoccupied with the coming festivities around an annual school event: County Fair.

County Fair was a tradition as old as the school itself, part fund-raiser, part communal celebration. Each class had its own project; for the eighth grade, it was a play to be performed for the other classes, under the watchful and adoring eyes of parents. There were two performances, with a complete cast from each class, chosen by the staff and faculty. Anticipation was fierce.

That spring, the play would be *Alice in Wonderland*, with a script taken directly from the Disney movie (without the singing), and directed with the help of the school's drama department. On the day of the casting announcements, we were all milling around the classroom. I was not really paying attention to the event, since I figured I would be relegated to some marginal role as an extra. So when Mr. Griffith returned to the classroom, I was amazed to discover I had been cast as the lead.

Nor was I was alone in my amazement. I heard mumbling that it should be my classmate, Lhotze, whose blond hair and blue eyes made her the precise image of Alice in every book I'd ever seen. I didn't disagree; it had never occurred to me that I could be Alice. One member of the class said I would have to wear a blond wig. Mr. Griffith heard the comment, and spoke up very calmly. "No, she won't. She'll be herself."

I took home the story of Alice from the school library to read again. It had never been one of my favorite stories, but now I had important reasons to study it. I could still barely believe that the teachers would choose me. I was excited and terrified. This wasn't like real school, where you studied and did your homework and got your grades. This was a public performance. I didn't want to stand up in front of all those people and be Alice in Wonderland. I didn't want everyone to look at me. I didn't want to be terrible, or forget my lines, or fall off the stage. But I didn't want to disappoint Mr. Griffith, who seemed perfectly nonchalant about my being Alice, and told me he thought I would be very good in the part.

Mama was excited about it, too. We wondered what to do about a costume, as I explained to Mama about the blue dress and the white pinafore Alice wore in all the picture books. That's when I remembered that the storybook I had was illustrated, and I opened it for Mama to the page where Alice sat on a mushroom.

"Oh, that girl's got on a plain blue dress. You got a dress like that in the closet," Mama said.

"But that's a flowered dress, Mama."

"Girl, bring me that dress here," she said.

When I got it and held it up, it was the same style of dress that Alice wore in the illustration. That weekend, Mama went to Woolworth's and bought a few yards of plain cotton in a royal blue just like the dress in the picture, and she bought a yard of white cotton for the pinafore. She ripped the seams loose from the other dress and used it as a pattern for the costume. As for the pinafore, she looked at the picture for a few days, figuring out in her head how she would make it. Then she borrowed a neighbor's scissors that made zigzags when she cut with them. The old pedal sewing machine was broken, so Mama had to sew the whole thing by hand. In two weeks I had my costume. For once, it was exactly the right thing to wear.

Rehearsals were terrible, though. There was so much anger among some of the girls that I had been picked to be Alice. No one ever knew why anyone got picked, but everyone said it was because I was the teacher's pet. Already fairly quiet, I became nearly completely withdrawn as the days went by. Monica still talked to me, of course, but other people were not nearly so friendly. At one particularly bad rehearsal, I heard a couple of the boys joking about me, calling me the Black Plague. That did it for me. I burst into tears and ran out into the hallway, and smack into one of the older girls, someone from the high school upstairs who was taking something to the auditorium. She had long brown hair and knee socks; I can't remember her name. She saw my tears and asked me what was wrong. I told her, and she put her arms around me.

"Let's walk back," she said. "You can't quit the play." She walked me back into the auditorium, advising me to dry my tears, reminding me that they were teasing me just to make me quit. That point got through to me; I didn't want them to think I was afraid of them or of doing the play. I *was* afraid of doing the play, but that was beside the point. They'd never hear that from me. No one ever called me the Black Plague again, but they didn't exactly welcome me, either. But by now I had too much invested in it. Mama would be coming. Mr. Griffith would be there.

On the day of County Fair, I felt nearly paralyzed. Before the curtain rose, I took my place on a platform beneath a spotlight. In the opening scene, I would twirl around and around as the spotlight blinked; the idea was to create the effect of falling down a rabbit hole and into another world. I wanted to hide, or run, or disappear. I couldn't remember anything I'd learned, or where to stand or what to do. I remember thinking that at least my costume was wonderful; even the other kids had admitted that. The auditorium grew quiet as the lights dimmed; our director wished us luck. I remember the blinking of the lights as we began.

Suddenly, it was over. The lights were up, and the audience was applauding. I stepped forward to take a bow, and the applause got louder. I looked around at the rest of the cast, and they were applauding, too, and smiling. As the curtain came down, I felt giddy, a little silly and strange. It was my first experience with public approbation. I walked out the stage door into the school gallery to find my mother amid the crowd. I ran over to her and hugged her, and parents began talking to her and to me about how good I was; I could hear the murmurs all around me. The cast was gathering near me to find their own parents, and the group grew larger. In the middle of all the excitement came Mr. Griffith, bearing a bouquet of flowers, an enormous smile on his face.

He swooped down amid my new admirers and kissed my cheek. As he handed me the flowers he said: "Congratulations. It's traditional for a leading lady to get a bouquet. You were wonderful." I couldn't decide what was more incredible: that Mr. Griffith had actually kissed me on the cheek, or that he had given me the first flowers of my life. Everyone smiled at me all day long; all day long, I smiled back. It was an absolutely wonderful day.

The days after County Fair kept on being wonderful. Girls who didn't really talk to me before suddenly did. Boys in the class who used to tease me just stopped it. A few of them even said hi in the halls. Now when I sat down in the lunchroom with my wrinkled paper bag, other people came to join me. I didn't really understand what had made everything different, but for once, I didn't ask myself about it.

I was sitting with my mother one night many years later, during one of my visits home, when I remembered those last weeks in Mr. Griffith's class, and my mother nodded. "Mr. Griffith said that would happen after the play," she told me. When I asked her what she meant, my closemouthed mother revealed that all my happiness had been part of a plan. She had known before I did that they would choose me as the lead in the play.

"The school called to talk to me about it," she said. "Mr. Griffith said you never talked to anybody except Monica, and that the kids wouldn't talk to you. He told me he wanted those kids to see who you really were. He told me, 'They don't know what kind of person she is, but they will.' "

Mr. Griffith did a lot more than show them what kind of person I was. He showed *me* what kind of person I was. Until then, I had remained ashamed of who I was. I knew I shouldn't be, I knew I didn't want to be. But I was ashamed, and all I could do was turn that shame into anger and silence, except in the classroom. Mr. Griffith helped me find my voice, glimpse my real self without shame. Doing that play in spite of how everyone felt about me, gradually winning them over, gave me a sense of confidence. I learned, too, that I was good on the stage—not Sarah Bernhardt, but credible—and that gave me confidence, too. The entire experience made me wonder what else I might be good at, and eager to find out.

Chapter 5

We were graduating from the eighth grade, and Parker, being a progressive school, helped us celebrate in a slightly different way. There would be no ceremony, but there would be a class trip: an overnight excursion to Hannibal, Missouri, where we could explore the backdrop of the Mark Twain we had been reading all year long. But I was excited because it would be my first trip to a hotel. And I was excited because I had just turned thirteen; I was a teenager at last, and could almost taste the four years left in my confinement. Four years from this moment in early June, I would be graduating from high school, leaving home to go to college, never coming back. I had only a little longer to tolerate my father's rage and distaste for me. Freedom was coming.

While I waited, I was working on my father to allow me to forgo summer school for a possible chance to work in the burgeoning presidential campaign of Robert F. Kennedy. Most of my classmates supported Eugene McCarthy. Some of them were going to work as gofers in his campaign. McCarthy was all right; he opposed the Vietnam War, as did most of us in those days. But in our house, as in many black households, the Kennedys were revered. Bobby Kennedy had shown himself to be an ally of black people in the preceding year or so. He talked sensibly about things that mattered to the people I knew—a big turnaround for a man who at one time had little interest in civil rights issues. But he was someone who had advanced the possibility of change, an example of conversion. He was, as my mother would say, a decent white man. Of course none of us could vote, but that was irrelevant. We cared, we wanted to act, even if we couldn't be part of the final decision.

A group of us—Monica, myself, and a couple of other girls—sat together on the bus, chattering about the differences in the candidates. We even talked about going to the Democratic convention in Chicago later that summer. Monica mentioned that lots of people would be camping in Grant Park near the convention site: maybe we could meet and hang out there. Another girl brought up the idea of becoming pages, and said her father might know someone who would be able to help us. I'd gotten used to this by now, these casual references of access to people and places that would otherwise be closed to me.

I was beginning to see what Daddy meant, about how white people paid more attention to who you knew than what you could do. He always said that lots of white people did business or hired people not because they were good at something, but because they both went to the same school, or their fathers belonged to the same club. I used to think he was just raving, but I started to get his point. I could tell my friends had never given it a thought—that one girl's father knew someone who could arrange things for us. I could tell they never wondered what happened to those who had no one to "make arrangements."

I decided on our arrival that I loved hotels. The Holiday Inn had a huge bed for each of us. There was a big bathroom with a shower in it, and something else I didn't have at home—a color television set. I turned it on and flipped the channels for a bit, long enough to be reminded that the California primary was that same night. After we were all settled, the rest of the kids jumped into the pool to swim. Mrs. MacGuiness, one of the school staff, noticed I was on the sidelines and asked me why I wasn't with them. She thought the other children's acceptance of me had diminished. But it was something much more mundane: I didn't have a swimsuit, and I couldn't swim. So she took me into town and bought one for me, and then she and Mr. Griffith tried to teach me how to swim. They succeeded in making me less afraid of the water than I'd been before. By the end of the day I joined the other kids and splashed around like a little fish, though mostly in the shallow end.

We went to bed early, in part because we were tired, in part because we had a full schedule for the following day. I didn't have any trouble getting to sleep, but I woke up in the middle of the night, something I usually did only when Daddy was on one of his rampages. It might have been the novelty of being in a strange bed. But that doesn't explain why I felt the urge to turn on the radio.

There was no music anywhere. On every channel along the dial, men were talking in hushed, eerie voices, speaking with the urgency that accompanies a great event. Half asleep, I couldn't tell at first what it was they were talking about. Finally, in a top-of-the-hour recap, an announcer made the unbelievable statement that Senator Robert F. Kennedy had been shot in the Embassy Ballroom of the Ambassador Hotel in Los Angeles by an unknown assailant who had been captured and was now in custody. Senator Kennedy's condition was not officially known, but the injury was thought to be grave.

I woke up Monica, who turned on the television. We couldn't believe it. Martin Luther King had been murdered two months before, practically to the very day. Was the country finally just falling apart? Were we all going to die, then? What had seemed like a childish fear when I was eight had become a chilling possibility five years later. I called the room of another girl to tell her what had happened; she was not amused to be awakened from a sound sleep for what she was convinced was a joke. I finally told her to turn on the TV in her room, and hung up. In a few minutes, most of us were awake and milling around in disbelief.

I don't remember much about the rest of the trip. I do remember, though, that my classmates were quite gentle and solicitous of my feelings. More than one of them spoke with me to console me. They were quick to remind me that he hadn't died; he was badly hurt, but he might have a chance. When I got home, our family spent much of the evening glued to the television, monitoring reports on Kennedy's condition. My father was blunt: he wasn't going to make it. Daddy was right; when I woke up the next morning, my mother told me Kennedy had died.

It seemed so unreal: another stretch of days spent watching the incomprehensible, seeing a much-admired man lying in state, listening to newscasters trying to explain what couldn't be explained to anyone's satisfaction, hearing the fear, the sorrow, the hopelessness in people's voices. It was as if someone had sucked all the life out of everyone I knew. The hope and enthusiasm, the sense of change and possibility—all these seemed to have been siphoned out of us in a great, vacuuming rush. I was angry; I wanted to do something, shake someone, make people listen and change.

At least there was the Democratic National Convention to look forward to. I grieved because my candidate would not be there, could not speak to issues that my family and I all felt were important. But the convention was drawing other spectators and demonstrators. The Black Panther Party and Students for a Democratic Society, along with the Yippies, had promised to bring their protests against the war as well as U.S. domestic policy, and dump them all into the convention's lap.

True to their word, a few members of my class planned to hang out at the convention. They were going to camp out in Grant

Park and Lincoln Park. On this, my parents drew the line. Daddy especially hated crowds of all kinds; even for something as innocuous as the annual Bud Billiken Day Parade, the black parade sponsored by the Chicago *Defender,* my father would allow us only to stand along the parade route. We were expressly forbidden to attend the party in Washington Park after the parade itself. Whenever that many people got together, Daddy figured, somebody was going to get hurt. The fact that he had always been right—someone was killed every year at the park—never kept me from wanting to go there, just as I wanted to go to the convention center. I begged, I pleaded, I stormed, I cried. But Daddy wouldn't budge. As far as he was concerned, I had spent too much time around those hippie white people anyway. No child of his was sleeping on the ground in a park halfway across town, or marching with hippies ANYWHERE.

The following week, we watched the Chicago police put kids' heads through the plate-glass windows at the Conrad Hilton. They're beating those marchers like they were black people, I thought to myself. I was sitting on the floor, my legs tucked under me. I was the closest to the television. Behind me, my father sat on the couch in his underwear, cursing under his breath. As I turned to see his reaction, he looked at me. "So that's where you expected me to let you go, huh?" For once, I had nothing to say.

The convention debacle came late in the summer of 1968, but I had already spent the summer embroiled in the adolescent search for identity, which, in my case, became enmeshed with politics. This self-examination had begun late in the school year, thanks to a talk by two speakers invited by a group of black students in the upper grades. The pair spoke about black cultural identity, and their immediate focus was every black woman's burden: her hair.

The hair issue is a cliché now, but in 1968, there may not have been a single more painful personal subject involving the meaning of being black. I had moved up in the world from a hot comb and Dixie Peach to straight hair acquired via a host of smelly chemicals that, if not carefully applied, could burn my scalp. This meant thirty dollars every three months, and hours upon hours in the beauty salon on a Saturday afternoon.

The two activists broached the previously unheard-of idea that whatever I chose to do to my hair, the idea that I chose to do anything was a statement in itself. My hair didn't naturally grow in thin clumps that stood out from my head of its own volition. Why did I straighten my hair? Was I trying to be white? The lecture itself had that same, slight undercurrent—the idea that these activists were speaking to us in a school like Parker meant that perhaps we wanted to be white ourselves. I wasn't terribly impressed with that kind of innuendo; I liked Parker, in spite of my rocky start there. I learned a lot, got exposed to all kinds of books and music I might never have encountered. I hadn't given up liking the Supremes or James Brown. Now, I liked the Beatles and James Taylor, too. I felt something in me growing broader and deeper, and I liked it.

But the question of my hair nagged at me, in part for purely practical reasons. It annoyed me to spend so many hours each month trying to make my hair do tricks it could not reasonably do. And once the question had been asked, it was hard not to ask others: Why was straight hair better? What good were bleaching creams? What else did I do just because the way I was wasn't good enough?

That spring I had been given as a graduation/birthday present a copy of a new anthology, *Sisterhood Is Powerful.* With all the excitement of the end of school, I hadn't had time to read it. But over the summer, I read every word, committing statistics and phrases to memory. Between its brilliant red-and-white covers I found page after page of harrowing facts and grim essays about the plight of women in America. Every page I read that summer gave voice to another set of questions about how things were—

this time, in the matter of gender. The more I read, the more I looked around me, the more I watched my mother's fearful deference to my father, the more sense feminism made, too. *Sisterhood* made a different point about the cultural obsession with the way women looked. It was an obsession I had observed in the behavior of my male classmates toward women whenever they saw one they considered worthy of their attention.

I had never experienced any such attention personally. As one of the few black women in the school, I had already begun to notice how asexually we were treated. The black men in school dated white women as soon as dating seemed permissible; white men, on the other hand, acted as though black women didn't exist. It might have bothered me more if it hadn't been for my father: regardless of race, Daddy wasn't letting me go anywhere, with anybody. So the length and texture of my hair, no matter what I decided, would affect only me.

But I wanted to be affected. I had come to believe that how you looked made a statement about who you were—not completely accurate, perhaps, but certainly in broad strokes. I realized that there were certain things I wanted people to know about me, just by looking. If I wore my hair naturally, people might know I was a black woman who loved the hair she was born with. If I wore jeans and loafers with my blue and white blouses, then people might know I valued freedom and ease of movement rather than sexual attractiveness. Most important, these seemingly minor decisions made a difference to me; they were a sign that I knew what I believed, and I was willing to act on it.

I had expected opposition from my parents on both fronts. They were the kind of people who still wouldn't let me get my ears pierced because that was something "fast" girls did. I was surprised, though, especially by my father. Daddy wasn't wild about the no-dresses-and-skirts stance. But he completely understood my desire to make a political statement about blackness by cutting my hair.

I went to the hairdresser one late-August afternoon and told her to cut off every inch of my permed hair. I had let the chemically altered part "grow out" so I would not be completely bald by the time school started. What was left was a thin covering of curly black hair, through which you could see the skin on my head. It was a brusque, no-apologies, no-frills look, one that matched my no-apologies, no-frills state of mind.

On the first day of my high school freshman year, we gathered again in the front hall. My classmates were amazed by my newly cropped hair. At least one of them asked what a dozen or so probably wanted to know: "You haven't become one of those militants, have you?"

I guess to them, I had. But I preferred to think of myself as gaining consciousness.

Virtually no one was hostile at school anymore. There were many people—some younger, some older—who liked me as I was. And in the months since the class play, I had changed, too. I had come to accept the circumstances of my life with a lot less embarrassment. I had begun to see in myself some of the resiliency that I had relied on, even without knowing it. And I had come to identify with larger groups of people than my classmates, or my family. I was part of a community of people of African descent; I was part of the family of womanhood. These were larger senses of identity than I had ever investigated before, and they felt powerful and good—much as I began to feel. Out of that sense of power, in turn, came a corresponding interest in, even fascination with, the lives and backgrounds of others.

When we all met as freshmen in Mr. Stephens's homeroom on the first day of the new year, I could see there were lots of new faces. Now that I felt more at home, and because I remembered the bitterness of my first day there, I was determined that I would greet all the new kids at least once. It wouldn't take long to figure out who might become a friend, and who might not. The two people I remember best were Mary Yoshimura, a Japanese American, and Leeber Cohen, a conservative Jew whose father was a rabbi at one of Chicago's oldest synagogues.

Yoshi and I liked each other right away, and I spent as much time with her as I did with anyone, even Monica. As we got to know each other, I learned that her parents had been interned in a California camp during the war and her three oldest siblings had been born there. Yoshi didn't know many details of the experience; her parents, like many survivors of the internment camps, spoke very little about what had happened to them. But from what she told me, I got my first direct experience with people who weren't black, but who'd still been treated unfairly by the American government.

Leeber was slightly shy, a little awkward—and very, very smart. He dreamed of becoming a surgeon, too, like Monica, only he went so far in his commitment as to play with rubber bands, manipulating them endlessly with his fingers in order to build the dexterity he would eventually need. I developed what was clearly a crush on Leeber, but he had eyes only for Yoshi, who thought of him as just a good friend. As a result of all this unfulfilled longing, we tended to travel in a pack, eventually using our free time to roam around the neighborhood.

Every high school student had a faculty adviser, assigned at the end of eighth grade, a teacher whose job it was to keep an eye on you until you were safely graduated. Monica and I were assigned to Marie Stone, the head of the school's English department and, for most of the students, one of the most intimidating presences at Parker. She was tall and thin, with rapid-fire speech and a precise mind. Our classmates, having been assigned more relatively benign advisers, felt pity for us. But Mrs. Stone became one of our staunchest allies. For both of us, she was part goad, part cheerleader. We were young women with minds, she told us, and she expected us to use them.

Freshman year at Parker brought a wealth of choices in curriculum, all offered in greater depth than in the lower school. I was more than ready to do as Mrs. Stone had counseled me. But I wanted other things as well. My summer reading had made me suddenly, acutely conscious of what we were learning in school—and what we weren't learning. I wondered out loud, after an early English class, why we were reading only books by white people. I didn't object to reading them, I just wanted us to read other things, too. This was not a controversial observation at Parker. Its motto, "A school should be a model home, a complete community, an embryonic democracy," was taken quite seriously by everyone. So it wasn't unusual to question your teachers, or the principal, for that matter, and there was an open-door policy that allowed for a decent amount of give-and-take. My teacher wasn't prepared to change the entire curriculum, but she was prepared to allow me to do some extra-credit work on a writer of my choosing. I chose Lorraine Hansberry, because of my budding interest in drama and because she was from Chicago, too. Looking back, I see that all of the class should have had to read Hansberry, not just me. But by my junior year, the English class reading list was astonishing in its variety—Chaim Potok and James Baldwin, N. Scott Momaday and Sherwood Anderson in the first semester alone.

It was experiences like these that reinforced my growing belief that I might actually learn to say the things I was thinking and not be shunned for my trouble. I began to believe it was possible to negotiate a way of belonging in this largely white, culturally very different world without abandoning the rest of my real life. For seven hours a day, I was the Rosemary who could hang out by the corner lockers between classes with a group that looked like the United Nations, griping about student government and arguing about local politics. For the remainder of the time, I was a young black woman who could feel herself growing farther away from Berkeley Avenue, but who still longed for it the way every child longs for home. My family could sense the changes in me, and yet they still saw me as Ro. It was more comforting than I could say.

I discovered, too, that one path to acceptance was to be really good at something. I knew how to do things—or how to bluff until I figured them out. So I joined student government committees and got involved in class projects. It was a way to prove myself, and a way to get out of my house; any late nights were permissible, so long as I was working on "school stuff."

My father was always pleased to see me immersed in schoolwork, so the growing stack of books I brought home every night delighted him. At the same time, he had doubts about the wisdom of exposing me too much to white sensibilities that he felt might one day hurt me. It incensed him to hear me come home from school and talk about "my friends," for I finally believed that some of the kids were my friends.

"Girl, you better quit letting these white people fool you," Daddy warned me over and over, propped up on pillows in his bed, the floor covered with the day's newspapers. "Those same kids call you nigger when they get home."

"Things aren't like that anymore," I told my father. "The world is going to be different when we all grow up. Everybody's going to talk to everyone, and understand everyone. People are going to accept each other for who they are, and everybody's going to love everybody."

Daddy lit another cigarette and grunted. "You don't know white people like I do. They don't love nobody but themselves. You keep living and see what I say."

I didn't agree with Daddy about most things, and I didn't agree with him about this, either. I already knew white people who thought being black was a cool thing to be, not embarrassing, or a disaster. It seemed obvious to me that if black people like me were willing to risk being ourselves among whites, retaining our culture and our slang and our worldview, and accepting them as they were, then whites should be willing to embrace the reality of who we were without trying to make us into something else. I learned the possibility of this most clearly in my sophomore year.

Our homeroom teacher was Mr. O'Neill, who had a charming Irish accent, a salt-and-pepper beard, a cheerful disposition, and an open mind. It was Mr. O'Neill's agreement to a class request that we be allowed to paint a gigantic sun on the front wall of our homeroom that caused my father to refer to Parker as "that hippie school." Mr. O'Neill's sense of fun endeared him to my mother, and the two of them became great pals from their first parent-teacher conference.

In keeping with my commitment to get involved in things, I had chosen to run as head of the sophomore class project, which was Christmas Decorating—another Parker tradition. The idea was to plan a theme and decorate the entire school grounds for the holidays; this included the painting of the school windows. I decided to create "A Black Christmas," which meant that major figures in the decorating scenes would be black people. For three years, I had looked at the glorious decorations in every school window—all featuring blond or blue-eyed people. I thought it might be a good idea to expand our notions of what Christmas could look like. I made sure to include Hanukkah windows, too, since a lot of my friends didn't celebrate Christmas. I had even solved the problem of how to get the appropriate skin colors: Glass Wax, plus food coloring, made an excellent, easily removable paint for the windows. I mixed colors for days before the presentations.

I didn't realize I would set the entire class to arguing about the appropriateness of such a plan. The class discussed the proposals in the lunchroom, on the playground, in the courtyard, everywhere, for days. It was the kind of situation that if it occurred today, would become a battleground. But all fifty-three members of the class talked about the differing projects with passion, yet also with great civility and attentiveness. When the votes were counted, it was found that the class was tied. The vote counters casually asked our class president, ineligible to participate in the balloting, whom he would have voted for. He said he liked my project best, that it was well organized and different from what the school always did.

And that is how I won—through a tie-breaking vote. Sophomores and parent volunteers filled the halls on that wintry night when we all decorated the school for the holidays. There were cider and doughnuts and music while we worked into the night (I myself could not draw and had to settle for mixing colors and running up and down the halls).

While we were waiting for Mr. O'Neill to give us a ride to the subway station, I walked across Clark Street in the frosty night to look at the front of the school. The lights were still on, and a few stray students and parents were walking through the gallery. But the glass-and-brick building had been transformed. There were Glass Wax murals everywhere: a black Jesus, a glowing menorah, a multiracial heavenly host. It was different and real and very beautiful. This is the world I want, I thought. This is what life should be like all the time.

It was harder for my friends to understand the other extracurricular activities I took part in, especially the fledgling Black Student Union. Many of the kids I worked with in other capacities felt left out. There wasn't much I could do about that; they *were* left out, to some degree. I had no language to explain my hunger for a connection to the culture that grounded the major part of my life. I needed the affirmation and the familiarity of other black students, the in-jokes that black people tell one another and that always require explanation when you tell them to someone else. I needed to see them and be with them. Scattered as we were all over the school, we needed this connection as much as the football teams needed to scrimmage or the chess club needed to play. We needed to work together toward making ourselves more clearly understood by white people who believed in civil rights, but were mystified by the new claims of black beauty and cultural pride that were so alive in black communities in those years. To bridge the gulf, we created programming for Morning Exercise, the daily forty-five-minute assembly in which all the school got a chance to see and hear events having to do with the issues of the day. We showed films, invited speakers, facilitated dialogues in which students and teachers could talk about these issues with us.

I did the same kinds of work with a women's consciousness-raising group in the high school. Just as black students found they needed the respite of speaking without having to explain every single nuance, young women at the school wanted a similar sense of shared experience. In many ways, the consciousness-raising group and the creation of a women's week of programming for Morning Ex (in which we discussed issues of feminism with a not-always-sympathetic audience) were a lot harder to do. But I was attempting to give flesh to all the issues I had become preoccupied with, issues that had everything to do with my own life.

Lots of teachers at Parker had the reputation of being demanding, even difficult. But my social studies teacher, Mrs. Moulton, stood alone. Mrs. Moulton was in charge of teaching the school's required American history class to juniors. She belonged to that most rare variety of Parker faculty—she was a disciplinarian. Class began promptly when the bell rang, but it didn't end until she had walked to the door and opened it—bell or no bell. Woe unto the eager student who leapt to his or her feet before Mrs. Moulton's hand turned that doorknob.

But that was hardly enough to secure her reputation as the toughest teacher in school. She assigned voluminous reading, and asked complicated questions about the materials, many of which were assembled from primary sources. I loved history and reading, so I wasn't particularly intimidated by her first assignment, a one-page paper about some aspect of the Revolutionary War. I read the assigned materials and wrote what I felt was a competent essay. But Mrs. Moulton's response to my work was much less satisfying: she gave me the first C I'd received in some time. My only consolation was that other members of the class did worse, as she was quick to tell us at the next class session.

Bewildered, I asked to see her in her office. She invited me to take a seat as I stumbled through asking her about why I'd gotten a C. Mrs. Moulton said: "Because you did C-level work, Rosemary. I know very well from the other teachers here what you're capable of doing. Why didn't you do that in my class?"

I was thoroughly confused, and said so. I didn't study for her assignment any differently than I did for any other class. That, Mrs. Moulton said, was the problem. She asked me how I typically studied each night. I told her I went to my desk and turned on some music, then read and took notes for a couple of hours every night.

"You have to concentrate to be successful in this class, Rosemary. You can't study with the radio on. And you can't skim. If you read something and you don't understand it, ask about it in class. If you'd read carefully, you could have gotten an A."

I absorbed her little talk, given in a matter-of-fact but friendly way. I think she liked the fact that I'd actually come to her to ask about my grade; most of the other kids were too nervous to do it. But I knew that junior year was the year that mattered most to college admission committees. Getting a C in this class could be a disaster for me. I resolved to try it her way for the next few weeks.

It was an exhausting time. Reading every word of Mrs. Moulton's assignments kept me up until one or two in the morning—no fun at all if you have to get up at six-thirty A.M. And the arcane language of the Revolutionary-period documents made for slow going. But after a week or two, I started to get a feel for the differing arguments and points of view. And in three weeks, when there was a pop quiz—her version of a pop quiz was an essay question you didn't expect—I got my A.

Now that I was less preoccupied with figuring out how to get good grades in the class, I found myself increasingly fascinated with the history I was learning and the documents we were reading. One of them, Thomas Jefferson's letter to John Adams discussing Jefferson's belief in a "natural aristocracy," was the source of a running joke all year. Those of us who consistently earned A's from Mrs. Moulton earned along with them our title as part of her "natural aristocracy," and it was fun to be part of a different kind of clique for a change.

But as I studied, I wondered, too, about all the contradictory behavior of the Founding Fathers, about Lincoln, about Daniel Webster, about the Great Question that, indirectly, had caused me to be here in the first place. Daddy had always placed great faith in the documents that built America. Now that I was reading them, and some of the thinking behind them, I shared his faith. And yet, I was astonished by what seemed like total duplicity. How could Jefferson write so stirringly about the importance of freedom, yet own slaves himself? How could Lincoln cherish the Union so desperately, knowing its foundation was built on the enslavement and the destruction of my ancestors?

It was only small comfort to me to know that Jefferson had been visited by second thoughts about his complicity, and his country's complicity, in something so fundamentally immoral as slavery. As I read the section from *Letters from Virginia* in which he writes, "I tremble for my country when I reflect that God is just," I did a little reflecting of my own. It was the spring of 1971, and I wondered whether these angry and tumultuous times were the ones that Jefferson foresaw.

At school, we were a microcosm of a new world: diverse, congenial, cooperative, and respectful of each other, if not of authority. But when I left Parker's manicured grounds each afternoon and emerged from the subway into my other world—the world of home and street and family—life was tense, skeptical, uncertain. The Blackstone Rangers and the Disciples still recruited quietly from our streets; the Black Panther Party sold its newspapers elbow-to-elbow with distributors of the Nation of Islam's *Muhammad Speaks.*

The Panther brothers and sisters in their black berets; the Fruit of Islam, with brothers in their sparkling suits and bow ties, sisters in their flowing garments—these made white people afraid. I knew this now because friends told me—their safe black friend—that the Panthers and the Nation scared them. They had reason to be afraid, I thought, though not of marauding Panthers running through the streets of Chicago shooting up the North Side, or the Fruit of Islam dragging so-called white devils out of their homes. The Panthers, the Nation, the dozens of other groups of black people intent on self-determination—they shared the common intention of changing the rules of the game. After more than two hundred years, they were responding with a revolutionary fervor, a willingness to fight for what they believed was theirs. How was that so different from colonists deciding to declare their freedom to King George, not ask him for it. My wish from years earlier—that civil rights people stop begging and start demanding—was coming true.

None of these brothers and sisters spoke much of loyalty to America, only of betrayal by America, and my problem was that, as far as I was concerned, they were right. I was in a first-hand position to see America's broken promises each night when I went home. And yet, in the morning, I would begin again on the other side of Chicago, the other side of the world, living and working and playing and studying in an energized, multicultural world, being part of a vision of what life could be like. What I couldn't figure out was the trajectory—the route we would all have to take to bring the two halves of my world together. It was a tension that would live with me long after I left Mrs. Moulton's class.

Chapter 6

Everything I knew about college I knew from the movies. There was always a certain scene in a forties college film, an almost standard shot of white girls in plaid skirts and cardigan sweaters, walking to their dorms across a broad sweep of quadrangle, some traveling in a giggling pack, the star—June Allyson? Kathryn Grayson?—linked with the boy of her dreams. I could easily skip the guy. What I lusted after was that long walk across open space, surrounded by libraries and dorms and freedom. I'd never met anyone who'd really been to college except my teachers. This was not so unusual in black communities—in 1960, only 7 percent of black women and men were enrolled in America's postsecondary institutions. It would be my generation that would triple that percentage within fifteen years, thanks to the desegregation of schools, the creation of scholarship and loan programs by the federal government and by individual schools, and the active recruitment of black students by schools all over the United States.

I started getting letters as soon as I took my Preliminary Scholastic Aptitude Test. The form asked if I was willing to be contacted by schools seeking minority students. I checked the yes box without hesitation. If schools were looking for me, I wanted them to find me. I had to go to college—anybody's college. As the catalogs and brochures began to arrive, I made piles of application materials from colleges, based on their geography. The goal was to find a school close enough to get home for Christmas, and far enough away so that my father couldn't just drop in on me. College was the vision of freedom I had nurtured my entire childhood, the goal that fueled my ability to hang on one more day in my chaotic household.

Daddy was not taking my plans for college very well. He had already announced that I wasn't leaving Chicago to go to school. He believed that leaving his supervision would encourage me to be, in his words, "a whore just like your mama." Our fights had grown more confrontational; no longer was I acting to protect my mother. With the false bravado of adolescence, I was deliberately provocative, daring him to hit me. One evening, after launching into a tirade about my incipient decline into whoredom, he turned to go back to his room, and I picked up a shoe and hurled it at his head with amazing accuracy. He leapt on me almost at once, and though I was frightened, and sore from his blows, I kicked him enough before my mother separated us so that it was worth it to me.

"You better come get this little bitch before I kill her," he told my mother, half in rage, half in disbelief.

"Kill me, then," I screamed back. "Go ahead. I'd rather be dead than listen to you the rest of my life!" I was hysterical at that moment, the rage in me unleashed for a time and honed in on its rightful target. What could any man offer me that would be worth a lifetime of this? I thought. My mother was appalled; she appealed to me to stop for her sake—the only plea that could reach me.

"Girl, he's just talking and you just keep going along with him." By now he had settled in his room again.

This was a common theme of my mother's, one I continually

resented. If the blood was still pumping, if I was not yet spent from the terror and excitement of the moment, I would confront her, too. "Why are you always making excuses for him? Why am I always the one who's wrong?"

Mama was mostly patient with this display. Once she got me calm enough to listen, she reminded me of something that, in my own rage, I had forgotten. As far as Parker, the state of Illinois, and the rest of the world were concerned, Daddy didn't exist. "He ain't got nothing to do with where you go to school," she reminded me. "He got nothing to say about it. I'm the one who has to sign them papers; they don't know nothing about him. You just go on and do your work and don't pay him no mind. I'll take care of this."

She was right; I knew that. But his constant torment, his continuing disruption of the household, and his taunts directed at me—these things were well within his power. When he was not threatening me about going away to school, he was announcing that I was too dumb to go to college anyway and that no one would have me. It was the kind of psychological torture that no sixteen-year-old is prepared to hear.

Later that night, I got up to go to the bathroom. I was unable to sleep, still churned up and angry from the melee. I found myself tiptoeing past the bathroom, into the kitchen where I knew there was a butcher knife. I picked it up, then moved to the door of my father's room in the dark. I could hear him snoring; as my eyes adjusted to the dark, I could see his outline under the pale sheets.

I wanted so much to be able to kill him. If he were gone, I wouldn't even have to go away to school. I could live at home with Mama and Brother and Linda and Terry, only none of us would be afraid anymore. If I could just sneak into his room, drive the knife through his heart, our troubles would be over. But I thought beyond the pleasure of killing him, to my mother and her sorrow—and to my own fear. Because I would surely go to jail, the one place I had promised myself Mama would never have to visit me. My half brother, J.D., my cousins—they were regular visitors to Twenty-sixth and California, the location of the Cook County jail. They loathed school as much as I loved it; they were adventuresome and fearless, always, it seemed to me, engaged in escapades involving stolen cars and joyriding, while I was too timid to end the life of the man who had rarely given me a moment's peace.

Yet I had made up so many stories in my head about my life, a long time from now and a long way from here. None of them included me behind bars. In all my stories, I wore a cap and gown, or I was rich and successful, traveling with my mother to California, where she had always wanted to go. I thought of those piles of catalogs in a corner of the living room, all those schools that might offer me a chance to get out of here for good, if only I could hang on. I put the knife away in tears, as angry as I was relieved that I could not do it. No matter how much sense it made not to kill him, I still felt like a coward.

I spent a lot more time reading college catalogs than I spent doing homework, especially my Spanish homework. My Spanish teacher was big on public humiliation for preoccupied students like myself. He especially liked to have the unprepared victim stand in front of the class and stumble through the homework exercises. On one particular morning, I wasn't in the mood to be singled out. So I did what any self-respecting senior would do—I searched for a way to miss class.

My salvation lay with a sheet of paper tacked on a hallway bulletin board—the college visitation list. Juniors and seniors had the right to skip a class to attend a college-admission conference that convened during class time. Quickly, I scanned the list to see what school was visiting during Spanish class. It was Yale, the first choice of my best friend, and an object of keen desire on the part of several other classmates. I had envisioned myself as a poli-sci major at Cornell, my first choice. But Cornell's seminar didn't meet until the next week.

The room was filled with juniors and seniors, most of them wearing the glazed look of desire common among aspirants to the Ivy League. As I listened, and glanced at the pictures passed around the room, the fantasy of Yale became more tangible, especially after I heard the magic word: *coeducation*. Unlike freshmen at Cornell, which had always admitted women, those entering Yale in the fall of 1972 would be in only the fourth class to include women as undergraduates. The school still had a quota for women: two hundred fifty, so as to preserve one thousand places for their commitment to train "a thousand male leaders." I asked the admissions officer how many women applied each year for those places. "About three thousand," he told me. I asked, too, about tuition; when he said it was four thousand dollars, my mind went blank. All year long, the five of us lived on about that much money.

I must have looked the way I felt, because the officer came up to me afterward and asked my name, and whether I was thinking of applying. I introduced myself and told him I didn't think I could beat the odds he'd mentioned. After all, my school's own guidance counselor had advised me to apply to the minority program at the University of Illinois so that I would be, in her words, "sure to have a place to go to college."

Later that day, the principal asked to see me. I showed up in his office, first puzzled, then relieved when he told me that the Yale recruiter had come to the office to ask about me. "He told me you said you weren't going to apply," Mr. Ellison said. When I told him I thought I wouldn't get in, he stopped me. "I think you have a good chance. Your grades are good, you have respectable SAT scores." (At least the verbal was; my math was dismal as usual.) "I think you should apply."

I considered it all the way home. It would be wonderful to go to a prestigious school. And though to my parents the very idea of college—any college—was a miracle, I knew I'd be better off graduating from Yale than from the University of Illinois. Even if what I learned was exactly the same, I knew people would think it was different. I had learned that much from being at Parker for the past few years. When I told people I went to Parker, their expressions changed; they took me more seriously. I wasn't just some poor little black girl with nothing. I was a poor little black girl with nothing but her brains. Daddy had drilled it into my head often enough: white people respected those pieces of paper. They might not like me, but they would like that Yale diploma. I sent for the admission packet that night.

All through the fall and winter, I filled out application forms and wrote essays and asked my mother a thousand personal questions about money—most of which I already knew the answers to. It was especially important for the sake of the Educational Testing Service's financial aid application, though that turned out to be the easiest form to fill out. When I reached *Amount you can contribute to applicant's education,* the answer was a big $0. I already knew that welfare and college tuition didn't mix.

Application fees could have been another stumbling block, but I was eligible for what were then called minority/poverty waivers: people of color and those without economic resources did not have to pay the application fees, which were twenty to twenty-five dollars for each school. I applied to nine schools on the basis of the strength of their political science departments or my conversations with recruiters—about the same number as my equally anxious classmates. That was about two hundred dollars, or a little less than two months' rent—just not possible for me without those waivers. Some things couldn't be remedied by government help: there was no way I could manage on-site visits to any of the schools outside Chicago. I could walk to the University of Chicago, and take the El to Evanston and visit Northwestern. But Yale and Penn, Cornell and American University and Wesleyan and the others—they would remain a mystery unveiled only by the talents of their public information departments.

That, in large part, was how Yale seduced me. It looked like COLLEGE, like every movie I'd ever watched on *Family Classics* or *The Late Show.* The coeds' cute plaid skirts were more stylish than June Allyson's, but the photographs of Cross Campus and Harkness Tower were right out of my fantasies. The University of Chicago was a good model, too, but it had the fatal flaw of being just down the street from home. No, to be perfect, the dream required distance.

Until the Yale materials came, Cornell seemed far enough away to satisfy my longing for space and adventure. When the packet did come, though, nothing else would do. I kept seeing the pictures of Cross Campus, with students looking appropriately committed and interesting, though not especially multicultural. (That would come later.) Throughout the catalog the emphasis was on opportunities. Yale, it seemed, had room for all kinds of people interested in all kinds of things. I had already heard of its president, Kingman Brewster, when he said that the Black Panthers could never get a fair trial in New Haven. It amazed me that the president of a place like Yale could make a statement like that; I felt encouraged.

Because I could not go to New Haven, my interview would have to be conducted by a member of the Alumni Schools Committee; no one was admitted to Yale without being seen in a personal interview of one sort or another. Because Parker routinely sent several students to Yale each year, a member of the committee was scheduled to spend a day at the school interviewing the seven of us who were applying.

The night before the interview, my parents began fighting again. I was doing my homework in the dining room and heard them start up as they battled from room to room. By the time I reached them in my bedroom, I could hear the strangled sound of my mother's voice. My father had his hands wrapped around her throat and was choking her. The sight terrified me. I jumped on him from behind and started hitting him, trying to pull him away, hoping at least to loosen his hold. Enraged at my interference, Daddy let go of Mama, turned, and punched me in the face.

He landed only a glancing blow—my father was a big enough man to have knocked me out if he'd really made contact. But he struck me hard enough for me to look, on the morning of my interview, as if I had been in an accident. The right half of my face was a complete mess. My eye was swollen, as was my lip: there were bruises along my cheek. The whole thing was turning a variety of colors, despite the ice I had put on it all through the evening. I was embarrassed and furious and miserable. I would have given anything to stay home. But the committee representative was there for only one day, and I couldn't get to New Haven in a million years.

So I dressed up in the good clothes I had picked out for the interview, and I went to school anyway. I ignored the stares of my classmates, though I did tell a few friends some story that approximated the truth. And I went to my scheduled interview with the representative, who was kind enough to talk with me about everything except my frightening appearance.

I decided that my chances of being admitted, already minimal, had disappeared after the interviewer got a good look at me. Yet one of my classmates voiced a different opinion about my chances for admission—and the reason. "They'll take you because you're black," he said. I looked at him, prepared to laugh at his teasing, but he was not smiling, and I realized with amazement that he really believed what he was saying. I felt weird for a moment. On the one hand, my guidance counselor was telling me that only a minority program at a state school would accept me. On the other hand, a competitive classmate decided that being black was an edge for being admitted to an Ivy League school.

I found myself wishing white people would make up their minds. For my own part, I wondered what made him think having enough money to pay for Yale wouldn't give him an edge. I knew that I was getting better grades than he was in the toughest class in school, so I wasn't worried about doing the work. I knew that many of my classmates talked about getting into their first-choice colleges because that's where their parents had gone to school, but I had no such reassurance to fall back on. The previous year, one of the Ivies had accepted a white student with a promising career in tennis, but what gifts I had were hardly athletic in nature. From where I sat, there were a thousand ways to get into college that didn't have any bearing on your grade point average or your SAT scores.

But what was even clearer to me was how little I cared about why I got admitted to college. I was in no position to care. They could take me because I was black, because I was poor, because the closest any of us had ever been to a college was when we drove by one in Daddy's car. They could admit me because of my essay, or my haircut, or because they drew my name from a hat. They could pity me if they liked, or congratulate themselves for their open admissions policy. It made no difference to me at all. The only thing that mattered was having one school, somewhere, say yes.

In its infinite wisdom, Parker was smart enough to declare spring break during the same week that seniors received their notices from college. Frankly, spring break for seniors began the day the last application deadline passed. We all knew college admission was contingent on successful completion of high school, and we knew we wouldn't flunk, but after the stacks of essays and forms and questions, we could be forgiven for not really being interested in mundane topics like world history and Spanish III.

It was April 17, my father's birthday. I was home pacing the floor while my mother cleaned an already spotless living room.

Daddy had gone over to visit his sister, my aunt Marie. From my perch at the front window, I searched the street for the sight of the mailman. College acceptance letters were usually received on April 15, but the date fell on Saturday that year, so we all knew that Monday would be our day of reckoning. Leeber and Yoshi and I had been burning up the phone lines all weekend long, trying to map out strategies. Monica was already in college; she and I had been offered a chance to accelerate out of high school and enter college a year earlier. I refused for several reasons. First, it would have meant staying in Chicago to attend the University of Chicago. That put me within my father's orbit and so was out of the question. In addition, I was already a year younger than my peers, and it had taken me a long time to get over it; I didn't want to be two years younger than everyone else. But Monica had been miserable for a while, even though her admission to the University of Chicago meant she'd become a doctor that much faster.

The doorbell rang, and when I answered it, the mailman announced himself. I froze at the top of the stairs and looked at my mother. "Oh, Mama, I can't; it's from schools. Suppose they all say no?"

My mother gave me her best I-can't-wait-until-you-stop-being-a-teenager look. "Girl, go get that mail and quit acting a fool," she said. The mailman handed me a stack of letters with my name and the name of my brother as well. At fifteen, he was applying to college, too, at least to those colleges that had allowed him to apply so early. I leafed through the stack, searching for the Yale logo, but there was nothing there. I was horrified; I guessed that if they didn't admit you, you just never heard from them again.

Northwestern sent a suspiciously thin envelope that contained a simple rejection notice, which stung. I didn't even want to go there, but it was the principle of the thing. They could have wait-listed me, at least! American University said yes, but they didn't give me enough of a scholarship to attend; neither did Penn. The University of Chicago said yes, but wanted me to go to summer school to bolster my grades in math, and Wesleyan had put me on their waiting list. Only the letter from Cornell held the clear and unambiguous answer I had sought—a yes, with money enough to go. It had been my original first choice, I told myself, and it was a good school. I breathed a sigh of relief.

I was in my brother's room—where our old Royal typewriter was—working on my housing application to Cornell, when the phone rang. Mama was asleep on the couch in front of *The Newlywed Game,* so I answered it. It was the Chicago area representative from Yale, calling to apologize.

"We're so sorry that there was such a mix-up with the mail," he said. "We wanted to call you before you made any decision to let you know you've been accepted to Yale."

I dropped the phone and started screaming. I ran around the living room, throwing the other acceptance letters into the air, waking up my mother and deafening the poor man at the other end of the phone. When I remembered that I had left the Yale representative on the phone, I calmed myself enough to pick up the receiver and apologize.

He was laughing as I asked him over and over whether he was sure. "I'm sure," he told me. "The letter should arrive tomorrow. Congratulations!"

I hung up the phone and screamed some more. My mother watched from the couch, making halfhearted attempts to calm me. Finally I collected myself enough to pick up the phone and call Yoshi. But when her mother answered the phone, she told me Yoshi wasn't talking. She was devastated that Yale, her first choice, had turned her down. The news took some of the joy out of my own acceptance. The two of us had fantasized about being roommates. And it hurt a little that she wouldn't talk to me; I had manners enough not to gloat.

It bothered me, too, that my brother was getting rejection letters from all the schools he applied to. I wanted so much to celebrate, but at least two people who were important to me were worried and disappointed about their own futures. Still, I couldn't help being happy, and Hiawatha dismissed my attempts at mournfulness.

"You're being silly," he told me. "I knew it would be hard getting into college at fifteen. I'll just have to work for a year and try again when I'm sixteen. You have every reason to be happy. Yale is a great school, and you've been dying to get out of here."

Even my father had ceased his constant badgering about my inability to get into school, faced now with the fact of my admission to several colleges.

"Where is this Yale?" he wanted to know, as I went in to say good night.

"New Haven, in Connecticut," I told him. I had found the catalog I'd gotten earlier in the year and I showed him some of the pictures.

"That's a long way from here," he said.

"A thousand miles," I said quietly. I had learned my lesson, made my decision a year earlier. I had no reason to get upset, nothing to react to—everything was all right now. No matter what he said, no matter what he did, as long as Mama and I could both draw breath until August, I was going to New Haven. Curiously, Daddy didn't start throwing fits, or screaming. He simply took the catalog and laid it in the bed beside him.

The letter came, as promised, the very next day. "Dear Miss Bray," it began. "We are pleased to tell you that we have reserved a place for you in the class of 1976. . . ." I don't remember the rest of the letter. The first words were the only ones that mattered. The scholarship was less money than Cornell had offered, but enough to get by. I walked around the house with the letter tucked into my pocket. I pulled it out to read to myself all through the day. I read it out loud to my mother until she threatened to burn it. I slept with it under my pillow at night. No matter how many times I read that letter, I never got tired of what it meant: I was free.

I was going to Yale in the fall with two other members of my class. One of the other kids admitted was the boy who'd said I'd get in because I was black. I have no idea what he thought, but he never again voiced that opinion to me. The other was a young woman from the popular group in school, pleasant enough, but not someone I knew well. We had never been friends, but now the three of us had something in common. It happened that way for many of us going to the same colleges; suddenly, it was time to move out of our established patterns and into conversation with our new peers. David and Julie and I agreed that we would attend the dinner given for prospective Yale students by the Yale Club of Chicago. The idea, I learned, was to convince those of us who were waffling that Yale would be an excellent choice. I was baffled by the idea that someone would have to be lured to attend Yale. I would have left Chicago that night if they'd wanted me.

At least that's how I felt until I got to the University Club on Michigan Avenue. There were dozens of people at this sit-down dinner, the vast majority of them white, male, and extremely old. But if they weren't delighted to see me, they did a fabulous imitation. I was met at the door by an area representative, introduced to several members of the club, buttonholed about my prospective major, regaled with stories about their good old college days, and urged again and again to come to Yale. I gradually gravitated toward the familiar faces of my classmates, feeling a sudden sense of panic I hadn't had since my early years at Parker. This place was all so formal, with paneled walls and thick rugs and chandeliers. I guessed Yale would not be anything like Parker.

My panic was full-blown at dinner, when I was escorted to a seat at a table literally covered with dishes and silverware. All those books I'd read as a child about etiquette were about to pay off; there were at least six pieces of silver on either side of the plate, including utensils I didn't even recognize. Frantic, I paged through the book in my mind until I found a crucial bit of advice: watch your host or hostess. I made a quick cross-reference:

hosts or hostesses are seated at the head of the table. I swiveled my head to the right and found one of our hosts, just as he prepared to pick up the spoon for the first course. And so I followed each movement of his, ready to mimic him for as long as it took for me to survive the ordeal, feeling the sweat gathering under my arms. It was a good thing I'd already sent in my acceptance form to New Haven; that dinner might have changed my mind.

I thought I would cry the night of my graduation from Parker, but I didn't. We didn't wear caps and gowns; instead, we wore suits or formal dresses. My mother made mine, a floor-length A-line cotton dress, white, with little red embroidered strawberries. I knew it wouldn't look anything like the clothes some of the other girls wore, but finally, all those things were unimportant. Yoshi was speaking to me again, talking about visiting me in New Haven; Connecticut College, the school she'd decided on, was in New London, only an hour away. As I laughed with Yoshi and my other friends, posing for pictures and talking about summer vacation, I realized that the night was just a formality; I'd left Parker, and Chicago, as soon as the letter from New Haven came.

Our "prom" was an all-night beach party in Michigan. Some of the other girls wandered off with guys in the class, out of sight of the parent chaperones, to neck and chase each other. I walked along the dark water, mostly by myself, thinking about my new life. I could hear giggling going on over the dunes, and I felt lonely. I wouldn't have minded having someone to chase me around the sand, just as long as he didn't want to get serious. But that had never been part of my life at Parker. I was the girl who was everybody's buddy, in part because I was short and dumpy, in part because I hated all the coy flirtation that seemed necessary to get a boy's attention. Besides, *coy* wasn't the first word someone would apply to me.

I had nothing against sex; in fact, having my first sexual experience as soon as I could get out of town and onto campus was part of my master plan. But getting serious, getting married, being stuck with someone who treated you like a child or worse—I had made myself a promise never to do it. I had waited seventeen years for my freedom. And I had yet to hear of a man who, once you got "involved" with him, would let you keep it. I planned to remember Mama's admonition: "Stay away from all these Negroes out here." More important, I planned to remember Mama's life. Hers were the mistakes I would not make.

Time crawled that summer. Thanks to the Model Cities program, a federally sponsored plan to renew and revitalize inner-city neighborhoods, I had a summer job with the city of Chicago that year as a day-care worker. It paid the minimum wage, but I earned enough money for my airplane ticket east, new clothes, and some of the books I would need. The first thing I bought was a big blue metal trunk; I knew from listening to my friends that I would need one. It sat in the living room, up against the wall near my mother's room. Each afternoon, after I got home from work, I would pull the trunk out into the middle of the floor and open it. My brothers and sister started to moan as soon as they saw me anywhere near it.

"Mama, she's in the trunk again!" And they would all start laughing.

"Girl, you ain't gone nowhere yet," Mama would say, laughing too as she watched me unpack everything that was in it. I kept there all the things that came to the house from Yale: maps of the campus and blue books with the course schedules, copies of *The Yale Daily News.* As I would buy clothes that I was saving for the fall, I'd put them in the trunk for safekeeping. And always, at the very top of the pile, I put the letter itself, to read again before I closed the trunk.

As the summer progressed, something else began to sink in: I was leaving home, and home was a lot more than Daddy. I wouldn't see Mama every day, or Brother, who had finally gotten into Knox College and was leaving not long after me. I wouldn't see Linda or Terry, or run to the store before dinner, or go to the park or the library with everybody. We were breaking up, it seemed to me. We would all be going in different directions. Suppose Mama got sick or hurt while I was at school? Suppose something bad happened while I was gone? What would I do?

"You'll go right on about your business," my mother told me one night, when I was worrying out loud. "There ain't nothing in Chicago for you. You need to go on to that school and get you an education. Everybody here will be all right." Mama didn't look worried at all, and I wanted to believe her. But it occurred to me that as much as I had thought about leaving home, I had never really thought about what it would be like. Maybe I wouldn't like it as much as I thought.

On the Fourth of July, Daddy violated one of his standing rules about public places and holidays. We went with some of our cousins to a barbecue at a park on the West Side. We didn't spend much time on the West Side, in part because the neighborhoods there were even wilder and woollier than the South Side. My brother and sister and I were playing with our cousins; not far from us, another group of rowdy kids were also playing. After a time, they began to taunt us and throw bottles at us. As the oldest, I felt it was my duty to get them to back off, so I started yelling at them and telling them to leave us alone.

My yelling only made things worse, and in a few minutes, a full-fledged fight was in the making. Just as quickly, my father was suddenly there—and the crowd of teenagers turned on him and began to beat him and kick him as he placed himself between us and the mob. They might have killed him if they'd meant him real harm, but they were not vicious so much as territorial. In the end, Daddy was badly bruised, and his wallet, containing the proceeds of a very lucky day at the track, was gone.

All of us were stunned and silent on the ride home. I had never seen Daddy lose any fight, but perhaps it was because there had never been enough of us at home prepared to hurt him. Mama wanted him to go to the doctor or the hospital, but he refused.

The hundreds of dollars he'd won and then lost weighed on him far more than anything the crowd had done.

I was sick with guilt, and confused. What made someone who spent his whole life hurting you step in to protect you against an angry mob of teenagers? Why, if he cared about what happened to me, did he treat me like dirt so much of the time? I had seen what it was like between girls who loved their fathers and the fathers who loved them back. Some of them lived right on Berkeley Avenue, where I'd grown up. They didn't have anything more than we did. But they acted different. The fathers had nicknames for their daughters: "pumpkin" or "li'l bit," not *bitch* or *whore*. They treated their girls with kindness and care; they supported and consoled them. Daddy was perpetually cruel, dissatisfied, terminally angry with me. But if he hated me so much, what made him rescue me?

About a week before I was to leave for school, Daddy, very quietly, walked into the kitchen, where my mother and I were talking about something, and handed me a hundred-dollar bill.

"You liable to need some things for that school," he said simply.

I looked at him and the money, then at my mother, and cried. I felt bad enough about all the money he'd lost trying to help me. And now he wanted to give me more to send me off to school. I went into the bathroom to cry; I couldn't touch the money. Through the door, I could hear the muffled sound of my mother's voice, trying to explain.

"She just feels so bad about the park," she said. "She knows you're still trying to make that money back." I didn't hear what he said. When I came out after a while, Mama met me with the crisp bill in her hand, and folded it into mine. "He knows you're sorry," she said.

On a sunny morning in late August, we all got into Daddy's Buick for the ride to O'Hare International Airport. I had already sent my big blue trunk ahead to New Haven, along with boxes of books and other things I thought I would need. I had a new pocketbook; inside it were my airline ticket and, folded carefully, the hundred-dollar bill Daddy had given me via Mama. I'd never been on an airplane; most of us had never been to the airport before. My brothers were having a wonderful time watching the planes take off and land.

Everybody had gotten all dressed up to see me off, especially Daddy, who stood holding his hat, looking mournful. Some Parker people who were already students at Yale would be on this flight, too. They were acting as unofficial guides, and some of them were already there. When the gate attendants announced my flight, Daddy started to cry. He grabbed me and hugged me tight; I hugged him back. I wanted to cry, too, but I thought I would be acting like a hypocrite. I couldn't wait to be gone, and yet . . . . Mama looked at me suspiciously and gave me a push toward the gate.

"We're all all right. Go on before you miss that plane."

Nobody else but Daddy was big on hugs and kisses, so there was no throwing my arms around anybody. I walked onto the plane and took the window seat I had asked for. When I looked out of the window, I could see the terminal where all my family stood, their noses pressed against the window, waving wildly at the plane in the hope that I could see them. I could feel myself crying as I watched them. The five of them looked so small and brown against those big plate-glass windows. For a wild, scared moment, I thought about getting off, but the plane was pulling away from the gate, so I cried and waved until they were out of sight, as the plane turned toward the runway and New York.

Chapter 7

Four months later I was in big trouble. It was exam period, right after Christmas, and I had a semester's worth of work to learn in two and a half weeks. I had exams in political science, economics, psychology, and music, and I didn't know much more about those subjects than I'd known when I got off the plane. The work was hard, but not much harder than my classes at Parker. All of my classes were lecture courses, and there was no real contact between my professors and myself, but they all had office hours I could have availed myself of.

I was flunking out of Yale because I wasn't studying. And I wasn't studying because there was too much to do. There was the freedom of waking up in the morning and deciding not to go to school. Or the unexpected pleasure of taking a walk in the middle of the afternoon without telling anyone where I was going or when I was coming back. I had keys for the first time in my life, and I was so unused to them that the campus police—responsible for admitting locked-out students to their rooms—already knew me by name. There were the twelve to twenty hours a week I worked at a local drugstore to make money for books and clothes and anything extra I ever got, plus the babysitting jobs I could wangle occasionally. There were parties and card games and movies and football games, television anytime I wanted to watch it in the TV room, free concerts at the music school.

But now it seemed I had paid for my sense of freedom with my academic career. I couldn't tell anyone about what I was doing to myself; I couldn't even tell me. I kept thinking I could handle it, get over being distracted by all this fun and get down to work in time. Even if I had known fully what I was doing, I couldn't have told anyone; the first rule of survival in my family involved keeping your troubles to yourself. When I walked into my economics final, and realized I couldn't answer a single question on the exam, I knew I'd run out of time. Of the four classes I'd taken that semester, I had flunked three. I could still read well enough to know from the Yale undergraduate academic code that three F's meant dismissal.

I was sitting in my room on a January afternoon trying to figure out how I would tell my parents. In New Haven, unlike Chicago, it never snowed that much; the East Coast had lots of dreary days with rain, and this was one of them. I was looking out of the window at the puddles of mud in the courtyard when the phone rang. It was the dean's secretary; the dean wanted to see me at once. By the time I reached his office, I had started weeping in shame. This was the worst thing that had ever happened to me—worse than anything my father had ever done, worse than any cruelty designed by hostile preadolescents. I didn't think I would ever have been Phi Beta Kappa, but I knew I could have graduated. Now I would have to go home in disgrace, and it was a disgrace I had brought upon myself.

Dean James Stewart Davie was a large, sallow-looking man with a very kind face. I remember thinking that perhaps he wouldn't humiliate me any more than I had already humiliated myself. He asked me to sit down, and handed me a Kleenex to soak up the tears that by now were leaking from my eyes despite my best efforts to contain them.

"Stop crying and sit down, Rosemary," he said, opening a manila folder with my name on it and looking over the papers inside. "You know, I know exactly what kind of person you are. You're one of those students with strict parents who spends her whole life studying, then comes to college and spends the whole time partying, am I right?" I nodded, and kept wiping away tears.

"Do you think if I put you on academic probation you might actually open a book next semester?" I found my voice and promised him through my tears that I would.

"Good," he said. Then he picked up the phone right in front of me and called each one of my professors to cut a deal. Before the start of the next semester, I would write a ten-page paper for each class on material covered in the course. If the paper was acceptable, I would receive a D in the class. Two of the three professors agreed; my economics teacher said that nothing I did could save me from that F. In my heart, I agreed with him; I wasn't sure I could write ten pages even about opportunity cost, the only concept from the class that I actually understood.

I couldn't believe Dean Davie was doing this; I wanted to ask him why, but I didn't dare. I only promised him to head for the library immediately and thanked him for giving me another chance. He smiled at me and said it might be a good idea to drop in on classes instead of sleeping through them, too. All I could think of in the next two weeks, as I wrote the papers that bought me that reprieve, was that I didn't have to go back home in shame.

As a freshman in Timothy Dwight College, one of Yale's twelve residential colleges, I resided in the basic freshman quad—a three-room suite, with two bedrooms and a decent living room with a working fireplace. The bedrooms had bunk beds, and simple desks and bureaus. A lot of the students talked about how ugly the place was, but I thought the rooms were adorable. My roommates and I were a motley group: Katherine, from Casper, Wyoming; Janet, from Wilkes-Barre, Pennsylvania; and Cheryl, from New York City. Cheryl and I, both black, were from big cities; Katherine and Janet, both white, were from small towns.

Janet was soft-spoken and friendly, but studied constantly. Once I started going to the library more regularly, I saw her there quite often. Katherine, it seemed, had a boyfriend from her old high school. Now that they were both at Yale, she spent a great deal of time with him. Cheryl and I grew to be good friends, in part because we had much the same background: strict parents and a life of unending study until we were emancipated by our admission to college.

It had been a long time since I'd been good friends with another black woman. The three other black women in my high school class were very different from me—much more social, for one thing. We all knew each other from the Black Student Union, but we had never been running buddies. It was different with Cheryl. She had an extremely agile mind, a lot better social skills than I did, and a raucous sense of humor that she encouraged in me. She was also incredibly beautiful, and the black men of the freshman class were constantly in our room on one pretense or another.

The black community at Yale was part of my first-semester seduction, but it was also part of my eventual education in a balance between work and play. There were only a few hundred of us at Yale, when you counted the sprinkling of blacks in the graduate and professional schools. For me, it was like finding a group of really smart, really raucous cousins I had never met. There were some who had college-educated parents; there was even that rarest of beings—a black man whose father had graduated from Yale. Most of us, however, came from families who'd spent their lives in factories or garages or someone's kitchen so that we could come to school in New Haven. Recruiters had plucked lots of us from less-than-ideal circumstances and encouraged us to come here, as part of the thrust of affirmative action on college campuses in the early 1970s. The policy of affirmative action began, after all, as a sop to more radical groups who for many years had called for reparations to the descendants of enslaved black people. The feeling was that compensation after all these hundreds of years might best be provided in a nonmonetary way—through opportunity and access. It was a sensible attempt to make up for the more than two centuries in which black people were largely barred from attending Yale.

It was a good idea for Yale, but not always good for some of us. Even for those of us who had attended integrated schools, there was the sense of being in an alien land. It was one thing to go to school with white people, and another thing to live with them. There was a persistent rumor that all residential colleges kept discretionary "psych singles"—extra rooms in the dorms—to cope with the inevitable personality clashes that arose. Some of those clashes were racial and cultural, not matters of personality.

I was most impatient with my roommate Katherine, whose only previous contact with black people included a member of her high school's track team and the woman who cleaned her parents' home. Having someone black actually living with her led her to interrogate me endlessly; she went so far as to ask whether my natural hair really grew "that way," or if I'd stuck my finger in a light socket.

What was most pervasive at Yale, however, was not its overwhelming whiteness so much as its overwhelming sense of entitlement. I thought I was familiar with it from my days at Parker, but it became clear I had mistaken privilege for entitlement. Yale was where I learned that leaders might be born, but more often they were made, nurtured in an atmosphere of success and expectation. Those of us who were black saw this complete sense of entitlement for the myth it was—we knew it would never be as easy as Yale made it look—but we were drawn to it just the same. It helped that many of the white kids we met weren't any smarter than we were. They were just more acclimated—to the nuances of class privilege, to a family tradition of being a doctor or a lawyer or a scientist or a writer.

Most of us learned to adapt that sense of entitlement to suit our own styles, modify it into a brash confidence that we would need in the world all our lives. But for a lot of black students the notion that we deserved our surroundings, our first-rate education, led automatically to the corollary that others did not, and that was a leap the rest of us could not take. To say such a thing would mean declaring our superiority to the friends and family we left behind in Chicago and Cleveland and Memphis and Baltimore and Oakland. Was I really better than my parents and brothers and sister, or was I better at playing the game of being absorbed into the elite? These were and still are questions at the heart of African-American notions of success, and I was only beginning to learn how complex the questions were. It was not for nothing that some of us feared giving up part of our true selves. Part of being black and successful—whatever your profession—involved learning how to make white people comfortable. And we all knew that white people were most comfortable when they could forget we were black. What we feared most was the possibility that we would forget, too.

This tension fueled the continuing popularity of the black tables in all of the college dining halls. We quizzed each other about our hometowns, and teased each other about their respective reputations. We reminisced about home, or made study dates, or played whist after dinner. At mealtime, we reveled in the respite from the stresses, both small and large, of integration. We felt the warm balm, too, of being adopted by the Yale staff of cooks and servers, janitors and groundskeepers. Like much of New Haven's population, they were black men and women who reminded us of the family and friends and neighbors many of us had left behind. They were glad to see us there, vociferously proud that we were there to study and not to work. It wasn't long before we knew each other, often by name.

White students resented this shared familiarity. On crowded lunch hours, when a long line of freshmen stood waiting to be checked in at Commons, I can remember passing to the front and waving to Miss Betty, one of the women working the desk. She waved back with a cheerful "Hello, baby," and checked off my name. It was something nearly all the black freshmen did, unless we were in conversation with a white fellow student and chose to wait in line with her or him. I recall a white student once asking me why so many black people refused to stand in line. I told him I didn't refuse; I just didn't need to identify myself to the woman on duty. Miss Betty knew my name, and she knew most of the other black students.

"If you ever spoke to her, she might know your name, too," I said. Many of the white students treated the men and women who worked in the dining halls as if they were completely invisible. These students never even looked up to say hello. And they rarely thought about what effect their actions might have.

One night in my dining hall at Timothy Dwight, a group of white students instigated a food fight. Mashed potatoes splattered against the wood paneling, peas rolled off the edges of adjacent tables. There were shrieks of laughter and hooting all around us. From a safe distance, the group of us seated at the black table looked at the white kids, and then at each other. Many of us were from homes where there was just enough food to eat, nothing extra to throw. And all of us were from homes where our mothers would have broken our knuckles at the first sign that we were lifting food any higher than our mouths.

It was a moment of great cognitive dissonance for us: being at Yale, with its aura of understated calm and its overstuffed chairs, watching white teenagers in bare feet hurl food that black people in the kitchen would have to clean up later. We were all silent for a moment, watching, until one of us said what all of us were thinking: "And they say we're savages." We all laughed, resigned to the label, but curiously reassured. If people like this thought they belonged at Yale, God knows we belonged, too.

One of the things I learned early on was that the personal style I had cultivated in high school—iconoclastic and plainspoken, unadorned and feminist—was anathema. I particularly remember an argument one night at dinner, when several of the men at the black table were discussing their plan to go "road tripping" to Smith or Vassar. The Yale sisters, they agreed, weren't being very cooperative sexually, and they were feeling a bit deprived. I found their expressions of horniness pretty insulting, and said so. Several of the men and I got into a fierce argument, and the confrontation ensured my reputation as a hostile bitch. Some part of me was hurt and grieved by this, and another part of me was pleased. I'd had a taste of popularity toward the end of my high school career, and I wondered whether I could expand it. But the part of me that didn't care if people liked me was actually entertained by the idea that I was scary to some of these guys. I couldn't imagine why they thought the black women they studied with had spent years writing papers and taking exams so that they could come to Yale and provide sexual relief for men. I wanted a man to sleep with myself, but some conversation afterward would be nice, along with some basic respect. These requirements, it seemed to me, eliminated all of the undergraduates. I would have to seek out a grown man.

I found him down the street, at the Yale Law School. Greg, a first-year student, was thin and frail from asthma, but brilliant and seductive. He was doing what I thought I wanted to do, and he found me attractive and desirable. That was enough to send me to the department of university health for my first gynecological exam and my first pack of Ovral-21, the birth control pills the student health service handed out like candy. Greg and I spent the weekends together: in the mornings we would walk back from his room in the Law School to my dining hall for breakfast, since the Law School dining hall was closed on weekends. My new relationship gave me a status I could never have anticipated. I suddenly seemed imbued with a mysterious and mature sexuality that baffled some of my peers. These men no longer sniped at me, but regarded me with a distant respect.

But my relationship with Greg had an effect on me that I hadn't anticipated: it was giving me second thoughts about my choice of career. All those weekends we spent studying together before bed, I could see firsthand the volume of study and preparation Greg had to undertake. The fact that he had so much to do helped me get a lot more of my own work done, but it also alerted me to the tedium and detail of the law. I saw, too, how the study of law affected his worldview. Once, during a date to see Earth, Wind and Fire, I found myself surrounded by first- and second-year law students during a delay in the start of the concert. By the time the show began, I had spent hours listening to my boyfriend and his colleagues discuss the possibility of filing a class-action suit on behalf of all concertgoers against Earth, Wind and Fire for the three-hour delay. If I go to law school, I thought to myself as the concert began, I'll sound like that one day, too. It was a far cry from the ringing eloquence I had always associated with the law.

Most of us had come to Yale to study law or medicine or engineering; it was important to be prepared for the revolution we were sure was imminent. Gil Scott-Heron's political music played on WYBC, the college radio station, and on the phonographs in rooms that had them, advising us all that the revolution would not be televised—it would be live. By the start of my sophomore year, however, Greg and I had broken up, and I doubted that I was fit for the law. A year of freedom from my parents had opened my mind to an unconsidered possibility: I might choose a career because I loved it, because it was fun. For the first time in my life,

I gave a lot of thought to what I loved, and discovered that my pleasures came from arenas I had always considered frivolous before.

I joined the staff of the college radio station as a producer on the afternoon segment *Black Spectrum.* I wanted to learn about radio, and I had just discovered jazz. I helped produce the news shows, and because I was a night owl, I eventually did the midnight-to-three-A.M. jazz show. I didn't have a license, so an engineer had to be on hand, but I did play the music I had learned to love—lots of Freddie Hubbard and Herbie Hancock in those days—and took requests. At least once, I called the campus police to walk me home after my show, after an enthusiastic fan said he wanted to meet me and promised he'd be waiting for me. He wasn't there, but I wasn't prepared to risk someone's actually trying to meet me. It turned out that someone on campus was a fan of my show, but I wouldn't learn about him for some time.

I had learned the rudiments of photography in high school, and bought myself a camera one summer. Since I'd come to Yale, I found that my residential college had a darkroom I could use for a nominal fee. So I spent a lot of free time my sophomore year locked in that small basement room, longing to become Henri Cartier-Bresson. I entered some local photography contests and even won a prize or two. But photography wasn't something I could easily major in at Yale; it would require becoming an art major, and my ability to draw or paint was nonexistent. To test the idea, I enrolled in an introductory drawing class, where the instructor placed cardboard shapes in the center of the table and asked us to sketch them. As I struggled over my drawing board, he walked through the room, looking over the shoulders of students, giving out praise and correction as he went. But when he reached my table and saw my misshapen squiggles, I noticed a pronounced silence as he stood just behind my shoulder. It was the nearly imperceptible shake of his head as he walked away that made me drop the course.

The other thing I loved was writing. Even amid all the pressures of school, it was still my great joy to sit with a notebook and sketch out short stories on lazy afternoons while I did laundry or didn't feel up to more studying. I was already taking English courses, but they were reading courses in the classics of English literature; they were not about the nuts and bolts of storytelling. In the second semester of my sophomore year, I took a class jointly sponsored by the English and Afro-American studies departments, taught by the writer and poet Larry Neal. He was an active and invigorating teacher who assigned us such exercises as retelling a Greek myth in contemporary terms. As I worked on assignments for his class, I could feel a sense of contentment in me that I never felt when doing anything else. By the time the class was over, I had decided to change my major to English. I would follow my first love; I would see whether there might be a way to make a living as a writer.

Even among my peers at school, this was not a well-received choice. By this time, Yale was entering what was popularly known as the era of grim professionalism, the wholehearted pursuit of a lucrative career in a traditional field. Black students were even more captured by this attitude. It was too hard to get into Yale, too hard to stay there, too expensive for our families, not to commit to a career that would pay back some of the enormous investment we had all made. So when I announced one night that I was thinking about abandoning my choice of the law for the more creative arena of writing, I was met with a goodly amount of scorn. One of my classmates went so far as to say that black America needed serious leaders with serious skills. He said I was as bad as the handful of our black classmates who wanted to sing or dance or make movies or act. "The last thing we need," he said, "is more singing and dancing black people."

Some part of me agreed with him. I recalled a moment in high school when one of the black students was performing at Morning Exercise, his bass voice filling the room. It was beautiful to hear him, but it was difficult, too, to watch the delight on the faces of white people. I was always so suspicious of their happiness as they enjoyed an expected spectacle—someone black doing what he was supposed to be doing. I sometimes felt that way when I saw black members of the football team. But I also knew that people couldn't help what their talents were, no matter how white people might seek to make that talent a prison. I knew that I had been writing most of my life. And I wasn't convinced that the white world was so comfortable with creative black voices, especially literary ones.

In fact, there were several black students like me who weren't rushing off to graduate and professional schools. I knew them very well, and as I thought more about what I wanted to do with my life, I found myself spending more and more time with them. In many ways, we were all pretty eccentric. We liked all the music our friends listened to, but we also liked classical music and Broadway show tunes and jazz. We frequented the Yale Repertory Theater as well as the local movie houses, and we even auditioned for plays put on at the Yale Dramat.

Some of these students were writers in training, like myself. Others were budding filmmakers and still others were actors. My friend Austin was the glue that held us all together. Attractive and urbane, Austin possessed a wicked sense of humor and a horror of the ordinary. Austin and I had met the first week of school, standing in line at the president's reception, and had been running buddies ever since. He had directed plays in dining hall productions at Timothy Dwight and Calhoun, including a version of Lorraine Hansberry's *To Be Young, Gifted and Black*. I was a member of that cast, and the play did so well that we performed it off campus for a short run at the end of sophomore year. The experience had helped to give me the bug—not necessarily to perform, but to create in some way.

Because Austin's great love was the stage, we were always trying to write something that would get us out of school and make us rich and famous. At the same time, there was a part of me that agreed deeply with the need for black professional people with a serious commitment to the future of black America. Once again, I felt at odds, and went home that summer with the idea of persuading my parents to let me take a year off to think it over. It didn't help that Yale was getting more expensive by the year, and the amount of my scholarship was decreasing exponentially. I figured that a semester or two off would let me think things through while I made some money.

Later that week, the Afro-American Cultural Center (known to all of us as the House) was giving its last party of the year. I went to say good-bye to people, find out about their summer plans, and get my mind off studying for finals. As I walked into the Enormous Room, a Stevie Wonder album was playing, and amid the dim red lights I could make out the figures of many of the folks. Some people were dancing, some were drinking, others were chatting in the halls, or were in the next room shooting pool. I started wandering toward the punch bowl when a man's voice asked, "Would you like to dance?"

The voice belonged to a guy named Bob McNatt. I'd seen him before; he was part of the artistic group I hung around with. But he rarely came to parties, so I was surprised to see him here. He was tall and dark and quiet; he held a lit cigarette between his fingers and kept it with him as we started to dance. We danced and talked about exams. I told him I was looking for a summer job and thinking about taking a semester off. Bob was hoping to put together a junior year abroad; he wanted to study at the London School of Economics.

"I thought you liked the theater," I said over the music.

"I do. But I'm an economics major. Besides, it would give me a chance to go to Europe."

We danced together the rest of that night, talking about acting and writing. When I told him I was thinking about being a writer, he said that was a good thing. And when I mentioned that a lot of people thought it was a waste of talent for the black community, Bob scoffed.

"That's nuts. Black people need art and music and good

books, too. Besides, if you don't try writing, how will you ever know if you're any good at it?"

We ended up walking home together, since his college and mine were right across the street from each other. At one point, he asked me if I was the woman he sometimes heard on the radio late at night. I said I was, flattered that he recognized my voice.

"Well, you have a great voice," he said simply. We wished each other a good summer, and I especially wished him well in London. His encouraging words about writing stayed with me on the trip home to Chicago. What a shame, I thought. I meet a nice guy, and he ends up going to London for a year.

My father, who by this time had grown accustomed to my being away at college and had had time to recognize the prestige attached to my attending Yale, would hear none of my plans about taking time off.

"If you drop out of school now, you'll never go back," he told me one evening after dinner.

"Daddy, I'm not talking about dropping out of school," I said. "I'm only talking about taking some time off. Kids do it all the time."

"I don't care what those white people do," he yelled. "White people are liable to do anything! You're not dropping out of school. You're not going to be some hippie roaming the streets. I sent you out of here to get an education. You're in the best college in the United States and you want to drop out!" He was beside himself. Frankly, so was I. He hadn't wanted me to go away in the first place, and now he didn't want me to come home.

Watching television later that evening, I stumbled across an old movie biography of Cole Porter, a Yale graduate, starring Cary Grant. I loved Cole Porter's music even before I knew he was a Yalie, so I settled down to watch it with a kind of knowing amusement. My father wandered in and sat down to watch it, too. By the time Cary Grant and Monty Woolley were returning to Yale for a gala concert, my father was completely engrossed in the story. At one point in the movie, one of the returning alumni voices a plaintive question: "I wonder whether Yale has changed."

I started to snicker under my breath as Monty Woolley replied that some things had changed, but not the spirit of freedom and commitment that had always characterized Yale. As he spoke, a chorus of Old Blues sang in the background, and the film showed a montage of campus scenes: Harkness Tower, the Old Campus, the Yale Bowl. As the last image faded away, I looked over at my father, who looked back at me with genuine puzzlement.

"How could you want to leave a place like that?" he asked me.

I stared at him, defeated. How could I tell Daddy that it was just a movie, that it looked that way, but that going to Yale didn't feel that way? Trying to explain it would be a waste of time. I tried to console myself with the fact that I had only two more years to go. Perhaps it wouldn't be so bad.

At the start of our junior year, it was Austin's idea to form a theater group with several of the other creative outcasts among us. We wanted to perform plays written by black authors as well as put on productions of other popular works with a multiracial cast—something that rarely happened on campus. We agreed to meet and talk it over at a dinner meeting in Silliman College, the dorm across the street from mine.

By the time our group had hashed out its fantasies, we had become a black repertory company called Shadowbox. We divided into two sections. One was to put on a stage version of *Casablanca*, written and directed by Austin. The other group would do a production of James Baldwin's *The Amen Corner*, directed by a sophomore from Chicago named Charles Jones. Charles was a member of the wrestling team, a serious opera fan, and a student of Russian. I had not decided which group I would work with, but for the time being, I agreed to be the company photographer, recording for posterity all the cast members of our productions.

Among the people who joined the group was Bob, the young man who'd been on his way to London the last time I saw him. It turned out that the London School of Economics was not as thrilled to meet him as he'd hoped, so he'd returned to Yale. But the quiet, gentle person I remembered from that night seemed to have disappeared. In his place was an arrogant and opinionated man who grated on my nerves in the worst way. I think it was because Bob was impossibly blunt in his opinions. If he didn't like an idea, it stank. If he thought someone didn't understand something, he or she was dumb. I thought he often acted like an intolerant snob, and I often told him so. He didn't know what to make of my not-so-gentle critiques of his style, and there were times when we would snipe at each other all through the meetings.

One evening I arrived at Silliman for an early-dinner meeting of the Shadowbox group and took a seat at our usual table, where Bob already was. To make conversation, I noted that I hadn't seen him around that weekend. He told me he'd gone home to see his parents, since it was his birthday.

"You should have said something to us," I chided him. "We could have taken you out for a drink, or gotten you a cake."

"Oh, I didn't think it mattered," he said carelessly.

I felt a funny little pull at the nonchalance in his voice. Of course it mattered, I thought to myself; he's one of us. For the first time, it occurred to me that Bob might be lonely. Whenever I saw him, I saw him alone. He'd gone home, I guessed, because he didn't want to be by himself on his birthday. I'd always thought he preferred his self-induced solitude. But now I found myself wondering about that, and resolved to be a little kinder to him.

Later that week, I was working on cast photographs for *Casablanca* in the common room at Calhoun. The drapes were open and I could see students passing as I worked. Bob was walking by—alone as always—and I waved to get his attention. He caught the wild motion of my hands as I beckoned to him to drop in. He ambled in, his knapsack on his shoulder, and asked me how things were going.

"I'm probably going to have to stop for the night; I'm nearly out of film," I told him, positioning one of the cast members against the wall.

"If you want, I could get some for you," he said, giving me a smile that made his face look quite handsome.

I thought that was pretty nice of him, and took him up on the offer. When he returned with three rolls of Tri-X and my change, something mischievous in me made me reach up for his face with one hand and pull him down for a gentle kiss on the cheek. The two of us were mildly surprised, and I went back to work, wondering what was up with me. I didn't ever do things like kiss guys on the cheek. Besides, I was sure Bob had a girlfriend. I'd noticed his frequent trips home, and the picture of a woman he kept in his wallet—"someone I know from high school," he'd once said. The fact that he didn't give more details made me suspect he was involved with her.

Bob stayed on my mind a lot, enough for me to transfer my dinner meals to Silliman several nights a week and sit at the round table with several of our friends, wondering if I might see him. He had a habit of placing his green canvas knapsack on a table near the serving line; it was how I knew whether he had already come to dinner before I arrived. If the knapsack was there, I scanned the room for his profile and to see whether there was an empty seat near him. If there was, I'd wander over with my own books and say hello. He would always smile and say hi, as I surveyed his tray to see how close he was to finishing dinner. He was almost always with people I knew, so it didn't feel especially strange to ask the general question, "Are you all going to be here awhile?" And almost always, the answer was, "Sure, go get your food."

So I would get dinner and pick at it while I listened to Bob excoriate Nixon as a liar and a traitor to his country (his resignation had occurred only a few months earlier) or talk about a recent play he'd seen on Broadway during one of his visits home, or a concert he'd been to. He seemed to know something about nearly every topic; he always had an opinion he was willing to defend. When I interjected a thought of my own, he listened to me seriously, even if he disagreed. What I had earlier considered arrogance in him, I now viewed as a passionate, often impatient, self-assurance.

By now it was clear to everyone what was happening—clear to everyone but me, that is. I persisted in the belief that Bob was just so much more interesting than the other guys my age. It was a pleasure to talk with him, that's all. If I never ate dinner in TD anymore; if I asked about Bob's whereabouts at the check-in desk so often that Mary, the middle-aged Irish woman who worked there, had taken to giving me status reports as I entered; if I tried out for a part in *The Amen Corner* (Bob had agreed to be assistant director) rather than work with my friend Austin on *Casablanca* as I had planned—well, it was just because he was so funny and pleasant.

I became the production manager of *The Amen Corner*, after losing the lead to a senior named Allyn, an incredibly beautiful woman with a singing voice like an angel's and an equally wonderful body. Her physical attributes didn't go unnoticed by Charles, the play's director. He offered me a secondary part, which I turned down, but promised that I would work on the nuts and bolts of the production itself. And so each night after dinner, I would grab my notes and walk across campus to the Cultural Center, which had provided us rehearsal space in a large open area on the second floor.

I was sitting on the floor in the House library one night after dinner, taking notes on a scene Bob was rehearsing with the main characters. I found myself watching him a lot more than I was watching the scene—the quiet, passionate way he spoke about the material, the way he moved his hands as he spoke. I liked watching his hands; they were large and graceful, with long fingers that, at that moment, were holding a cigarette, which he waved to emphasize a point. It suddenly came to me that I was feeling something very different about Bob than I thought—and the revelation plunged me into despair.

I had no way of knowing that I was even on Bob's radar. I wanted to pursue him, pursue the feelings I had, but I was too afraid to say or do much of anything. My feminist sensibilities were appalled; I knew I should just say something to him about my feelings and take the consequences. But the rest of me was too insecure to be direct. Suppose he didn't like me? Suppose he laughed at me? Suppose he gave me that most terrible of all speeches: "I think you're a very nice person, but . . ." The best thing to do, I decided, was to live with the feelings and say nothing while I considered what to do.

But once I had realized that I was attracted to Bob, it became harder and harder to act nonchalant. We all had a habit, after each rehearsal, of walking back together and stopping at Durfee Sweet Shop for a snack. Now I searched for ways to delay my departures with the rest of the cast, maneuvering so that Bob and I would end up walking a little behind the others, taking stock of the evening's work and trying to figure out what might be left to do. It didn't take more than a few evenings for this to become a kind of ritual for us. Even after I'd run out of excuses to lag behind, Bob and I walked each night along High Street alone, toward Old Campus, talking sometimes about the play, sometimes about school or our families. I realized during our nightly talks that we were becoming friends.

One evening at the House, rehearsals were especially tense. A rivalry for the affections of the lead actress in *The Amen Corner* had been brewing for a while between the director and the male lead. Finally, as Charles rehearsed the scene, a fight broke out between him and Pierre, and Bob had to break it up. I had never seen Bob angry before—neither had anyone else—but it was an episode to remember. He delivered a blistering speech on the collective responsibility of actors in a small production, excoriated everyone involved for their immaturity, and dismissed rehearsals for the night. We were all so shocked to hear Bob raise his voice that everyone scurried to disappear. But when he looked at me, he said only, "You almost ready to go?"

As we walked back along the darkness of High Street, the only sounds I could hear were our footsteps and the distant clacking of typewriters from open dormitory windows as students worked late into the evening. Finally, Bob spoke—he wanted to know if I thought he'd gone too far. I demurred, on the grounds that I was just the production manager and it didn't matter what I thought.

But Bob disagreed. "It matters to me what you think," he said. "If it didn't, I wouldn't have asked you."

The blood came to my face in a rush of pleasure. It just so happened that I thought he'd been quite right to read everyone the riot act, and I told him so. "Actually, you probably should have done it a while ago," I said.

"I know," Bob told me. "But I was hoping things would work themselves out. Now, we probably won't even have a play."

"Oh, that's not true," I said, in a rush to reassure him. "They know they were wrong. And it's not like you jump up and start throwing fits every night. Everything will be fine by tomorrow."

"You think?" he asked, and I could tell he was worried about it.

"I really do. It'll be all right."

It was, too. The next night, Charles and Pierre apologized to the cast and crew, and rehearsals went on a lot more smoothly. Later that week, while Charles and I were meeting before dinner about production details, I decided to tell him about my new crush. He didn't seem all that surprised.

"Do you want me to find out what he thinks about you?" Charles said.

I was panicked that Charles would do something horrible and

embarrass me for life. So I cautioned him to be as subtle as possible in his inquiry. I wanted to know for sure who that girl in the picture was. And I thought it would be nice to know whether Bob had ever considered thinking about me "that way."

Meanwhile, I was gathering up my courage to ask him out on a date. I had noticed in *The Yale Daily News* that an off-campus movie theater was showing one of Bob's favorite movies, *Love and Anarchy,* directed by Lina Wertmuller, along with Bertolucci's *The Conformist.* I had made up my mind to suggest our going together as soon as I heard from Charles that Bob was a free man. I got my answer in a few days.

"He likes you," Charles announced to me one night before dinner in the Silliman common room.

"What do you mean, he likes me?" I asked, with growing horror.

"I mean he likes you. He told me so himself," he said with great pride.

"How did he come to tell you that?"

"I asked him," said Charles. "It seemed like the best way."

I let out a scream that caused heads to turn, then lowered my voice to hiss at Charles. "You told him? How could you tell him? How I can ever look him in the face again!" I was absolutely mortified. But Charles was unsympathetic. He herded me toward the check-in desk, where I absentmindedly said hello to Mary. She smiled back and said in a confidential whisper, "He's here already!"

I moaned in despair while Charles laughed. "Rosemary, stop worrying. It's not like it's a big secret or anything."

"Why, did you tell everybody else, too?"

"No, we all knew anyway. You're always coming here for dinner; you hang on to everything he says. It was impossible not to know. I'm telling you it's all right."

I could have died. But I couldn't leave now; I didn't have a good enough excuse. So I decided to get a grip on myself long enough to make it through dinner. There was, for once, no rehearsal that night, so I could go back to my room and cry for a couple of hours.

There was a seat right next to Bob, saved for me by my thoughtful friends and meant to complete my humiliation, no doubt. Bob was in the middle of talking to someone else when I sat down, but he turned to me and gave me his usual quiet smile. Perhaps it wouldn't be so awful to be near him if he wasn't going to treat me like a lovestruck fool. In a few minutes, he turned to me again and asked me about my day. I made some mindless comment about it being uneventful, and tried to keep my eyes on my plate. At the other end of the table, someone had started discussing what movies were in town the next few days, and I found myself blurting out, "*Love and Anarchy* is playing at the Lincoln."

Bob said, "Well, I guess we'd better go see it, then."

I'm sure I looked completely stupid as I asked him, "What did you say?"

The smile Bob gave me that time was not quiet at all, but very sweet and knowing. He said, "I said, I guess we'd better go and see it, don't you think?"

I smiled back at him. "Yes, I think we should."

I've always intended to rent those two movies so that I could actually see them; all I remember about that night was sitting next to Bob in the darkened theater, conscious of his arm draped casually across the back of my chair. Later, as we walked home in the fall New Haven drizzle, he put his arm around my shoulder to steady my steps over a puddle—and left it there. When we got to my back gate, he kissed the top of my head and said good night, then ambled toward his own room.

I didn't know what to think. I'd prepared myself for the usual wrestling match at the door. Part of the fallout from the movement toward sexual liberation was that women often had to justify why they weren't having sex with a man who'd asked. But Bob didn't even ask, and that threw me. I didn't know if he'd had a terrible time. I didn't know if he'd want to go out again.

We saw each other a lot, in fact. There was still the play to work on, and the same group of us still met for meals and went to parties at the House. But more and more, he and I spent time together alone. One night, he climbed with me to the roof of Silliman College, through a skylight in the ceiling of one of its towers. It was a brilliant night, and Bob was showing off his knowledge of astronomy by pointing out all the constellations he could see amid the hazy lights of campus and downtown. No matter what we did or where we went, our time together ended the same way. We'd talk, we'd laugh, we'd have a wonderful time—then he'd say good night and leave. It was beginning to make me worry: was there something wrong with me? After a few weeks of this, I made a decision to come right out and ask him. I knew him well enough by now to know that he would tell me the truth. And no matter what he said to me, he wouldn't be mean or hurt my feelings.

He'd come over one afternoon to pick up a book I'd promised to let him read, and for once he was planning to have dinner at TD with me. Standing in my living room, I asked him point-blank. "You've never once tried to sleep with me. Is it because I'm not attractive?"

Bob looked a little surprised that I'd just blurted out my question, but mostly he looked thoughtful. After a pause he said, "It's not that at all. I guess I'm still not over my old girlfriend. And I guess I didn't want to start sleeping with you until all of me was with you, not just my body. You understand what I mean?"

I had never heard a man say anything like that in my life. I said I understood completely and left it at that. What I understood most was that I was irrevocably in love. Another young woman might have found this revelation exhilarating, even a cause for celebration. But I had always imagined myself alone; no, I had promised myself that I would stay alone. Men were for convenient sex; involvement was something to shun like the plague. I was so frightened by this overwhelming rush of feeling that I was thrown into a major depression in the days that followed. I did a minimal amount of schoolwork to keep myself from falling behind in my classes, and I put on a reasonable facade in front of others, even Bob. But I cried myself to sleep each night. In my heart, I was terrified.

Thanksgiving was coming up, and I couldn't afford to go home before Christmas. So I would be having Thanksgiving dinner in the Commons with the other students too poor or too alienated to see their families. Bob explained to me that he had to go home, but that he would be back to see me as soon as he could. I chafed a bit at his not asking me to come home with him, but how could he do that without making it look as though I were his girlfriend? Part of my annoyance stemmed from the fact that I didn't know what I was to Bob. I guessed he would just drift along with me until he recovered from his last heartbreak, but he gave me no clue as to how long that would be.

The upshot of my lonely weekend was that I had worked myself into a fine state of hurt and rage by the time Bob returned to campus Saturday afternoon. We went to the movies, but I met his conversational overtures with terse answers or stony silence. Finally, he'd had enough. On the walk back home, he asked me what was wrong, which only infuriated me more. What was he, blind? He asked again, and I exploded with all the hurt feelings and loneliness of the past week and a half. Bob looked more baffled than upset, and when I had finished, he walked me upstairs to my room.

"I didn't think you would be upset; you told me you would be here for Thanksgiving, and I told you I'd be back as soon as I could. And I'm here," he said gently.

"Well, I didn't think it was going to bother me as much as it did," I confessed. "It was lonely without you here."

"But I'm here now," he reminded me, and finally got around to kissing me for real.

We were lovers by the time school was back in session. I felt completely transformed, sure that everyone could tell I was in love by gazing at my radiant countenance. I was happy, confident, filled with all kinds of energy. On the nights when I did not see Bob, I sat with my friends in TD, listening to their agonies and triumphs with a kinder ear, joining in without defensiveness as I talked about my writing classes. On the nights when I did see him, we were together the way we had always been—not pawing each other in public, since it was not our way—but being silly together, with lots of teasing and very bad jokes. My observant friends noticed that we always had breakfast together on Sunday morning. It was my favorite time of the week. Bob would rise from the narrow bed we shared to go to the local newsstand and buy the Sunday *New York Times.* I'd be dressed by the time he got back. Together, we would take the front section, the Arts & Leisure section, the Book Review, and the Magazine, and walk in to brunch.

We sat at the black table most of the time, but just a little apart from the others; it left us more room for the papers and our breakfast. As we ate waffles or omelets, we each took a part of the paper. Bob usually reached for Arts and Leisure; I alternated between the Book Review and the Magazine. We ate and read parts of the articles and reviews to one another out loud. We would spin great fantasies about Bob's headlining a brilliant show on Broadway while I wrote incisive articles for the *Times.* At some point, Bob would rise and bring over a fresh pot of coffee, and refill my cup and his own. Our friends would join us now and then, teasing us gently. But neither of us minded very much. For the first time in my life, I considered the notion of happily-ever-after as something other than a misogynist plot.

Chapter 8

Falling in love sent me back to the feminist movement. In theory, I had never left it, but college life and all its freedoms had proved a lot more seductive than activism. I had abandoned my involvement in most things political to pursue the personal life I'd never had. But now, awash in all this happiness, I began to think. Suppose Mama and Daddy had loved and respected each other? Suppose, instead of meeting someone like my father, she'd met someone like Bob? What would the world be like if women could be in love and be themselves? I had always imagined my choices rested between being alone and happy or being with someone and suffering. I'd never considered the possibility of a third way: love between equals.

Among the black men and women at Yale, I had noticed signs of a disheartening traditionalism about gender. I think it especially grieved me because I thought we ought to know better. Men who understood perfectly the ways in which ideas about race circumscribed their life and choices drew a total blank when it came to extending that understanding to women. Only a handful of men I knew were patently different, and Bob was one of these. Not overtly political in the way I was, he seemed to think the equality of women was a matter so obvious that people who thought differently were simply not worth serious consideration. I felt, in contrast, that they were precisely the people who had to be taken seriously.

I had time for all this rumination, in part, because Bob chose to accelerate out of Yale after his junior year. Only two credits shy of graduation, he elected to save his parents thousands of dollars by taking those credits at CCNY in New York. We'd discussed it all spring. I knew he was right to do it, and I understood he wouldn't be with me for my last year at school. But it hurt just the same, and I was afraid. How could I be sure that distance wouldn't make him change his mind about us? Bob gave me one of those quiet smiles of his, and reminded me that he was not so easily dissuaded by seventy-five miles. He promised to visit every two weeks or so—a promise he largely kept with the help of Trailways, which had its New Haven bus terminal across the street from my dorm. I spent a lot of Friday nights meeting the ten-thirty bus from New York—with a big silly grin on my face.

As for the rest of my time, I'd gotten involved with the Minority Women's Political Caucus on campus in the spring of my junior year. It was a group composed of African-American, Caribbean, Latina, and Asian women. There were no Native American women on campus in those days, and even the one or two Asian women who had been with the group drifted away after some months. Those of us who remained found ourselves acting as a kind of support group for each other, and as a voice that challenged the more traditional feminism of white women on campus. I knew about the Yale Women's Forum, and was friendly with some of its members. But I vacillated about joining the group because their focus seemed so narrow, even antithetical to interests of my own. This felt especially true in subsequent months, as a series of incidents in my senior year revealed.

A rapist had begun preying on women living in Yale dormitories, and many of us were extremely frightened. At least three women had been attacked by the man, who was described as a black man in his late twenties with short hair. Such a vague description led to some very predictable consequences—the questioning of nearly every black man in the vicinity of the Yale campus. At a school in which student freedom of movement around campus was a given (unlike many other colleges in the mid-1970s), this level of surveillance was noticeable. In light of a historic tension between black men and police authority, these events were especially insulting at Yale.

I never had any great love for authority, and growing up in Chicago instilled in me a lifelong distaste for the police. The Chicago police were legendary harassers of black people in general and black men in particular. It was rare for a month to go by without complaints from Daddy about the police who stopped him. Once the police even stopped my parents when they were running an errand together. The officers were so rough with my father as they took him from the car for a "routine" search that my mother began hitting the cops with her purse. According to my mother, the officers were so stunned that they let them both go without giving them a ticket.

My own first encounter with police occurred when I was in junior high school, during one of our family's summer trips to the library. We were walking our usual route one Saturday afternoon when cops in a squad car stopped us and wanted to know why we were walking around. I told them that we weren't doing anything wrong and that we could walk wherever we wanted to—in retrospect, a pretty dangerous thing to say to two men with guns. I can remember, too, my mother cursing out half a precinct for detaining my baby brother on his way home from school because he looked like a suspected rapist. The fact that he'd been in school at the time of the attack seemed not to affect their judgment in the slightest.

These incidents were hardly unique to me; the lore of black womanhood includes the fear of police intimidation of the men in our lives. Faced with the real threat of an on-campus rapist, those of us in the caucus lived with all the same fears that white women lived with, plus a few bonuses. We knew both a growing anger at the climate of suspicion that surrounded our male classmates, and a deep frustration with women's groups for whom no police presence could be too extreme. We were just as vulnerable as anyone else, just as afraid. But we also knew most of the black men on campus as individuals, as guys who had walked us home from parties or stayed up studying with us for killer finals. Some of these men were our boyfriends—in one or two cases, our fiancés. At the black tables in every college, the brothers would tell their latest stories of being stopped by members of the Yale police, forced to show ID and account for their whereabouts, even taken in for questioning.

Even Bob was subjected to the scrutiny of the police, a scrutiny that was especially intense because he was no longer a Yale student. He had such trouble gaining access to TD on his weekend visits that I reported to the maintenance office that I'd lost my gate key and needed a replacement, a replacement I passed on to Bob so that he could move freely.

The Minority Women's Political Caucus found itself in conflict with white feminists over the harassment of innocent men based in large part on race. As one woman told me during a heated discussion, "Well, if they're innocent, then what's the problem?" The problem was that, for all its flaws, this was still America. Even black men, I told her, had the right to be protected against unreasonable search and seizure. At the black table, one bitterly angry man told of being stopped for the tenth time by the campus police, and blamed the hysterical rantings of women's libbers. I reminded him that rapists didn't ask women about their politics, and that I wanted the man caught, too, whoever he was.

It was my first direct experience with the convoluted, sometimes contradictory politics of race and gender, but it would hardly be my last. In the end, nothing was resolved. The attacks stopped as suddenly as they began. The rapist was never found. The communication gap between women of color and white women grew ever wider, and a woman's right to move safely and freely in her world—a core issue of feminism as far as I was concerned—was still at risk for all of us. The weeks of tension left me feeling torn in two. It occurred to me that when it came to issues like this, black women might always find themselves in a no-win situation.

I had a lot to be anxious about that year. Graduation was coming in a matter of months, and I had no idea of what to do next. I had toyed with the notion of graduate school in creative writing; one of my teachers, the poet and essayist June Jordan, had encouraged me to apply. But I had to be realistic; I couldn't afford any more school. I needed to make a living, and didn't know how I might do that except by writing as a journalist, not a poet. The usual paths to a job after graduation—an internship at a paper, or years on *The Yale Daily News*—were closed to me. I'd decided far too late that writing was the path I would choose, and I didn't even have clips to send to a prospective employer.

When I heard that a new weekly paper, the *Advocate,* was starting up in New Haven, I decided I had nothing to lose. I just walked into their offices one afternoon and told them I wanted to write for them; I added that I could take pictures. The editor, a nondescript and harried-looking man, regarded me for a moment and then said, "Stokely Carmichael is speaking at the Afro-American Cultural Center tonight. Cover his speech and write me the story. Get a picture, too."

I turned in a short piece, along with negatives I'd developed, in a couple of days. He ran the story and a picture, and paid me the princely sum of ten dollars. I was hard-pressed to decide which was better—seeing my name in print, or getting paid for something that was essentially fun. I gathered up several copies as the first entry for my clip file, and kept going to the *Advocate* offices every week. Sometimes they'd have an assignment for me, usually something local and straightforward. More often, as the months passed, I'd turn to my own preoccupations for inspiration.

The Equal Rights Amendment was a hot topic in 1976, and I'd discovered that the author of the original 1923 version of the amendment, Alice Paul, was alive, very frail, and living in a Connecticut nursing home. With the help of a friend who transported me to the nursing home, I did a long interview that turned out to be one of the last Ms. Paul ever gave. She was still quite lucid when I met her, and quite angry with contemporary feminists. It was ridiculous, she felt, for modern-day feminists to focus on issues like abortion and sexuality, rather than on basic constitutional protection such as that to be provided by the ERA. She saw sexuality as a fatal distraction, allowing the antifeminist forces to misrepresent the purposes of the amendment, and told me it would lead to the ERA's ultimate defeat. She didn't live to see how right she was.

One of the best things about being at Yale was the many opportunities to meet the men and women who shaped public policy and public opinion, even made history. My college, Timothy Dwight, was host each year to the Chubb Fellowship, a week-long seminar during which public figures lectured and spent time with students. Jimmy Carter spent a week at Yale before he ran for president; Jesse Jackson wanted to meet with as many of the black Yale students as possible during his week. Someone prominent was always striding through the dining halls with a tray, or showing up at a Master's House Tea, or speaking at the Yale Political Union, debating the hot issue of the moment.

The Equal Rights Amendment was still a hot-button topic after Alice Paul had weighed in on it. In fact, the Yale Political Union sponsored a debate on the amendment, between Karen

DeCrow, then president of the National Organization for Women, and Phyllis Schlafly, president of the Eagle Forum, a small right-wing group in Alton, Illinois. Most of the students knew little about Phyllis Schlafly, except that her demeanor was reminiscent of the headmistress of a Dickensian orphanage: severe, unsmiling, and very glum indeed. I didn't know much more about her, but I did know that she didn't just pop up one day to save the women of America from same-sex bathrooms; she had long been a darling of the anticommunist right wing. Something about her was fundamentally sneaky, a real contrast to the let-it-all-hang-out ethic that was a legacy of the 1960s and still very much alive in my world. She would appear on television perfectly coiffed, perfectly reasonable, dressed in smart little suits and little earrings, looking for all the world like the Beav's maiden aunt. But this was a maiden aunt with a law degree from Harvard, at a time when women with such degrees were rare; she was also a woman with six children and a husband no one ever saw or heard anything about. It was still too early in America's political life for the deeply personal vendettas that would come to dominate the political arena, but I can remember wondering, even as a student, if the life she advocated in her public appearances was really the life she led.

So when one of the members of the Yale Political Union, who was also active in the Women's Forum, asked if I'd be interested in joining a small group for dinner with Mrs. Schlafly, I accepted at once. It was hardly a fancy occasion. Though we ate the usual dining hall food, we were able to commandeer one of the "fellows' rooms" for quiet conversation. It was a very instructive meal. Some of the women there were feminists, but others were profoundly opposed to feminism, as were the men who accompanied them. Most of the men who attended were members of some of the stranger political parties represented by the Political Union—who could have envisioned meeting Tories in 1976?

I listened a lot more than I talked, mostly out of amazement.

A lifelong Democrat by inclination, I knew there were people who were Republicans, but the Republican Party of the mid-1970s had not yet devolved into the distasteful assembly it is today. There were moderate and liberal Republicans, and then there were the John Birch Society Republicans, but even my father, fairly paranoid in his own right, believed they were few and far between.

But this small gathering was a glimpse of the future. I didn't understand fully what I was seeing that evening, but I knew in the pit of my stomach that their vision of this country wasn't good for me, or for people like me. The people gathered around that table were angry, vengeful, appalled. Their America was being destroyed by feminists, civil rights activists, radicals of every stripe. I was the only black person in the room—and I felt it—but their displeasure far exceeded the sense that I had moved beyond my "place" in their world order. No one was rude, no one was hostile—on the contrary, they were unfailing in their courtesy. I was simply an unfortunate individual, a perfectly decent young woman, of course, who was part of an unhappy band of malcontents hell-bent on undermining the fundamental liberties of Americans.

Mrs. Schlafly sat at the head of the table, presiding over the dinner conversation in a pale pink dinner suit. Her makeup was flawless, her hair colored ever so delicately and pinned in a chignon that accentuated her icy eyes. At some point, during a conversational tangent that touched upon the government's increased support for higher education for students who might not otherwise be able to attend college, Mrs. Schlafly turned those eyes upon me.

"You're here at Yale on a scholarship, aren't you?" she asked me.

And thrilled to be here, I thought, but contented myself with a simple affirmative reply.

The small tight smile she gave me was brushed with annoyance. "Now, you see, my children didn't get a scholarship to college. Why should we be penalized because we have more money than your family?" She turned toward a young man who erupted into a tirade on the murder of individual initiative by the interference of the federal government.

I was speechless. My silence in that moment began with hurt; why would she choose to single me out for public display when she didn't even know me? How could she so quickly judge my life in those few seconds? But as the conversation around me went on, I remained silent. I had met people that I didn't like before; I had met people who were selfish, and mean. My father was brutal and violent, and college was my escape from his unstable presence and from the constant fear he provoked in me. But all those things were different from my sense of the room at this moment.

If I had still been a practicing Catholic, it would have been a moment for me to call a priest. I could feel something warped, even evil, invading the atmosphere. This was worse than anything I felt watching Southern racists on television; worse than the free-floating contempt I sometimes felt in passing encounters with white people; worse than my father's snarling disrespect for my mother. There was something fundamentally dangerous about these people. In the face of such unexpected danger, I was frozen into silence.

This was my first exposure to people I would come to regard as the enemies of this imperfect, but vital, democracy, and it would awaken in me a curious patriotism that I had always considered maudlin. I would resist these twin impulses—enmity and patriotism—for many more years. I would try to talk myself out of the instinct to demonize this small group of people whose vision of America was so antithetical to my own, and remind myself that given the relationship between black people and the American government, America was not so much my country as where I happened to live. I would console myself that what I had seen that night at dinner was simply a room filled with very smart, very conservative, very privileged people venting to the converted. But that small gathering would never leave my memory, and in some ways it would cushion the shock of what appeared, by the early 1980s, to be a permanent shift to the right in American politics.

The woman who invited me to join the group came up to me with pity in her eyes, apologizing for what she viewed as Schlafly's rude attempt to humiliate me to make a political point. The remark she'd made stung, to be sure, but the fear that lingered had little to do with what she'd said to me directly.

At the debate that night, Mrs. Schlafly faced Karen DeCrow, who showed up in jeans and a shirt, living up to every stereotype of feminists ever created. I was always a low-maintenance woman myself, and agreed with the notion that looks were often irrelevant. But for me, the operative word was *often*. I was also an African-American woman who knew that what you wore, how you fixed your hair, even your shoes telegraphed a host of messages. I would never have appeared before a public body in jeans and a shirt to debate an important political issue. Where I came from, the way you dressed was a respect issue: I would have been representing my people as well as myself, and how I looked would matter to those for whom I hoped to speak. For me personally, the way I dressed would also be a strategic issue. I would never allow an audience to be distracted from my message because they were too busy wondering why I didn't put on appropriate clothes. That night it didn't seem to matter: DeCrow, representing the pro-ERA side, won the debate. But I could tell from the practiced way that Schlafly worked during the debate that she and people like her were determined to win the larger war. I could also tell that the stakes we would all be playing for were a lot higher than the fate of the ERA.

People who'd been working for the *Yale Daily* all the time I was changing majors had already scooped up internships in their junior year. By the start of my last semester, I had begun to panic.

I was stuffing envelopes at my work-study job in the dean's office one afternoon, sharing my pre-graduation anxieties with Marnesba Hill, one of the deans and one of the few black women in the Yale administration. I'd kept doing stories for the *Advocate,* and I'd expanded my writing to include work for *The New Journal,* a monthly campus publication that had just started up. But my job prospects were growing much more slowly than my clip file. I'd never done an internship, and the only ones available in the coming summer were unpaid—a complete impossibility for me.

Dean Hill said that she might know of a job about an hour away, at the New London, Connecticut, *Day.* It was a small paper in a small town, she told me. I couldn't have cared less. Any job I got would have been in a small town anyway; I was afraid it was going to be some small town out west or down south, where I knew no one and where, frankly, I feared going to live alone. After making a couple of calls, Dean Hill confirmed that they were indeed looking for a general-assignment reporter. She gave me the address of the paper's managing editor and told me to send him a résumé and clips. I made copies of my work and my résumé with lightning speed, and sent them off with a prayer. In three days, I got a call from the managing editor, wanting to talk to me about the job.

A friend drove me to the offices of the New London *Day,* where I met with John Foley. Foley sat with my clips in front of him, asking about a couple of the stories I'd sent him, and every now and then he'd nod, and look at me, and say, "You went to Yale, eh?" It was a strange interview, though not at all unfriendly. He told me that he'd be meeting with the publisher and that I'd have an answer in two weeks. And he added that I'd have to provide my own car for the job. I told him that wouldn't be a problem, as long as I could start work toward the end of the summer, to give me time to make money for a car.

Two weeks to the day after my interview, John Foley called to offer me the job beginning in late August. The pay was nine thousand dollars a year, which sounded like a fortune to me. At dinner I told my friends that I'd gotten the job, and then recruited them for my next big task. I'd told John Foley that I'd need time to buy a car. What I didn't tell him was that I'd need to learn to drive the car before I bought it. That's where my friends Sue and Donna came in. They were underclassmen in Timothy Dwight, but we'd hit it off right away, and they'd been rooting for me to get this job and stop whining every night at dinner about my soon-to-be-ruined life.

Sue, a black woman from New Jersey, owned an enormous Ford Torino given to her by her parents. Each night after dinner, she'd take me out in the streets of New Haven and teach me how to enter and exit expressways, how to make hand signals, and—hardest of all—how to parallel park. I banged up fenders all over New Haven as Sue sought out the most difficult spots for me to practice in. This was part of the grand strategy. Sue alternated lessons with Donna, a white woman from upstate New York who owned a tiny yellow Ford Pinto. Both Sue and Donna reasoned that if I could learn to be proficient in Sue's behemoth, Donna's Pinto should be a cinch. They were right: nervous as I was, I passed on the first try. Now there was nothing left to do but pass my courses and graduate.

The only damper on my feelings of relief and success came courtesy of my father. My mother was happy for me, simply because I was happy. But Daddy was outraged that I would be writing for a living. He had never taken my love of writing seriously. Even in junior high, when I would come home ecstatic about creative writing class, he would interrupt me in a rage. "Nobody wants to hear about that bullshit! What did you do in your math class today? What did you do in your science class today?" As in most things, the simplest way of dealing with Daddy was simply not to tell him anything.

It was my silence that allowed him to delude himself into

thinking I would come to my senses and go to law school, or at least come back to Chicago to live. When I called to share what I thought was good news, and told him what I would be making, there was dead silence, then the explosion: "You spent four years at Yale to make nine thousand dollars a year?" Then he hung up the phone, and wouldn't talk to me for three months. My mother gave me her typical good advice: "Don't pay him no mind; you know he's a fool." I knew she was right, and 90 percent of the time, I was glad for the job and the chance to stay on the East Coast. The other 10 percent of the time, however, I caught myself wondering whether Daddy would ever approve of anything I did.

There was only money enough for one airplane ticket, so Mama came alone for graduation. I was nervous, because it also meant that Bob's family and my family—at least the most important part of my family—would finally meet. I watched them all together with a great longing during the dinner at Class Day. Bob's mother was gracious, as usual, and deeply proud of her younger son. My mother was just as proud of me, and as warm, charming, and direct as I knew she would be.

My mother thought the entire McNatt family was wonderful, but she saved her highest praise for Bob's father, a handsome and courtly man with a knack for putting everyone at ease. All weekend, he held doors open for my mother, helped her with her jacket at events, pulled out her chair, and complimented her on what a good job she'd done in raising a daughter like me. It was a chance to see firsthand where Bob's quiet charm had come from, and I smiled to think that, thirty or forty years from now, the two of us might be at Yale for our son or daughter's graduation.

For I had succumbed by now to the dream I had scorned all my life: I wanted to marry Bob. After years of declaring that marriage was the closest thing to legalized slavery, after years of watching my parents' combined misery, knowing Bob and being with him had changed my mind. A few rare souls among my classmates were living out my particular fantasy: graduating on Wednesday and getting married on Saturday. As Mama, Bob, and his parents talked together, I thought of how wonderful it would be if this were the nucleus of my new family. We could send for my brothers and sister and Bob's brother, and life could be complete and wonderful.

Bob, however, refused to cooperate. He was not remotely ready to marry, he'd told me, and he didn't think I was, either. I think that was the real source of my tears that day, as I marched with my class and received my diploma. As tradition held, there was no rain on commencement day. Most of the downtown streets were blocked as the entire graduating classes for undergraduate and graduate schools paraded to the Old Campus. The procession was kind of a kick for me; it was so much more traditional than anything Parker would have done, but satisfying in a way that less traditional ceremonies lack: this was the recognizable end of things. I wasn't sorry to be leaving Yale; I was thrilled. Sixteen years of school were over and my real life could begin; I was free, black, and twenty-one. What could be better?

New London was lonely.

I'd spent one last summer in Chicago, after a summer job in New Haven fell through. I got a job as a waitress in a neighborhood pizza joint, saving my meager pay and tips to buy my first car—a used Toyota that I named Bianca, but that my mother called Putt-Putt because of its noisy engine. Bob flew to Chicago in August to help me drive my car back east. He arrived right after my last big blowup with my father—a fight that was all my fault, and that crystallized his opposition to my desire to write.

For almost a year, I had attempted to publish a short story I'd worked on in college. In retrospect, it seems an undistinguished piece, influenced by magical realism and focusing on a chance encounter at a Chicago concert in the park. I'd sent it to *Essence* magazine, and just before I was scheduled to move to New London, the piece was published.

Daddy was rendered speechless when confronted with my name in print. He bought a copy of the magazine and took it into his room to read. He came out much later and found me in the living room. I had never seen this particular look on my father's face before—a look of genuine curiosity, as though he didn't understand who or what he was seeing. And then he said to me: "Where did you get this from?"

At first, I didn't understand the question. He repeated it. "Where did you get this from? Where did these people come from?"

I was contemptuous, tired of his making fun of me and of my writing. I answered honestly enough, that I didn't know where they came from, I just made up the people in my head. But I answered his honest question in that snappish, smart-ass way I had long ago perfected in conversations with him. He bristled, as he always did, and cursed at me; I shouted back something defiant and angry, and the moment to really answer him was lost forever.

I found out later from my mother that he had gone to a newsstand and bought every copy of *Essence* they had, and put them in the glove compartment of his car. Whenever he ran into someone he knew, he would stop the car and pull one out, turning to the two-page spread with a photographic illustration of a nameless woman and say, "My daughter wrote this story. That's even a picture of her!"—even though I looked nothing like the woman in the photograph. Apparently, he bragged about me everywhere and to everybody—except to me.

My job at the *Day* was a wonderful introduction to daily journalism, and the editors were extremely patient with me, considering I had no idea what I was doing. On my first day, the city editor brought me a stack of press releases to rewrite.

"I'll need a take on this one, two graphs on this one, a graph on this one, and see if you can get two takes out of this," he ordered as I scribbled notes to myself about what he wanted. After about fifteen minutes of reading the releases and deciding I shouldn't start out bluffing, I went back to the editor and pulled him aside to ask quietly, "What's a take, and what's a graph?" He was very kind, if a little nonplussed; he told me that *graph* was short for paragraph, and that a *take* was a page. After that translation, my early months went smoothly. Eventually, I moved to night side as a town reporter, covering meetings and elections in two tiny bedroom communities, Salem and Colchester, Connecticut.

I was two and a half hours away from Bob; I was working nights and beginning to chafe at small-town life. I had never lived alone, and suddenly there I was in a three-room attic apartment on a quiet street in a too-quiet town. I was the only black reporter at the *Day;* indeed, I was the only black employee other than the janitors, who treated me like a favorite niece. The only other black people I saw were the men and women of Electric Boat, the submarine builders. Part of the reason was the hours I worked: four to midnight suited my body clock, but made it murder to meet other people. Mostly I saw folks in Dunkin' Donuts, where I inevitably stopped on the way home. It was good just to sit in there, have a cup of coffee and a doughnut, and listen to other people talk, even if they weren't talking to me.

I filled my days with wandering through malls—my first experience with them, really—and shopping at yard sales, which I loved. Most of my colleagues at the *Day* didn't live in New London. They had apartments and homes in Mystic and Stonington, by the water, in the woods. They loved small-town life; they hiked and swam, or were raising families and wanted lots of room for their kids to grow up in. None of this was part of my life, though. I missed jazz and theater, so I especially loved the weekends, when I could meet Bob in New York for a play or a concert.

A series of muggings in downtown New London that would have been a squib in any metropolitan newspaper was worth a week's headlines and a special news meeting to discuss ways to enhance coverage. At the time, it seemed ridiculous to make such a fuss about an incident so commonplace in 1977 urban America that it didn't bear mentioning in most other places. But I was too naive then to understand how important those events were in the life of a small community. The truth was, I wasn't really part of the community there. I had reverted to a schizophrenic life. This time I was covering school board fights and zoning meetings during the week, then jumping into my car and zooming toward Teaneck on the weekends, where Bob still lived with his parents while he worked as a stock analyst.

While I was not adjusting to life in Connecticut, the rest of my family was living through a shock wave: Daddy had cancer. For all his hell-raising, my father had never been well. For years his night table had been covered with brown and white bottles, prescriptions from Walgreens courtesy of his various clinic doctors. We were forever being summoned to bring water so that he could swallow his medicines. So when he complained all summer of not feeling well, I did what I always did when it came to him: I paid him no mind.

By the fall after my graduation, he had captured my attention. Mama told me he confessed to having lung cancer, a natural consequence, I supposed, of smoking three packs of Chesterfields a day for nearly fifty years. Some part of me never believed that he could actually die. One of our family's mythological underpinnings was that only good people died. Evil people, it seemed, lived on forever. How else could it be that John and Robert Kennedy were dead, while George Wallace was still around? What was true in politics surely was true in life. Mama would be the first to confirm how evil Daddy was. "He's so evil, he don't even want his pants to touch his ass," she told us once, sending everyone present into fits of laughter.

The last time I saw him alive was in April. It occurred to me that I should go home for his birthday; it was increasingly clear that it would be his last one. He was back in his room, gaunt and obviously ill, just as disagreeable as ever, but in a lot more pain. He would not eat at all. He would order these vast, elaborate meals, which my mother would dutifully cook, then eat three bites and put the food aside. One night he really wanted spaghetti and a beer. I went to the store to get him a Budweiser. When I returned the spaghetti was done, and I dished it up and poured the beer into the glass for him.

I entered the room and stopped at the foot of his bed—right by the door—where I had stood so many times, usually in fear. He waved me in with a thin hand, and motioned to a TV tray, where I put the spaghetti and the beer. He drank most of the beer, and took a few halfhearted bites of Mama's food. But it was clear he couldn't eat any more. Asking him how he felt was pointless. I knew how he felt from the constant moaning that penetrated the walls of my room each night, along with the faint rustle of the paper as he tried each day, unsuccessfully, to read the *Tribune.* His bedside table was so thick with vials and pills that there was barely room for his lamp or his ashtray or his cigarettes—for, despite what the doctors said, he kept on smoking; what was the point of stopping now?

I had the feeling each day he wanted to tell me something, but I'm not sure even he knew what he wanted to say. I do know that on the day I left to return to Connecticut, he got himself up from bed, as thin and weak as he was, to walk me to the front door. He hugged me as hard as his frail bones would allow, and cried as he said good-bye. I kept thinking I would say something to him for those moments he held me tight. But all I had were questions, thousands of questions, none of which he would have answered even if he'd been well. So I went back home, to go on with my life, and waited for word from home.

It came on an afternoon in June. I was on a back road, on my way from Salem to New London with a list of real estate that had changed hands that week. It was part of my job as a town reporter to make sure readers could spy on each other's real estate transactions. As I drove along, the thought appeared clearly in my mind, a simple sentence: Daddy died today. I put it away as just a morbid fantasy. Still, people in my family knew things. Years earlier, my father woke up one morning and told us he dreamed his mother was going to die that day. I didn't believe him, but my mother did. At eleven-forty P.M. the phone rang. It was Daddy's brother, my Uncle Gus. Their mother was gone. I considered this ability the gift of the previous generation—intuition as a substitute for book learning. But I had been to college, and suspected the gift was lost to me.

When I got to my desk, I almost missed the note tucked into my Royal typewriter: "Call your mother." I picked up the phone and dialed. My mother answered, and asked how I was, and whether I was at work. After I had told her all these things, she just came right out and said it.

"Daddy's dead. He died about three this afternoon."

She was so calm. I was relieved. In many ways, it had been easy for me. I had not watched him die by inches; that task was left to my mother and sister and brothers. They lived with him as the cancer ate his bones and gnawed at his brain until he began to hallucinate. I only heard the weekly reports on his failing body during my Sunday phone calls, and even then my first thoughts were grateful ones: he was too sick to hurt or threaten anyone. My colleagues were sympathetic; though I never talked much about Daddy, they'd known about his illness and wanted to know if there was anything they could do. I thanked them, and said simply that I needed to go home and help my mother with the arrangements.

I don't know what I expected to find when I arrived home—the whole house lit up in neon, maybe, glowing in the dark from the amazing news. I figured since everything was completely different now, there ought to be some kind of sign. One thing was certain: the house smelled the same. Daddy's room still smelled of him—of Chesterfields and the motor oil ground into his work clothes, of iron shavings and the thousand manual tasks he had harangued us about avoiding in favor of education and a job that used our brains instead of our hands. Only his good clothes had been disturbed; Mama had them hung over doorways and draped them on his bed, choosing things he might have wanted to be buried in. It surprised me that he had not picked out his own exit suit.

Mama waited for me to arrive before making the arrangements. Metropolitan Funeral Home, it seemed, was the establishment of choice; the small burial policy Daddy had would be accepted there. The funeral home was a huge Gothic limestone house; the oily representative who greeted the five of us had eyes, not for my mother's grief, but for me. Time after time, as we walked through the display rooms, he lingered near me in an effort to tempt me, it seemed. I couldn't envision being cornered in a room full of caskets, so I spent the time maneuvering between the mortician and my mother.

Mama wandered through the rooms, stoic for the most part, but suddenly weary as she looked at an elegant casket of pearl gray. That was the one she wanted, and the funeral director made his notes. It was a lovely casket; that was important. After all, the whole family on both sides would be there, at the wake and at the funeral, judging and evaluating as well as saying good-bye and offering their condolences. There was a right way and a wrong way to bury your husband, even a husband like hers.

I did what I always do in times of crisis: I work and plan and organize and orchestrate—the occupational hazards of the oldest child. Brother was his distant self, even in sorrow. My sister, who was closer to Daddy than anyone, was distraught. But my baby brother was closest to me in feeling, as I discovered the night of the wake, when he rode with me to get more pop from the store.

"I feel like I ought to cry, but I can't," Terry told me as I drove up Drexel Boulevard. "I'm not sorry he's dead." The task of protecting my mother had fallen to him after Hiawatha and I went away to school, and he had adopted it with a certain viciousness. Once, when Daddy decided to act out, Terry punched him in the nose. Daddy chose to retaliate, the story goes, by shooting at Terry as he ran down the stairs. They periodically felt the need to slug it out, and Terry's budding adolescence had as much to do with that as his duty to my mother. Still, Terry, in his way, was as close to Mama as I was. The death of the man we regarded as an impediment to her happiness was not exactly cause for either of us to mourn.

All the relatives came to the wake, along with friends of mine from school, particularly Monica, some of our neighbors, and a host of the old running buddies who kept up with Daddy after he had forgone his life of profligate gambling and what he called chippie-chasing. The funeral home had done as good a job as possible in restoring the face of a 190-pound man reduced to 70 pounds in death. It didn't look like him, but no mortician could have accomplished that. Fleetingly, I remembered a college class about death where I learned that an open casket was not typical, except in what the book had referred to as "certain ethnic communities." But how else would you know the person was really dead? We had to tear my sister away from his coffin. Linda simply would not leave him there. I watched this from far away, in confusion and a little bit of astonishment. My sadness was reflexive, a drag on my emotions, something I felt because everyone around me felt so bad.

Back at the house, visitors drank and told stories about Daddy so wild and crazy they had to be true. My mother was a serene presence amid the mourners and revelers in her living room. At one point someone came to console her. She looked at the person and said distinctly, "Free at last, free at last, thank God almighty, I'm free at last." She was not gloating; hers was a heartfelt thanks. Mama had done her duty and, in return, had been released from bondage while she was still young enough to appreciate it. The person she said it to was shocked; I knew exactly what she meant.

At the funeral, my cousin Niecie—whom Daddy had always liked—sang his favorite hymn, "Precious Lord." Mama and I had arranged for two limousines to carry us and my father's sister and her husband; Oakwoods Cemetery was a long, long drive. We were taken to a plot far from the cemetery's center. It was completely nondescript; I suspect that it was land freshly annexed by the cemetery. Daddy had no gravestone to mark his resting place. Someone among us asked how we might find his grave again, and we were told by an official that there was a kind of map, demarcating where every body lay. Someday, the man told us, when we wanted a headstone for the grave, we would of course be able to find it. I didn't tell them that I planned never to look for the spot.

Mama cried a little when they lowered Daddy's casket, and hung around awhile to see whether they would actually bury him in it, or dump the body out into a pine box and resell the pearl-gray one. Years earlier, Daddy himself had told the story of standing at the newly dug grave of his mother and instructing the gravediggers to cover his mother's coffin with dirt then and there. He loved to recount the gravediggers' stalling and his own response—that he had paid to have his mother buried in that particular coffin and he intended to stand right there until they buried her in it. He stood, he told us, until the last shovelful of dirt was tamped down, and then he went home.

None of us had Daddy's endurance; when the limousines were ready to return, we went back with them. None of us really knows whether they turned Daddy out into that hole in his good suit and his Dunlop hat and his Florsheim shoes. "Don't worry," one of my brothers said. "If they did, Daddy will come back and haunt their ass"—something my father had always promised he'd do when he died. Irreverently, we howled with laughter. He had threatened especially to disturb my mother's peace, but she told me later: "I sleep sound every night."

I'd been at the *Day* nearly a year, and even before Daddy died, I'd been restless. I knew I belonged in New York, and had made some fledgling attempts to get there. Earlier that spring, I'd taken a day off to visit New York employment agencies that specialized in publishing jobs. At least two agents said they'd call if something "appropriate" came up. But I could tell from their expressions that my being black made me too inappropriate for that occasion ever to arise. Next, I tried calling and making appointments for preliminary interviews at the agencies. On the phone, my credentials and Ivy League education made me a promising young woman. In person, opportunities suddenly vanished. It was such an old story, I wasn't even angry. It was happening to all my friends from college in one way or another. We traded horror stories whenever we met for drinks. One young man, especially tall and especially dark-skinned, was told by an interviewer that he should retire the navy blue suit he'd invested in, since "navy blue is a power color, and you don't want to give the wrong impression." He was so impressed by her advice that he went out and bought two more just like it—"so they'll be clear about the impression I want to make," he said defiantly.

Only one of the many agencies I visited actually interviewed me when I showed up. The employment counselor arranged an interview for me with Scholastic Magazines, which, as it turned out, had been seeking for some time to diversify its workforce—hence my warm welcome at the employment agency. I was excited: not only was it a job, but it was one with a company I knew as a consumer. St. Ambrose students read the rival magazine *My Weekly Reader*, but every girl scraped together her pennies to buy books from the Tab Book Club. The books were peopled by carefree blond girls whose parents owned houses and had office jobs, girls who spent their summers drinking lemonade and volunteering in hospitals and going to the town pool looking for nice boys. Their fantasy lives had been the source of many happy summer evenings for me. It seemed right to be able to return the favor in some way.

The job turned out to be as an assistant editor for a social studies magazine for high school students who read below grade level. The editor, a man in his late thirties, was suitably impressed by my Ivy League credentials, and made clear to me that this was primarily a writing job, and a specialized one at that: sentence and paragraph length was strictly formulaic. Did I care? It was a real magazine job in New York. I accepted with pleasure.

I was planning to stay only two years. I didn't like the idea of actually living in New York City but I didn't have much choice. If I wanted to work in publishing, I needed to be there. All that spring, as I perused the want ads and the real estate sections, I had set a goal for myself: to be working for a national magazine by the time I was twenty-five. I had more than three years to make the grade. But first, I had to be where the jobs were.

I found my apartment on a Fourth of July weekend; it was a tiny one-bedroom on the Upper West Side, with a working fireplace. Bob and I had spotted it in the Sunday *Times,* and it was he who warned me to take it right away if I liked it. On July 22, 1977, Bob pulled up in front of my new apartment in a rented U-Haul, with me following in my ancient, shabby blue Toyota. We unloaded my minimal possessions, including my oak four-poster, which barely fit into the bedroom, and collapsed into an exhausted sleep. Finally, things were working out the way I'd always planned them. I had a cute apartment, a wonderful job, and a good man who loved me.

One Sunday night in early fall, I was in my new apartment with the television on. I was hanging curtains on the sole window in my narrow living room; a fire was burning in the fireplace and dinner was cooking in the closet-sized kitchen. I was standing on the ladder, adjusting the curtain hooks, when the theme music from *Kojak* came on. I felt an ache in my throat. *Kojak* had been one of my father's favorite television shows, right up there with *The F.B.I.* and *Mission: Impossible,* which he loved passionately (though he hated that Barney Collier, the only black character, was always scrambling around behind a wall with a screwdriver).

I hated *Kojak;* it was just another dumb police show to me. But hearing the music made me remember that Daddy would curse you out for not waking him up when it was time for the show. A thousand memories of him followed in the wake of that music, and for the first time, more than a year after his death, not all of them were bad. I was focused on the fuzzy memories of girlhood, the fleeting moments when I was afraid of the dark, of thunder, and he—not Mama—was the person who made me feel safe. I thought it might be homesickness that was plaguing me. I hadn't seen my family in months, though I talked to them every week. But that music from *Kojak* was not conjuring up memories of my mother or brothers or sister—only of a tall man with rough hands that used to lift me high above his head, hands that, before they grew accustomed to beating me, had once tucked me into bed. Once, a long time ago, I was his little girl, and that time would never come again. It was that realization that made me come down from the ladder, crying for the father I suddenly wanted but would never have.

Chapter 9

My father's death in mid-1977 was only the beginning of what proved to be a depressing slide downward. Though I'd come to New York in pursuit of my writing career, I'd also come to be near Bob, who was going through a few changes of his own. My arrival only exacerbated the tensions that had sprung up between us since graduation. Bob was miserable as a stock analyst, and he horrified his mother by renewing his commitment to a life in the theater, applying to drama schools all over the country. My greatest fear was that he'd get accepted by the American Conservatory Theater in San Francisco, thus separating us forever. He'd applied to Yale Drama, and to the acting program at NYU. I'd gently tried to persuade him to apply to the Goodman Theater program in Chicago, so that if he was accepted I'd have a great excuse to follow him there.

I was spending an April weekend with his family in New Jersey, and we were sitting around trying to figure out what he might do if he was rejected by all the schools. ACT had already said no, much to my secret relief, but we hadn't heard from the others.

Suddenly Bob's mother remembered that a letter had come for him from NYU. Bob leapt from his chair and dashed upstairs, with me in hot pursuit. I ran into his room just as he opened what proved to be an acceptance letter from NYU. We danced, we screamed, we hugged and kissed and screamed some more.

For once, Bob had done something his parents did not approve of. There were very few black stock analysts on Wall Street in those days, and he was abandoning what might prove to be a promising career for something insecure and largely unprofitable. His mother appealed to me to talk some sense into him, but she was asking the wrong woman. How could I think of asking him to go on doing something he hated and give up one of his great passions? I remembered those long night walks on campus, with Bob reminding me that I had the right—even the duty—to try writing if that was what I wanted. Loving him as I did, how could I not have the same faith in him?

I might not have been so noble if I'd understood what graduate school would mean to our relationship. By the time I settled into my Manhattan apartment, expecting the two of us to spend more time together, he was immersed in the artistic equivalent of boot camp: class after class during the day, driving taxis at night. The first-year program at NYU was intense, and disturbing to Bob in ways so personal he would not share what happened even with me. Always the quieter half, he became more silent and introspective than usual. I was accustomed to knowing and understanding large parts of what was happening in his life, and so his reticence hurt. Our infrequent weekends grew strained. Toward the end, the only thing the two of us shared was a sense of anger. Bob was angry that I wouldn't leave him alone; I was angry that he wouldn't tell me anything; and both of us were angry at our own helplessness: we couldn't seem to stop our downward spiral. We loved each other, I knew we did. But love was not enough.

One weekend evening, everything was all wrong. We couldn't decide on a place for dinner. Once we compromised on something and the food came, neither of us liked it. We sniped at each other all through dinner, and when Bob made some cutting remark that reduced me to tears, I gathered my things and walked out of the restaurant toward home. He caught up with me, I thought, to apologize, but instead began to yell at me for being possessive and clingy. I yelled back about his chilly and withdrawn nature. We fought all the way back to my apartment, even though neither of us could pinpoint the source of our rage. Finally, Bob grabbed his jacket to leave, and I went to the door to stop him.

"Look, this isn't good," I said, near tears. "We need to talk about things; you can't just leave."

"Rosemary, I have to go," he told me, and the desperation in his eyes was terrible to see. "I can't deal with this right now. I'll call you." It was the first time he'd ever lied to me; I knew it would be a long time before I saw or heard from him again.

At twenty-two, I was truly on my own—just as I had always wanted to be, and it hurt more than I'd have thought possible. I tried to console myself by becoming immersed in the novelty of my new job, attempting to find refuge in work, just as I'd once used school as a safe harbor. *Search* was a magazine of world cultures designed for "reluctant readers"—high school students who read at fifth-grade level. I spent much of my time researching and writing stories with a fixed number of words per sentence and a limited number of sentences per story. At first, it was difficult; I tended to write more complex sentences than the magazine ever ran. But after a while, I could look at a sentence and tell if it was too short or too long.

My editor (I'll call him David) was a good fifteen years older than I. He seemed fair and reasonable enough, even jovial in casual conversation. The other staff member was Bryan, the associate editor, very friendly and funny. Bryan introduced me around, dropped into my cubicle to say hi, and became a confidant in the first weeks on the job. The three of us put out this magazine every few weeks, and the mail we constantly received from readers told me that we were pretty widely read.

I was largely oblivious to the first sign of trouble. It came at an issue-planning meeting, in which David presented his outline of a dozen or so future issues of the magazine and then asked for feedback from Bryan and me. Accustomed as I was to the free flow of ideas, I believed that he really was asking for feedback. When it was my turn to comment, I said in my best, thoughtful, Catholic-school-girl voice that the issues were fine as far as they went, but there were no women to be found in any of the forthcoming issues, and no black (or any other nonwhite) people. Since this was a magazine about the cultures of the world, I asked, shouldn't we actually include some of those cultures?

The room got very quiet. When David recovered, he remarked that because I was new at this, I couldn't possibly know that the average readers of our magazine were, as he put it, "little white boys in Iowa." I didn't know that, I said to David, and I was glad he'd told me. But didn't that make it even more important that we have lots of different people in the magazine? Wasn't that the kind of information little white boys in Iowa needed to have? He acknowledged that possibility, and quickly moved on to something else.

Looking back, I can't believe how dense I was, how oblivious to the nuances of office politics. My only defense is that I had spent much of my life talking to people who for the most part respected my talking back, people who in fact had trained me to question authority—everybody's authority. Even my father, as angry as I made him during our political brawls, used to laugh grudgingly and say that I would be hell in a courtroom. Throughout all those indulgent years at Parker and at Yale, I had somehow gotten it into my head that an employer also would respect a principled disagreement with his—or her—employees, especially if he initiated the discussion by asking for comments. I couldn't have been more mistaken.

After that meeting, my work began to suffer—at least David's perception of it did. Copy that once would have earned a passing "Good job" now required an astonishing amount of rewriting. At first I complied without comment, understanding that newspapers were different from magazines, that writing for adults was different from writing for children. But my editor's comments became more pointed; his tolerance for my ideas in story meetings disappeared. We disagreed on story emphasis, we disagreed on topics; he didn't like anything I did. Bryan noticed it almost as soon as I did, and would drop by my desk to cheer me up after some of these miserable afternoons.

At my ninety-day evaluation session, David's assessment of my abilities was stark. After three months of working with me, he had come to the conclusion that I couldn't write, couldn't edit, and really had no future in the publishing business. In addition, he said, he was concerned about my arrogance. He felt I wasn't receptive enough to direction, and believed me closed to new ideas. I had three months to turn my work around or be fired. I sat silent through his monologue—delivered with not a little relish—and felt the tears burning my eyes. But something told me that crying in front of this man would be a mistake, and I had made too many mistakes already. At the end of his tirade, David asked me whether I had anything to say. I replied that I had nothing to say at all, and left his office.

It didn't occur to me for months that he might be wrong, that he might be more angry and vengeful about my frankness in meetings than he was right about my talents. I didn't consider that he resented my consciousness of race and ethnicity and gender, that my bringing up such hot-button issues was taboo, that we might just be two conflicting personalities. I felt stunned, because I had no experience with people who thought of me as incompetent or as a failure. And I didn't see any hope of changing his mind, because I didn't know what was wrong with the work I'd been doing.

I began to feel more self-conscious about my story ideas. Topics I wanted to propose now made me nervous. I didn't know how he'd perceive them, whether he'd take them seriously. I found myself censoring myself, something I'd never really learned how to do, and the knowledge that I was not contributing my best bothered me. Occasionally, however, I would overcome my reluctance and champion pieces that I thought had to be done. The National Women's Conference in Houston, Texas, that year was one such topic.

There was an informal women's group at the company, and some of us had discussed ways to write about what we considered a very important moment in women's history. Some of the women worked for the company's science magazines, for example, and a straightforward story about the conference was not feasible there. But I knew our magazine was the right place to talk about some of the issues the women's conference would raise. I decided to propose an article that was a mock debate about the Equal Rights Amendment between two of the youngest delegates to the convention. One of those two delegates was white; one was black. One was politically liberal, one was conservative. One of them supported the ERA, one opposed it. My idea was to interview them by phone, separately, then create a mock debate between them using their own language. Finally, we would ask the readers to write in and tell us what they thought about the ERA as a result of what the two delegates had said.

David was not hostile to the idea of the piece, but he wasn't doing cartwheels either. I could read in his eyes a kind of exasperation, a look that spoke of weariness with what he considered constant harping on this women's stuff. (I would grow to be familiar with this weary look on the faces of white men about many of the topics I cared for most.) I might have gotten more static, but the chairman of the company—a man with four daughters—had begun to think about the women's movement in very practical and personal terms. He wanted to meet with several editors about the conference and discuss whether Scholastic might want to send people to cover it. Imagine my surprise—and David's displeasure—when I was asked to attend the meeting. Some of the women I'd been chatting with all those weeks were influential in the company, although I didn't know it. It was their idea, after hearing me wax enthusiastic about feminism and women of color, to invite me to brainstorm with them. I knew that my being black was a key reason for the invitation; I knew I made them look enlightened and fair. I also knew that they could make me look good, too. The way things were going between David and me, I would need all the friends I could acquire.

By the time the meeting was over, a decision had been made to send representatives from several magazines to Houston, and to have articles about the conference appear in as many of the publications as was feasible. Needless to say, the piece I'd proposed to David was approved. David was even less thrilled when he found that I had been selected as the person from our magazine to attend the conference; after all, I was the junior member of his staff, and no one had consulted him about any of this. But to my way of thinking, this was an opportunity that I had tripped over, and I was going to take advantage of it. I figured my work in Houston would be an opportunity for me to make a good impression on my very cranky boss, though I didn't have much hope.

The trip to Houston was exhilarating. It was glorious to see those thousands of women from all over the United States spilling out of every hotel and restaurant in the downtown business district. The city clearly was unprepared for the number of people who showed up—not just the delegates and the press, but the antifeminist groups, led by a familiar nemesis, Phyllis Schlafly, who were convening at the Astrodome several miles away. I interviewed dozens of women and girls, sat through every plenary session, listened to all the speeches, and felt renewed. I was especially thrilled by the passage of a resolution in support of women of color, a rather delicate endeavor that at one point seemed jeopardized by great differences in opinion and some insensitive moves by white feminists. But some massive behind-the-scenes maneuvering went on, and ultimately a resolution was passed that marked a moment of détente between these two often oppositional groups. I made lists of dozens of article ideas for the magazine, even though I knew I was kidding myself. Most of them would never see the light of day.

It seemed that no matter what I did, David wasn't happy with me, and I was running out of ideas. I thought I ought to ask for some advice, and I did—from the division's editorial director. A Harvard graduate, he often teased me about my having gone to "that little school in Connecticut," while I shot back with comments about "that little school near Boston." I asked him out for drinks one evening, and took him to the Yale Club, where I was sure that we could speak privately. He was sympathetic when I spoke of David's growing disapproval, but remained noncommittal.

He was, however, extremely loyal to the chain of command, which I had violated with a vengeance. I'm sure that's what inspired him to go to my boss and relay the details of our conversation. The effect was electric. David called me in for a second conversation. Perhaps conversation is the wrong word; he did most of the yelling, accusing me of using my job as a steppingstone to a loftier position in the company, and of attempting to undermine his authority.

With David as angry as he was, it seemed clear I'd be looking for a job again, so I called the agency that had placed me at Scholastic. My counselor listened to my story, then told me to listen to her very carefully.

"You have to get through probation," she said.

"But I don't know what to do," I wailed, at the end of my patience.

She was an eminently practical woman with a simple suggestion: Do whatever he wants you to do.

"Even if I think it's wrong?" I asked.

"Even if you think it's wrong."

Sitting in my little apartment that night, I found myself thinking of Daddy. All those stories he used to tell us in his better moments: tales of walking off jobs, punching out his supervisors—they all came back to me in a rush of fear and regret. I finally had something I really needed to ask Daddy, and he was gone. He would know what I was talking about; he could have told me what to do. I tried to imagine what he might do in this situation, but dismissed that idea at once. Punching David in the face would only speed my descent into unemployment, though the idea held an undeniable appeal.

I couldn't call Mama about this; she would only worry. I suppressed the desire to call Bob, though in some ways I missed his calming presence most. The silence had lain thick between us for months. I was just angry enough to shun seeing him until I recovered from our breakup and created a life without him. My mother's words, delivered one Sunday night when I'd confessed that Bob and I were history, echoed in my head. "Girl, let him go. There are two things you never run after—a man and a bus, because there's always another one coming."

That might have been true about my love life, but I wasn't sure about my career. Publishing jobs were hard to find, and I was my sole support. Yet I didn't want to pretend this man was right, or affect a confidence in his judgment that I didn't feel. The truth was, I did question his judgment about pieces for the magazine; sometimes I got the feeling that his only taste was in his mouth. And since I'd never yet learned to mask my true feelings about anything, it was possible that my countenance revealed that I was less than impressed. The problem was that even if I was right about his taste and judgment, it wasn't his job on the line, but my own. So I decided to conduct a little experiment for myself.

I started by addressing the issue of my writing and my editor's comments. I looked though old files of stories and noted his comments and my responses. It occurred to me that I had treated his queries like queries—to be answered on the basis of fact, or in favor of my own judgment, based on the research I'd done. I realized that though he posed questions on the copy, he wasn't asking me—he was telling me. I wrote my next assignment in the usual way, then waited for feedback. David sent it back with several questions, much as he always did. This time, though, I answered them differently. Questions of fact were nonnegotiable; for those, I included a relevant citation. But most of his questions were subjective, and so I began to address them in terms of what I guessed he felt about the topic. Once I put my mind to it, he was laughably transparent; all the clues I needed were right in the margins. I changed my copy to reflect what I imagined he wanted to read. I retyped everything neatly, turned it in, and went home.

The next day, David came over to my desk to compliment me on the latest story. It seemed I was finally getting the hang of things at the magazine, he said. And he encouraged me to keep up the good work. That night, I went home and cried all evening. What was the point of coming to New York, learning to be a writer, when all I'd learned so far was that my editor was a frustrated writer who wanted every story to read the way *he* would have written it?

One of my few consolations was a new friend, Renita. We'd met thanks to Womanbooks, the feminist bookstore on Ninety-second and Amsterdam. About three blocks from where I lived, the store was my second home. I liked reading the bulletin boards, and one day a posting on a three-by-five notecard caught my eye. Its author hoped to organize a black feminist writing group, and gave a number in Brooklyn. Renita told me later that I was the only person who answered that ad. But it was a bigger stroke of luck for me than for Renita. She was a Wellesley graduate, a stockbroker, and a closet writer who envied my proximity to the career of my dreams. Both of us were wild about Toni Morrison, and we discussed her book *Sula* for hours on end, along with every other black woman's work we could forage from the shelves of Womanbooks.

As I learned to mimic David's voice in my writing, the tension at the office decreased markedly, but it was Renita I turned to, because I felt I was losing my mind. One night, in despair, I confided to her my conviction that I would eventually become a hack. It was she who told me about a short-story class she was about to take, offered by a local arts group, the Frederick Douglass Creative Arts Center.

"You might feel better if you were writing stories just for yourself," she said. "David wouldn't have anything to do with this class." I hadn't been in a writing class for more than a year, and the idea cheered me up, so I registered.

Each night after work, I hovered over a short piece for the workshop's first meeting. In the first session, when the workshop leader asked who had brought something to read, I made myself raise my hand and read my new work. Members of the class had lots of comments. At least one member didn't like the way I'd handled certain scenes. Another thought one of my characters was patently unbelievable. But all the comments were thoughtful and real, and I was buoyed by the ensuing discussion. Over the next several weeks, the class became a refuge for me. In that room, I was a writer growing in my craft, searching for my voice. That, along with Renita's steadfast friendship, was the only antidote to the hypocrisy of my daily work.

By the time my six-month review came up, I was nervous, but not unduly so; I had the feeling I had psyched David out. Sure enough, he beamed as I walked into his office. Now his praise of my talents was as expansive as his earlier pronouncements of doom. Rarely had he seen someone turn things around so quickly, he told me. I was happy to keep my position, but still miserable for myself. I felt like a fake, an obsequious little sellout.

"Yes, baby," Renita reminded me, "but you're a fake with a job."

One evening, riding the bus home from work, I read about a conference being sponsored by Avon, the cosmetics company, and *Essence* magazine about women and work. The theme was risk taking, and the evening seminar was free. I made up my mind to go, since the site of the seminar was within walking distance of my office, and because the editor in chief of *Essence,* Marcia Ann Gillespie, would be on the panel.

There must have been a couple of hundred women in that auditorium—all of us black, all of us ambitious, and more than one of us a little concerned about what our next career move would be. When the moderator announced that the panel would accept questions from the audience, I figured this would be my chance to get some career advice.

After about fifteen minutes or so the moderator called on me. Suddenly nervous, I stood to address my question to Marcia. "Well, I took a risk a few months ago, and I think I made a mistake," I began. "I'm a writer, and I left a job in Connecticut to come here and work. I found a job, but the editor I work for said I didn't have any talent . . . and I don't believe him, but he doesn't like the way I write, and . . ."

As I spoke, the strain of the last few months became very real to me. My boss liked my stories, but I thought they were dumb; I was sad and lonely for Bob, and I thought New York was the worst place I'd ever lived. Before I could stop myself, I had started to cry. I kept trying to talk through my crying, but I really couldn't. And now my misery was compounded by acute embarrassment, for almost to a woman, the room filled with soft exclamations of pity and sympathy. I flopped back into my seat, mortified. Into the hush of the auditorium came Marcia's voice through the microphone. It was straightforward and supportive, as she recalled her early years in the business at a conglomerate where she, too, had been judged untalented. "When all this is over, I'd like you to step up here and talk to me," she said, and the moderator called on the next woman.

Those sisters in the audience were wonderful. I didn't know any of them, but they all acted as if they knew me and what I was going through. Some handed me Kleenex and patted my shoulders. Several of them came up to me as the meeting broke up, to smile at me, or hug me and tell me to hang on. Several more told me to ignore the guy, and shared their own horror stories with me. A couple of women wrote down their phone numbers and gave them to me, admonishing me to call them anytime, and not to let New York get me.

As the crowd thinned, I worked my way to the front of the auditorium where Marcia stood, talking to other fans of her magazine. I lingered quietly, feeling shy in that odd way people can be in the presence of someone they admire. But she saw me, and motioned to me to come closer, and as she finished talking with another woman she slipped one arm around my shoulders in a hug.

"You know what you need? A chance to relax," she told me. "I'm having some people over to my house for brunch on Sunday. Why don't you come?"

"Okay," I said, surprised again. She didn't know me from Adam, after all, and I had already learned from my months in New York that nobody ever invited strangers anywhere. But my being a new face didn't seem to bother Marcia, as she wrote her address and phone number on a piece of paper and handed it to me.

"Do I need to call first?" I asked. "Should I bring anything?"

"Just yourself," she said, and smiled. "Don't you worry, my sister. Everything's going to be all right."

Brunch at Marcia's Upper West Side apartment was lovely. Her friends were welcoming and very funny. As she told them the story of how we'd met, they slipped into stories of their own early careers as writers and scholars. Some of their sufferings made my life look blessed by comparison. I was still young enough to feel slightly out of place, a little awkward. But if Marcia and the others noticed it, they said nothing. By late afternoon, the champagne and the quiche were gone, and I thought I ought to go home. Marcia walked me to the door. "I'm on my way to Jamaica for vacation," she said. "But I'll be back in two weeks. Call me; I want to talk with you about something."

It all sounded appropriately mysterious—but it took a lot longer than two weeks to get through to her. It was almost two months before she and I could solidify a lunch date and actually meet. But after we'd ordered food and talked about how things were going at my job, it was clear the wait was worth it.

"We have an opening for an associate editor at *Essence;* I think you would be perfect for it," she said. "Do you know how to edit?"

I remembered the words of a drama teacher I had at Yale, who taught the class as though every one of us planned a career in the theater. "There will come a moment when you'll be at an audition and the director will ask whether you can do a certain thing. When that moment comes," he cautioned, "always say yes."

"Of course I can edit," I told her.

She gave a satisfied nod. "When we finish lunch, come back with me to meet our managing editor; she'll have an editing test for you to take home with you over the weekend. After that, we'll see."

I picked up the test and spent the entire weekend with scissors and tape and blank paper, reconstructing one of the worst articles I'd ever read. By Sunday night, I had tried a dozen ways of dismantling the piece and putting it back together. I was so weary of fiddling with it that I didn't dare touch it again. I just dropped it off on the way to work and counted down the days. It didn't take long, really. In a few days, I heard from the managing editor, who invited me to lunch at the Algonquin. I asked my colleague Bryan, who knew I was job hunting, whether that was a good sign.

"I don't think they'd be taking you to the Algonquin for lunch as a consolation prize," he said, laughing at me.

He was right; the managing editor, Daryl, offered me the job on the spot, complete with a small raise. I felt like sinking to my knees in the middle of the Oak Room and kissing the carpet. I waited a few days for a confirmation letter, then went in to see David. The temptation to behave badly was enormous; my first impulse was to call him everything but a child of God. After that I could point out his complete inability to help or mentor, his condescending way of talking to everyone but especially to me, and close my exit interview with, as my mother once put it, an invitation to my behind. But the habits of a good Catholic girl die hard; I had to content myself with secret satisfactions. I said only that I'd been offered a wonderful opportunity as an associate editor and that *Essence* needed to see me in three weeks. If David was upset about losing my services, he kept his regret in check. He wished me well, I thanked him, and in two weeks, I was gone.

I'd built in an extra week for vacation so I could go home and see Mama; it was my first visit since Daddy's funeral. My mother and sister were beside themselves with pride in my new job. Even my mother, who typically read only the *Sun-Times* and the Bible, knew about *Essence*. On the way home, my head was filled with plans. I had bested my own personal timetable—I was an editor at a national magazine, and I was just turning twenty-three—by two full years. My mother, after years of servility in an abusive marriage, was free. I planned to talk to her about what she wanted to do next. I figured she could certainly go back to school, the way she'd always wanted to, though she'd have to cut back on the day work she'd been doing sporadically for some elderly white woman on the North Side. My brother and I could teach her how to drive, something she'd never been able to learn, because Daddy never had the patience to teach her. In a year or so, maybe we could finally take that trip to California. In my wildest fantasies, I even imagined that Mama might meet someone who was worthy of her, a man who would treat her well and look after her. I could have a stepfather!

It was strange to come home to a house I had never lived in. One of the last sensible things Daddy had done was to hustle his way into buying the foreclosed property my mother now lived in, the first house we ever had. He had been well enough then to restore the plaster walls and ceilings in the front rooms, badly damaged by water, but he'd begun to fade before he could start on the flooring. He lived just long enough to sell the house to my mother, for some nominal fee to make it legal, so that she wouldn't have to worry about where she would live. It was something else to add to the small list of things I respected about him.

Still, it was home because Mama was there, and if I felt the familiar tightening of my chest and the ache in my stomach, it was only a reflex born of habit. I reminded myself that no one here could hurt me; we were all free now, and Mama and I could make plans for her during my brief stay. But my mother had made plans—and a life—of her own; they had little to do with the scenarios in my head.

Now that all of us were grown or on our own, she had abandoned the Cook County Department of Public Aid. She had no more children to feed or take to the doctor, and her needs were simple and few. She had decided to expand her daywork job, which she'd started after I got to college, into the role of full-time caretaker. Her employer (I'll call her Mrs. Taylor) had been after Mama for some time to work more, but Daddy wouldn't have allowed it; once he was sick, Mama's commitment to take care of him took precedence.

A widow for several years, Mrs. Taylor was exceedingly rich. She lived a life of understated ease in Water Tower Place, a complex of enormous apartments, restaurants, theaters, and department stores like Lord & Taylor. But she was frail and depressed—at least, until my mother got hold of her. No one else could cajole Mrs. Taylor into walking through the mall; no one else nagged her to eat, or refused to let her lie around in bed all day. I had heard about Mrs. Taylor during my trips home from school, but I never thought my mother would actually want to work for her all the time.

When Mrs. Taylor's health first began to fail, her two sons debated the wisdom of putting her into a nursing home. It was my mother who fought them. In one of my phone calls home earlier that year, she told me: "So long as God gives me strength, they are not going to put her in a home. She doesn't want to go to a home, I promised her she wouldn't go to a home, and she's not going to no home. Now that's how it is."

And that is how it was. My mother informed Mrs. Taylor's sons it was ridiculous for them to dump their mother in a nursing home when they had enough money to hire people to care for her around the clock. Like most people confronted with my mother and her made-up mind, they saw the wisdom of the plan, hired the necessary people to assist, and turned Mrs. Taylor's care over to my mother.

Mrs. Taylor, in fact, urged my mother to live in, but at that request my mother drew the line. She agreed that she would go home only on weekends during the winter months, when my sister or brother could come to drive her home. But she didn't move her things to Water Tower Place, and she did spend Sundays at the church she'd recently joined—a small Pentecostal church on South Michigan with an elderly pastor who nonetheless had the spirit of God working in him, Mama said.

Mrs. Taylor's apartment was astonishing in its size, certainly too big for one woman and her companion. Most of the carefully decorated rooms were lined with books, filled with mementos of Mrs. Taylor's family and important events in their lives—commemorative coins, the framed menu of her wedding dinner, dance cards from country clubs of another era. It was opulent but not garish, and Mrs. Taylor and Mama reigned undisturbed over their kingdom on the fortieth floor.

As my mother and I talked that night over hot tea at the kitchen table, I found myself touched by my mother's commitment to this frail old woman—and angered, too. What had Mrs. Taylor ever done to deserve my mother's attention? Why should my mother again put aside her dreams of an education, of freedom and mobility, to care for a rich white woman whose own children were prepared to throw her away? I tried to sound Mama out about her future, but I was getting nowhere. I couldn't even get her to commit to a trip to New York to visit me and meet my friends.

"Ro, it's hard to get away, baby. Mrs. Taylor is sick and by herself up there. I would have to see about getting some of the other workers to watch out for her," she told me. "I have to see how things are going to go."

I could feel the sting of jealousy as she spoke. How dare this woman—this white woman, a relative stranger—lay claim to my mother's loyalty? Yet when my mother came home from work one evening a couple of days later, and asked if I could come by the apartment because Mrs. Taylor wanted to see me, I masked my displeasure and agreed to pick Mama up the very next evening.

When I arrived, I stopped in the driveway long enough to ask the doorman to direct me to the Taylor apartment. The doorman was a graceful older black man, the kind hotels use in their advertisements to suggest the elegant service of a different era. He knew me right away as Mary's daughter, the one from New York. Mama had told him I would be coming for her, but it wouldn't have mattered; being Mary's daughter meant being welcome anywhere my mother had preceded me.

"Don't worry about your car," he assured me with a smile. "I'll keep an eye on it. Just go on through that door and stop at the desk." At the desk, an imperious blond woman asked my business. I told her I was going to the Taylor apartment. She looked me up and down and asked if I was there to see Mary.

"I'm here to see Mrs. Bray, yes," I replied in *my* imperious voice, the one I used when I wanted white people to pay attention. "Please tell her Rosemary is here." She announced me, and I went through another set of doors to a hallway and an elevator that took me to the fortieth floor.

I got off and walked down more plush hallways, in search of

the apartment. Before I got my bearings, however, a door down the hall opened to reveal my smiling mother, dressed in white. It was not the white dress or separates that she habitually wore to church, but the white uniform of the household help.

I was exasperated. "Mama, why are you coming to the back door? And what are you doing wearing that?" Not a decent hello, to be sure, and my mother beckoned me with a look I had not seen since adolescence.

"Get in here," she whispered. "And don't start that mess. What's wrong with this uniform?"

Exasperation had changed to outrage by now, as I entered the gleaming kitchen where my mother had resumed her task of folding towels.

"Mama, you look like the maid."

"I'm not the maid. I don't cook no food, and Mrs. Taylor got people to do all that. That woman pays me good money to make her some lunch, and make sure she don't fall out of bed when she tries to get up. I'm just folding up these few towels 'cause these other folks don't half work when they're here. So you can just cut it out."

Mrs. Taylor had been grieved not to meet me all these years. She had already met my siblings, or talked to them when they called to check up on Mama each night she stayed with Mrs. Taylor. Mama had promised to bring me over the next time I was home, so that the two of us could talk. Mama led me through the kitchen into the "maid's room"—easily as big as a normal-sized living room, with a view of the Chicago skyline to match—and had me put down my things.

Before we could make our way back into the kitchen, I heard Mrs. Taylor's voice echoing through the apartment. "Mary, is your daughter here?" I could feel the wave of unnerving anger wash over me. It was an anger I barely understood myself. I truly hated hearing white people call my mother by her first name. For me it was the height of disrespect toward a woman who ought to be, I figured, ensconced in reverent security every day for the rest of her life. Mrs. Taylor had no condescension in her voice, just blessed assurance. For both her and my mother, everything was exactly as it should be. I was the one with the problem.

"She's here, Mrs. Taylor." Mama talked as we walked. I followed her into the elegant, commodious living room with its wall of windows, to face a woman dressed in a simple housecoat, seated in a wheelchair. She held out her hand to me, the soul of graciousness. "Welcome," she said. "I've wanted to meet you for a long time."

"It's nice to meet you," I replied, shaking her hand. She invited me to sit in the chair across from her, while my mother retreated to her work in back. It was where my mother had spent all of her life, in back rooms, in kitchens, behind doors, doing the shitwork, the endless, life-maintaining tasks that no one else wanted to do—not even me. I hated my presence here, I hated this sense that I was out in front, going places, doing things without my mother, things she had made it possible for me to do by retreating to the shadows of everyday life. How funny: her name might be Mary, but her whole life was one long stretch as the New Testament's Martha, left in the kitchen to serve alone, missing continually what Jesus called "the good portion."

But I had never wanted to plow ahead without her, to sit in rooms having conversations with people who suddenly found me worthy while my mother stood aside. What fun was it for me to do the things I'd done so far—get an education, find a real job as a magazine editor, perhaps finally get a handle on the life I'd always imagined—when I realized I might be leaving behind the most precious person in the world?

While I was fixating on these questions, Mrs. Taylor was attempting to make conversation. She pointed out that she and I had an additional connection of sorts. Her granddaughter, it turned out, had gone to Parker, my high school, though years later. She drew me out about Yale, about life in New York, telling me how many years it had been since she'd been there. It was her hope to be well enough soon so that she could go. "Maybe I'll take your mother with me," she said.

Mama came out of the kitchen then, to check on the both of us, perhaps. Mrs. Taylor asked me if I wanted a drink. "Mary, get Rosemary something."

"Oh, no thank you," I said with a stammer. My throat was dry, and I could have used some water, but the day would never come when I would let my mother wait on me in a white woman's house. "Mama, I'm worried about us getting caught in rush hour," I said as graciously as I could. "Do you have much more work to do?"

"Oh, I was hoping you could stay and visit for a while," Mrs. Taylor said in protest.

"I'm sure I can come back and visit again, Mrs. Taylor," I lied as well as I could. "I just don't want Mama and me to be out so late."

Reluctantly, Mrs. Taylor conceded that Mama had nothing to do that couldn't wait until tomorrow, and cautioned me to drive carefully. "I don't know what I'd do without Mary," she said, looking at my mother with genuine affection. I knew just how she felt.

I was angry and upset all the way home, though I was determined not to let my feelings out all over her. Instead I asked Mama about looking into an adult education program I'd heard about that would allow her to get her grade school diploma and then her GED. Mama shied away from the idea, and when I asked her why, she said: "I'm too old for all that now, Ro. It's too late for that."

I thought about Mama's answer as I lay in her bed that night, listening to her snore from her makeshift bed on the couch downstairs, the couch she refused to let me sleep on. "I get some of my best rest on the couch, girl," she said when I protested that she was too old to be sleeping anywhere but her own bed. "You not used to this old thing. Just let me get my pillow from up there."

I was lying in the dark, in the quiet of this unfamiliar house, with no ghosts to haunt me but the ones I brought. I remembered another moment like the one at Mrs. Taylor's house. It was the occasion of my eighth-grade graduation at Parker, during a celebratory party at a classmate's house. We gathered early one evening, with food prepared by several mothers. Parents as well as us kids and our teachers stood around talking in groups of two or three. About a half hour after the party began, I realized that Mama was nowhere to be found in the yard, so I left my little group to look for her.

It didn't take long to find her. She was in the kitchen, heating food, dishing up plates, marshaling the awkward efforts of other mothers to get the culinary part of the party in order. I was enraged. Hadn't anyone told my mother that this was 1968, that black women didn't have to spend their whole lives helping white women at dinner parties? Didn't she see all the other mothers talking outside? Why did she always have to work wherever she went?

I remembered her first visit to Yale, nearly five years later. I brought her to my dorm room at the start of Parents' Weekend in my freshman year. She put down her bags, hung up her coat, looked around until she found our broom in one of the closets, announced that I still didn't know how to clean house, and began sweeping the living room. She met all my roommates and got them to tell her their life stories. She even ironed a shirt for one of the guys living upstairs in the dorm who had come to our room to borrow an iron before his parents arrived.

I could admit in the quiet dark of her bedroom that night that my dreams of Mama's new life were my dreams, not hers. All of my life, Mama fixed, cared, organized; cooked, washed, soothed. But it hurt me to see her in Mrs. Taylor's kitchen, it hurt me to recall her in our own shabby rooms for all those years, boiling water for us to bathe in, lighting the oven to keep us warm. I had become, in the intervening years, all too conscious of what she had become. Folding those towels in Mrs. Taylor's kitchen, her short, ample body dressed in the uniform of service, she was transformed into Aunt Jemima, the embodiment of white fantasy caretaking. Ducking my father's blows, scurrying to cook something Daddy might eat instead of hurl at her, Mama had come to embody every trapped and unappreciated wife.

I wanted more for her; I wanted her to want more. But I had to face the fact that the life I feared for my mother was the very life she sought, especially after my father died. She loved to work, to help, to care; that would always be her art. My fears for her wasted life turned out to be projections onto my own future. I loved my mother fiercely, but just as fiercely, I knew I could not bear to be her. The appreciative look in white people's eyes that has always warmed my mother's heart chills mine. It has always been my fear of "Jemimahood": once you become something specific and recognizable in white people's eyes, you can rarely be anything else. I feared with all my heart being trapped in white fantasies of the ideal black woman—an ample bosom holding a loving, open heart; a selfless concern for the fulfillment of others' dreams; a warm laugh and a devilish sense of humor. For me, it was too narrow a pedestal on which to rest.

I was already embarked on my life's work, already learning to work out my own compromises, already deciding how best to represent myself and my own dreams. But they were my dreams, not my mother's dreams. All my life, she had endured the nearly unendurable, just so I might one day have the freedom to create myself, stake out my part of the world's territory. She had done it for me, because in her mind, that is what mothers did, surely what she would have wanted her own mother to do if she'd ever known her mother's love. I, who knew my mother's love for me all too well, had no excuse for trying to live her life for her. She'd had enough of that from my father. Mama had always said that I was more like Daddy than I wanted to admit. It pained me to think that she might be right, in this of all things.

I hated to hear her say it was too late. But she did not mean it with the same sense of futility and loss with which I heard it. Mama said it with the acceptance she has used on every occasion of her life. She had found a place for herself, a place where she felt loved and honored. She had no feel for the larger political ramifications of a caretaking black woman in domestic service, ramifications that made me squirm. I could tell this was a battle I would lose, if I were foolish enough to pursue it. Mama would not follow me to college, would not earn a degree in marketing and become a successful retailer in her sixties. Those were my fantasies for her life. It seemed ironic that I would have to correct my perspective about the woman who spent her whole life making space for me to be who I really was, allowing my decisions and discoveries about myself to stand, even in the face of my father's threats and anger. If I really loved her, I realized, I owed her the same courtesy. It was the only way to repay an immeasurable debt.

Chapter 10

If my father's death marked the start of a horrible time in my life, coming to work at *Essence* marked the start of a rich and fruitful one. It wasn't just the opportunity to really learn how to be a magazine editor, to become really good at it and to fall in love with words again. It wasn't just that I'd kept a promise to myself about working at a national magazine. In many ways, my years at *Essence* were a spiritual experience—though I would never have said so at the time. For the only time in my working life, the lives and experiences and hopes of black women, and the articles we generated from them, were regarded as blessedly normal.

In editorial meetings, in conferences with Marcia or other senior editors, I found myself working both for myself and for millions of women who relied on us to capture some of the truth of their lives. Unlike my editor at Scholastic, the women at *Essence* taught me what I needed to know. They wanted me to grow, to hone my skills, to take more responsibility and generate more ideas. Working each day in the company of others who believed in black women, in our inherent worth and power, was a balm to my damaged spirit.

As I learned more, I was filled with energy and purpose. I edited all kinds of pieces: fiction and feature articles, even poetry and recipes. I learned more about fashion and beauty than I'd ever cared to know. I realized that art directors and editors saw the same page in very different ways, and I learned to negotiate that delicate territory gracefully. As I read the letters to the editor that came in every day by the dozens, I came to understand more fully what *Essence* meant to the women who read it. Readers relied on us, trusted us, looked to us to affirm them and support them when no other magazine could or would.

It was a good place to make friends, too. There were several junior editors there, all about my age or a bit older; all of us were single black women trying to create a life for ourselves in New York. I grew closest to Denise, a young woman from Louisiana who shared my ambivalence about the city and my love of literature. Unlike me, she was a wonderful poet. Also unlike me, she was a fabulous cook whose first act upon arriving home was to put a pot on the stove. It wasn't long before we were fast friends.

Only my heart seemed beyond repair in those years. I dated a lot, even met a man I thought I might get serious about, but he moved away and I gradually spent more and more of my waking hours at the office. Denise knew about Bob, and had even met him on one of the rare occasions when he and I would meet for a drink. She thought I was masochistic, and I had to agree. Still, I couldn't help wanting to know how he was. I was glad to know he'd survived the first year of the acting program. I was appalled to know he was still driving taxis at night and living in a dismal studio apartment in the East Village.

Denise went with me once to visit him on East Fifth Street. Bob was proud of his very own apartment, but as I looked around at the gated windows and the grubby hallway, complete with a perpetually unlocked front door and some very distasteful neighbors, I grew more and more depressed. I'd brought him some chicken I'd cooked as a kind of housewarming gift. When I opened the refrigerator to put it in, I saw only a couple of juice bottles and a pot of congealing spaghetti sauce. That was enough for me; I was convinced he was taking far too literally the notion of a starving artist. Denise and I took a cab home, with me sobbing about Bob's living in a slum and despairing for his safety. Denise reminded me that he was a grown man, and he didn't look as though he was starving. I was unconvinced, but I knew that there was nothing I could do about it. He'd shut me out of his life, and I didn't know how to get back in.

So I was surprised when, a few weeks later, he invited me to a student production of an Adrienne Kennedy play he was appearing in. Another friend told me I should stay away after the way he'd just disappeared, but nothing could have kept me from going to see him. I once dreamed of sitting in darkened theaters, watching him and cheering, meeting him at the stage door afterward to go home together. I watched him onstage that night in a small role, and understood why he wanted me to come. He'd been working hard, and it showed. He was a better, more polished performer, and I was one of the few people in the world who would have been able to tell.

As he walked to the front of the stage at the play's end, I couldn't help cheering with abandon. I'd never been good at hiding my feelings, and when it came to Bob, I'd always found it impossible. Afterward, he came to the front of the house to look for me, pleased that I'd shown up. Though I'd promised myself to be reserved, I couldn't help hugging him and telling him he'd been wonderful. We went to Phebe's on the Bowery at East Fourth Street. A horrible restaurant with cheap food, it was an unofficial hangout for students in the drama school. We were there for a long time, talking.

School was harder than he'd thought; he was the only black man left in the acting program; he was thinking of taking a leave of absence to make some more money. I had a friend, an editor at *Black Enterprise* magazine, who needed some editorial research done. I offered to put the two of them in touch. Bob asked me if I was dating anyone, and I said I was, but that it was a casual thing. I asked him the same question, and he gave me the same answer, along with the quiet smile I remembered.

It was the middle of the night when he walked me to the corner, then struggled to get me a taxi. Standing on an uptown street, we were having the usual trouble getting a cab to stop for a black couple. An African driver finally stopped, and Bob opened the door for me. "I'll call you," he said.

"That's what you said before," I said, giving him a knowing look.

"I really mean it this time," he said. He slammed the taxi door and waved.

He did call, and in the next few years we rebuilt the relationship we once had. Bob enjoyed working for *Black Enterprise* so much, he decided to leave school and become an editor there. My heart ached for him when he told me he planned to quit school, but I could understand it when he said he'd had enough. The strain of constant rejection in the theater, being told no over and over as he found himself auditioning for parts he didn't even want, the monotony of parts for black actors in the early 1980s—thugs, pimps, and more thugs—all these things took their toll. So did being broke. Besides, I hated his driving a taxi, especially whenever a New York City taxi driver got robbed and killed, which was fairly often.

I'd spent four years at *Essence* by now, and had been promoted to senior editor. Marcia had moved on to other projects after nine years at the helm, and I missed her. Daryl Alexander had taken her place for a time, and eventually Susan Taylor, our fashion and beauty editor, was named to replace Daryl. Susan and Marcia were very different people, and though I liked Susan very much, our interests diverged greatly—enough so that ideas that might have been greeted with excitement by Marcia were often turned aside by Susan. I could tell that the magazine was headed in a direction that didn't interest me. The emphasis was gradually moving away from a combination of the political and the personal, and toward more personal issues, particularly relationships.

I loved a good relationship piece as much as the next reader. Such pieces are the bread and butter of the women's service magazines, and I'd assigned and written more than my share. But I found myself more interested in broader political themes, and especially intrigued by what I considered a threatening political trend. Ronald Reagan had been elected president over Jimmy Carter, and I was just elitist enough to resent that a second-rate actor could wrest the presidency from a graduate of the U.S. Naval Academy. I understood Reagan's charm from the moment I heard his speech during the Republican National Convention. If I hadn't spent an afternoon in the library reading about his history as governor of California, I might have been fooled. But this was a man with a profound indifference to civil rights movements at best, and outright hostility to these efforts at worst. He wasn't any better on issues related to women, and he had long been part of that band of rabid anticommunists who felt America was in greater danger from Moscow than it was from the reactionary maniacs on its own soil.

Reagan had effectively eliminated and snubbed any African-American presence in the White House or its environs, except for the economist Thomas Sowell, whom my brother regarded as brilliant and I regarded as turgid. But I was more interested in the trend I had seen in my excursions to the college bookstores. On the racks at Papyrus and at Shakespeare & Co. stood obscure academic journals containing the names of writers I had never heard of before: Sowell, Glenn Loury, Walter Williams. These were black men who had entered the conservative embrace and suddenly appeared as spokesmen for Afro-America. I was just as struck by the fact that there was not a woman among them. I thought *Essence* ought to try to track this mini-phenomenon, or at least acknowledge it. But I couldn't transmit my sense of excitement to Susan. She was not convinced that this was anything more than a few opportunistic black men who had made a pragmatic decision to position themselves on the winning side.

It was moments like these that helped me identify my own restlessness at *Essence*. Eventually, I went to work at New York University as a conference organizer for the Institute of Afro-American Studies, planning conferences with academics as well as social activists, and even designed an exhibit on the history of black American inventors and entrepreneurs that was a magnet for students in the tristate area. Some of the projects I worked on were a kind of accommodation to the changing spirit of the time, with the emphasis on black economic achievement and the downplaying of more overtly political issues. I didn't abandon writing. I wrote freelance for *Essence* and *The Village Voice,* among other publications, and grew more attached than ever to the Harlem Writers Guild, the workshop I had belonged to since my early, miserable days at Scholastic.

Bob had joined the Guild by this time, and so I had the pleasure of seeing him every two weeks, listening to his quirky short stories with delight and secret pride. Surrounded by words and ideas, we were falling in love again. But I was a different woman than I'd been five years earlier. I had watched friends marry for reasons other than love, or seen them lose out on relationships because of the wrong kind of stubbornness. I knew I didn't have to marry to be happy, and I knew that unless it was Bob, I probably wouldn't marry at all. But the truth was, I wanted to marry him, and though I didn't talk about it continually, I was very clear with Bob that marriage was what I wanted and expected at some point. We discussed the issue sporadically, and whenever the topic came up, I simply restated my position. On one occasion, I even announced: "You might as well marry me now, Bob. You're going to marry me eventually anyway!"

Bob alternated between laughter and fury. "You are absolutely the most arrogant person I've ever met in my life," he said, looking astonished. But I held my ground.

"I don't think I'm any more arrogant than you. I'm just clear. If you looked a thousand years, you'd never meet anybody who'd be a better wife to you than me."

Bob shook his head in disbelief, but he didn't propose. That came a year or so later, after I returned home from my best friend's bridal shower in a foul and envious mood. Bob was feeling talkative and solicitous, but I had nothing to say. My silence escalated his anxiety, and before long we were having a full-fledged argument. Right in the middle of it, however, I was suffused with a sense of deadly calm—the calm of surrender.

What was the point, I reasoned with myself, of wanting to spend your life with someone who didn't want you? In the middle of our fight, I went to one of the two walk-in closets in my bedroom, which Bob used to hang his stray sweaters and other things he left when spending weekends with me.

"What are you doing?" he asked me.

"I'm folding your clothes so you can take them with you when you leave. I'm through. If I find anything lying around, I'll mail it to you." I think it was my icy calm that got his attention.

"But you can't do that," he said. "I think we ought to get married."

"I have no intention of marrying you," I told him, folding the last sweater and adding it to a tidy pile on the bed.

For the next half hour, Bob persisted in his proposal. I resisted, reminding him haughtily that a couple couldn't save their doomed relationship by walking down the aisle. "We're not doomed," Bob said. "I'm just nervous. So, are you going to marry me or not? How about Wednesday?"

"Excuse me; you think I waited all these years to get married so I could run off to City Hall? If we don't have a real wedding, my mother will kill me," I said.

Bob was raised Unitarian Universalist, and asked if we could be married in a UU ceremony because it would mean a lot to his parents. Since I wanted to be married in a church, but had no intention of promising to raise any future children as Catholics, I was happy to agree. I hunted down more freelance work so that I could buy myself a serious wedding dress, and looked at bridal magazines for the first time in my life. My friend Denise, having just gotten married herself, was my constant companion as I agonized over whether to wear white.

"Wear what you want," she advised. "You're only going to do it once." She was right about that; no matter what happened, this was it.

None of us had money for an elaborate reception, so we decided to do it ourselves, with the help of my cousin Niecie, who counted catering among her many skills. Bob wanted roast suckling pig ("It just feels like a party kind of food," he said), so we had to find one for my cousin to cook in our oven; a March wedding in Chicago made an outdoor spit impossible. We promptly named the pig Wilbur, which grossed out my cousin so thoroughly that she threatened not to cook at all. We found a local photographer who agreed not to take stupid pictures of us feeding each other cake, and my mother and brother found a baker who would provide a three-tiered masterpiece to feed what would turn out to be 125 people. We spent the week before the wedding moving furniture to the basement and filling the empty space with rental tables, decorating the first floor with crepe-paper streamers and bells. It was absolutely corny, and both our families were thrilled.

My appearance on our wedding day rendered Bob speechless for the only time in our lives. Dressed in a tuxedo with a red bow tie, he stared at me in my billowy white dress and tiered veil, whispered, "You're so beautiful," and dropped into a folding chair: exactly the effect I'd imagined. I walked down the aisle on the arm of my oldest brother, but instead of giving me away, our families affirmed our mutual commitment. I read some Elizabeth Barrett Browning; Bob read a Shakespeare sonnet; we said an Apache wedding prayer; the soloist sang "One Hand, One Heart," from *West Side Story.* Our friends were resigned to our eclectic ceremony, but my mother was more blunt. "I know you're married," she said, when it was all over. "But what kind of ceremony was that?" We walked down the aisle, newly married, and Bob waited until we reached the alcove before bursting into tears in his brother's arms.

I was so happy. Surrounded by my family, old and new, by friends from all over the country and nearly every phase of my life, I saw the day as a single perfect sphere, my whole world in order at last. The magnitude of what I had done didn't occur to me until the last of the guests were leaving, about ten P.M. We'd cut the cake; two of the guests had treated my bouquet like a jump ball at an NBA game (we had to split it in half to placate them), and not a crumb of food was left in the house. I had changed into regular clothes, and we were headed for the Drake Hotel for our wedding night. As I walked into the living room and looked at my mother, I started weeping. My mother sighed.

"Girl, what is wrong with you now?"

"What am I going to do? I'm married!" I wailed.

The remaining guests broke into laughter. "You should have thought of that before three o'clock," my uncle said. "It's too late now."

Bob came downstairs and put his arms around me. "She's just tired; she'll be all right," he said, smiling at me with a familiar fondness. It was his smile that calmed me down. When all was said and done, this was just my wedding day; my marriage began from this moment on. I looked at that quirky smile of his, saw in it a safe harbor. It was a smile I trusted, coupled with that look of his, the one that said, "I know all about you, and you're cool with me." I knew I could count on that look for the rest of my life.

We returned from our Caribbean honeymoon to our new apartment in central Harlem, a glorious floor-through with its woodwork and high ceilings restored to pristine elegance. It was the middle of the go-go '80s, and black middle-class singles and couples were flocking to Harlem for their last shot at a piece of Manhattan schist. We considered ourselves privy to a great secret: we were young, in love, and living uptown, where the rent was cheap by New York standards and the renovated brownstones were phenomenal. It was a far cry from the rest of our lives.

I had spent six of the worst months of my professional life at the New York *Daily News* as a copy editor, the first black woman with such a job in anyone's memory. My female colleagues (and there were precious few of them) were pleasant enough, but most of the men on the desk were walking stereotypes. They made thinly veiled racist comments in my presence, gave me the worst work on the desk, and refused to speak directly to me for any reason. I went home crying every night; the only thing that saved my sanity was the knowledge that I would leave as soon as I could figure out something else to do.

I finally jumped ship for *The Wall Street Journal* shortly after our wedding. I had friends there, and though there weren't many black people working on the national news desks, I was no longer the only one. My unease in this world of financial journalism was of a completely different kind. Before this, I'd had an intellectual distaste for business, and listening to my husband talk about financial journalism was interesting, but not really compelling. Now, as I watched the machinations of investors and companies, my distaste grew. It astonished me to realize, as I read the daily predictions of stock analysts who were bullish on the market one week and bearish the next, that they were guessing. No one had the slightest real idea of what the market would do; a man who used Fibonacci numbers to predict trends did about as well as a woman who charted everything by computer.

But it was not simply the uncertainty, or the casino-like quality of the subjects and stories I edited. These were the early days of the Reagan era, and accompanying the enthusiasm for the market and for profit was a corresponding disdain for the poor and the vulnerable. I knew I was working in Republican territory early on; a victory party held in the newsroom to celebrate Reagan's second term was a pretty clear signal. The editorial page had always been far more reflective of the people who wrote for it than of the newsroom downstairs. We would sit and laugh each day at some new atrocity written in defense of the indefensible. But it was the other stories in the *Journal* that let me know how great the gap was between the things I believed in and the things the paper believed in. The front-page stories detailing the unraveling of the safety net for the poor and sick, the deliberate stonewalling by Republican ideologues that kept disability benefits out of the hands of people who genuinely qualified for them—these things were being celebrated on the editorial pages, less than a dozen pages away. I got a good, though schizophrenic, lesson in competing social and economic policies while I worked at the *Journal.* And the lesson was all the more chilling considering where Bob and I lived.

In the morning, in the evening, you could see them on the horizon, at the end of Lenox or Seventh Avenue, rising above the treetops of Central Park. In the morning, the tall buildings emerged from a kind of haze, presenting themselves for inspection, luring the workers and seekers downtown. In the evening, those same buildings glowed like beacons as the sheltering night fell. Their stately structures, their glittering presence seemed so far above the worry and the burdens of another world, the despair resting below them and along the broad avenues at the other side of the park.

At the other end of the glorious, gleaming city was Harlem: tattered, battered, bruised, nearly destroyed. Its elegant boulevards had changed their names. Lenox Avenue became Malcolm X Boulevard; Seventh Avenue was Adam Clayton Powell Boulevard. But those proud names were no compensation for tangible losses, little consolation for the economic devastation and the very human damage on display at every corner. Facile in one world, at home in another, some days uneasy with both, I became, in my years in Harlem, a traveler between these worlds.

Like the black tables at Yale, Harlem was a kind of respite for many of us. All day, every day, Bob and I were two of millions of blacks whose daily contact with whites was subject to a steady stream of what the sociologist Joseph Feagin of Florida State University calls "microinsults"—the clutched purse of a white matron as you board the elevator, the pointed questions of a new client curious about how it is that you are handling his very important business, the shocked and often barely hidden look that flits across the faces of new colleagues when you've taken on a job you—and they—have yearned for. By the end of the day, we weren't in the mood to help white people work out their racism and ambivalence. The sporadic hostility we would feel in Harlem was of a completely different character, rooted in class warfare and a clash of values—the regular, run-of-the-mill stuff.

Another year passed before we bought for ourselves not a brownstone but a narrow, unimpressive brick townhouse, exempt from the historic district and unoccupied—for good reasons. Owning an old house was a litany of irritations and frustrations and rage. The first winter, we lay next to each other in the dark, listening for the next impenetrable sound of disaster—the pipes bursting again, the boiler flooding the basement, the stray cats fighting with our gentle Abyssinian after sneaking through an undiscovered hole in the basement, a chunk of the roof falling like a bomb onto the fourth floor. On nights when it was cold, the feelings were just too familiar. I would get Bob to call his parents in Teaneck and announce our imminent arrival. Once Bob asked me what the big deal was. "We have an electric blanket and safe heaters. We're not going to freeze to death." I knew he was right, but it was a long time before I could tell him that huddling together in the cold dark was something I could never bring myself to do again. For Bob, an icy night was an adventure. For me, it was a flashback.

The house was my idea from the beginning; I had never lived in a house, ever, and I had created another fantasy for myself, this time as a married woman with a house. Of course my initial fantasy included living in a house in Chicago, or Philadelphia, maybe Atlanta. But that was long before I knew who I'd be sharing this house with—a city-loving man with an affinity for noise and concrete and an allergy to grass. Our particular money pit was a private purchase from a neighborhood lawyer and real estate mogul who never quite told the truth about any part of the deal. He ended up dying in a welter of conflicting claims on all his assets, including the mortgage he held on our little piece of heaven.

Harlem was never the hellhole so many people imagine, a place where white people never dared to tread except to buy their drugs. On the other hand, it was no paradise, either. On my way home each night, it took a while to get down the block. At their corner outposts, the young drug dealers stared; they knew me as part of the opposition forces, one of the folks most likely to call the police. I stared back, reminding myself that they could be dangerous, as young as they were. But I also lingered as I walked, because my neighbors were there, on stoops with their children, the old men in lawn chairs or leaning on canes, groups of two or three talking as night fell. It felt good to say hello, and ask after grandchildren, and listen as they complained about the shooting, or the noise.

One of my neighbors always greeted me the same way. "No babies?" she asked me, as soon as the weather got warm. "What you waiting for, girl?" I was waiting until it was safe for my child to play in front of the house, until there were more than two or three mothers who watched their children, until the school on the corner had books enough for every child. I was waiting for reinforcements. They never came.

Some part of us suspected that our stay wouldn't—couldn't—be permanent, though we took turns feeling lonely and traitorous. Some nights, I would head up my block toward Lenox Avenue for milk at the corner store, and watch the life around me—its messy, loud discomfort, the sweet fun of children dancing in the spray of a hydrant, the card games and the fights and the laughter of friends. I would argue with myself, hoping against hope to re-create a community I knew in my blood. Bob and I wanted to stick it out, along with our conscientious neighbors. We knew we could hang on if only there were a sign, just one sign from the Emerald City downtown: one real grocery store, market-rate housing near the park, a real drugstore that filled prescriptions and stayed open late enough for working people to shop there. If the city would only renovate one building on this block for the working middle class, if they would help us strike a balance among the desperate, the marginal, and the ambitious, we could work it out. The renaissance we dreamed of never arrived while we were living there. It was an era of urban disregard, even abandonment; it was a time of low expectations and even lower results. Even the economic development agencies that ostensibly worked on behalf of neighborhoods like ours seemed to be frozen by a lack of vision. They had set their sights on massive, impressive projects—hotels, office complexes, condominiums. The workaday basics that might have helped to stabilize our part of the world—small retail and service businesses, anchored by one or two larger chains—never seemed to materialize.

I had a bird's-eye view of the failure of trickle-down economics in those years. I'd go to work and read stories about America's economic recovery, then come home at night to live in the midst of its decline. We were doing better personally, but those around us could not make that claim. The Reagan Revolution had passed Harlem by, and the dissonance between what I saw and heard all day and what I saw at night was increasingly hard to bear. I missed writing about and editing things that mattered to me. The pay at the *Journal* was good, but the price was higher than I cared to pay. So when *Ms.* magazine called me and asked (for the second time) whether I would consider making a move, I squelched my immediate reaction and, after meeting and talking with the editors, agreed to join the staff. I took a pay cut to do it, but as I told Bob, it was good for my soul. People at the *Journal* were pleasant enough, but I knew I had no future there, and the fault was as much mine as it was theirs. I didn't love it enough; nothing that happened there set me on fire. What excited me was writing and editing for people whose passions matched my own. I had become an advocacy journalist, for better or worse. It wasn't everybody's editorial cup of tea, but it was mine.

The block association on my street is more than forty years old now, with some two dozen dues-paying members. Most of them are old enough to be my grandparents, even my great-grandparents; Mrs. Evans (not her real name) is hitting ninety years old. There is a core group in the association, made up mostly of its founding members, men and women who grew up on the block. They remember the street and Harlem the way it used to be. Sleek and clean and quiet, the brownstones and apartment buildings once housed the great and the near great of black America. One of my neighbors could remember playing, as a boy, in Fats Waller's car as it sat at curbside while Waller visited friends on the street. Others recalled flowers planted in gardens beside the stoops, neatly trimmed hedges crammed into small spaces in front of their buildings, on the basement level.

It was this way for a long time, they all told me; even the 1960s didn't change it much, though many of them changed. People who were tired of city life moved on, of course, out to Long Island, over the bridge to Englewood and Teaneck. But more people stayed than left, unwilling to ride commuter buses, or sit in traffic, committed to seeing the same faces when they left their houses each morning and returned to them at night.

It was the 1970s that changed everything. A creeping recession created an economy so sluggish that families turned single-family homes into rooming houses. Older residents began to die, leaving the buildings to children who'd spent their lives there and now wanted to be anywhere but home. And drugs, always a peripheral issue in black communities before, began their infamous rise in popularity. More than any single thing, the miserable economy that left young men vulnerable to the infection of drugs caused the fabric of communities to unravel.

The block associations watched their beloved streets begin to crumble, house by house by house. People who once confined their activities to summer block parties and holiday bus rides now found themselves having to organize around a host of issues with which they were completely unfamiliar. The language of local politics began to infuse their conversations; community boards and their casts of characters began to provide running themes for neighborhood arguments—social services facilities, transitional housing units, rehabilitation centers. Block by block, central Harlem, along with a few other neighborhoods, had become the institutional dumping ground of New York City. A host of programs designed to meet the needs of the city's poorest people—the city's takeover of near-abandoned buildings, for example—had the unintended effect of destabilizing blocks. Folks who had known each other for years, who lived across the hall or across the street from one another, were leaving, to be replaced by people with no ties at all to the community already there. Two parallel sets of lives began to emerge; two separate but unequal paths, always there before but never so starkly emphasized, became plainly visible.

None of these things was clear to me in that first year after we came to live in our house. I only knew we were thrilled to learn of an active block association; it meant we need not try to guess which of our neighbors would share our desires for a particular kind of city life. The association met each month in a church at the very center of the block. I found that a promising sign, the church opening its doors to the people. It seemed a harbinger of commitment by the pastor and the congregation—a notion that I later learned was true only in its minimal sense. (It took me years to learn that the pastor and most of his congregation lived far away from the church building; the pastor's official home, in fact, was in Mount Vernon.)

At my very first block association meeting, the heated discussion focused on a presentation from a private social service agency, which hoped to explain why thirty-two units of transitional housing for homeless families would be a good use for a building on an adjacent block. I didn't like the idea all that much, particularly after someone had enumerated the other "institutional neighbors" we had, including an alcohol rehabilitation center and a sixty-bed jail.

Over and over, both longtime and newer residents asked why the agency had chosen this particular building in this particular neighborhood at this particular time. The questions were consistently met with an explanation that focused on needs—specifically, the need for homeless families to have a roof over their heads, the need for them to learn the skills necessary not to be homeless again. I felt ambivalent. The men making the presentation were right. But so were people in the neighborhood who were tired of seeing their lives disrupted not only by new people, but by the institutions that sponsored the presence of the newcomers. True, it was a turf battle. But it was a battle that also went beyond turf, to the heart of cohesive community and what it takes to maintain it. It is a battle that I learned gets short shrift in places like Harlem. Neighborhoods in which most of the residents are poor and black are automatically ruled out as genuine communities, or classified as utterly dysfunctional. There was, in the minds of all too many, no way for a place like central Harlem to get worse than it already was. In fact, there were several ways for central Harlem to get worse—and all of them were being tried.

But these are thoughts with the benefit of hindsight; at the time, I was more intrigued by the block association's existence and its members. And even my perception of the association changed with time and exposure, as I learned how many people on the block knew about the group's existence but refused to attend meetings. Their refusal, it turned out, was rooted in an old-fashioned class rivalry between residents of the block who owned their homes and residents who rented rooms or apartments. The woman who was president of the group, I learned, was one of its founding members. She believed that only homeowners would be interested in association membership; worse, she believed from her own years as a landlord that all tenants were the enemy.

Tenants who occasionally turned up at meetings over the years were not exactly shown the door, but they were made aware by comments from the leadership that their presence wasn't exactly welcome. By the time Bob and I had come to live on the block, however, at least one more reason existed to be nervous about nonhomeowning members of the association. Younger, more streetwise people who suddenly evinced a pressing desire to "do something about the block" were just as likely to be spies for local drug dealers as they were to be citizens overcome with civic virtue. And even older people, longtime residents of the neighborhood who found themselves without a job or other means of support, turned into informants of sorts, in return for a few dollars under the table.

Were we ever sure about the informants, about who they were? Not really. We only knew that if information about the latest drug locations was publicly discussed at a block association meeting, the people who talked about it would later find themselves being harassed. Their phones would ring, but when they answered, only silence greeted them. And at least one member was confronted directly about what an unwise thing it was to get in the way of people doing business.

I knew about all these problems, at least in theory. But I didn't truly understand their complexities until, through a weird set of circumstances, I became president of the block association. In my mind, it was fairly simple: preside over the meetings, organize some bus rides to raise money, restart the neighborhood block patrols that had been suspended after it was realized that local drug dealers had electronic walkie-talkies and base units that allowed them to overhear our conversations as we walked the block, notifying police of questionable activities. To some degree, I did all those things. But I found myself, in addition, doing things I never intended to do with people I never intended to know.

I attended meetings of the association as often as I could those first several months, though I was putting in long hours at *Ms.* But at the same time I was deeply disturbed because no sooner had I arrived at *Ms.* than I began to hear rumors of the magazine's imminent demise. That would have grieved me—and not only because of the paycheck. As with my other alma mater, *Essence,* I had been reading *Ms.* since its inception and had written for it as well. More than one so-called postfeminist had declared its worldview obsolete by the mid-1980s, but so long as there was such a thing as patriarchy, I figured there would always be a need for us to exist, to bring feminist analysis to bear on every area of women's lives.

On a practical level, however, I couldn't afford to be out of work, and the scuttlebutt was enough to make me start looking. I'd been editing our special men's issue, and working with a *New York Times* editor named Brent Staples. A stylish and elegant writer, he'd done a wonderful essay for me on the ways in which the presence of black men alters public space. In the course of our work together, we'd become friends, and I mentioned to him that I needed to consider moving on. He suggested I get a packet together and he would shepherd it through at *The New York Times Magazine*, where he had it on good authority that there was an opening. I couldn't believe my timing; it was especially sweet to imagine that after ten years as a journalist and editor, a college fantasy might become real. I went in to speak with the editors there, and even prepared a portfolio of sample ideas for future stories. But after my initial contact with them, there was silence—months of it.

One Friday evening, I walked into my bedroom after work to check my answering machine for the day's messages. All of the messages were mundane, except one. Mitchel Levitas, the editor of *The New York Times Book Review*, had called and left his number. "When you call me back, I'll tell you what I'm calling about," he said, then hung up.

I was puzzled. Why would I be hearing from the *Book Review* when I'd been having very preliminary conversations with the *Magazine*? It made me crazy to have to wait until Monday morning to return the call. On Monday I went into my office at *Ms.*, closed the door, and made myself wait until ten-fifteen before I picked up the phone. The secretary answered and put me on hold. In a matter of seconds, Mike picked up the phone and cut to the chase.

"I know you're talking with the *Magazine* about a possible job, but I was wondering if you had ever given any thought to working at the *Book Review*," he said.

Oh, hardly ever, I thought to myself—only every Sunday of my life since I was nineteen. But I was cool. "I didn't know there was an opening, but it's certainly an opportunity I'd be interested in."

"Well, when could you come in to talk?"

"I'm pretty flexible; what would be good for you?" I didn't want to push, but I needn't have worried. Mike had my sense of the immediate.

"Can you come over this afternoon around four?" I checked my calendar, then looked at what I was wearing and thanked God that I'd worn something respectable enough to be interviewed in.

"That's no problem; I'm looking forward to it."

The offices of the *Book Review* were tucked into a corner of the eighth floor of The New York Times Building on Forty-third Street. Small, relatively modern, the place looked at first glance like a cross between a library and a bank: cubicles at half-height of nondescript gray, and books as far as the eye could see, covering every flat surface, with carts and shelves besides. Pearl, Mike's secretary, led me back to a good-sized office with a stunning curved desk. Behind it sat Mike, who looked like an old-style newspaperman dressed in professor's clothes; he had a formidable head of hair and a good firm handshake. On the other side of the desk sat his deputy, Rebecca Sinkler, tall with graying hair and an open, friendly face.

The three of us talked for about an hour. Becky asked about my experiences at *Ms.*, and we found we knew several of the same people. I told her that I'd been doing the lion's share of book excerpting and reviewing at the magazine, and my only regret was that sometimes I wanted to talk about books that had nothing to do with feminism, but we couldn't devote precious space to things that weren't directly related to our mission.

Mike wanted to know why I wanted to work at the *Book Review*—a question I'd had all weekend to think about. I had a feeling the two of them would appreciate directness. So I told them how Bob and I used to fantasize about my working there, how I'd read it for years, how much I loved books. I told them, too, that I thought it was important to bring as many ideas and perspectives as possible into the public debates that shaped the intellectual and political ideas of the nation.

"I know you're a feminist, but what if the book you're previewing doesn't believe in feminism? We have to be resolutely centrist here," Mike said. I replied that I didn't think liking a book should have anything to do with deciding to review it. Sometimes it was important to review a bad book, too, to bring to light the notions contained in it, for good or ill. And I didn't think I had to win every argument every time, I told him, just as long as ideas were getting out to the wider world.

I had to audition for the job, Mike explained. He needed to know if I could edit, and whether or not I had good judgment about books and reviewers and how to bring them together. "I can teach you the way we do things here at the *Review,* but I can't teach you judgment," Mike told me as he gave me a stack of uncorrected galleys. "You either have it or you don't."

Mike called me two days after I turned in my report on the books with a review of his own: I had the judgment. It took another month of interviews with a succession of higher-ups, but in the end, I had the job, too. When I called my mother to tell her about my new job and my serious raise, she congratulated me and laughed as she relayed the news to my sister and brother, who were visiting that afternoon. "Ain't this something! Ro finally found somebody to pay her to read!"

Mike would have been happy to have me report the next morning, but I had to give notice at *Ms.*, and I needed a vacation so I could go home and see everybody. It was late March, 1987. I decided to start work on the first Monday in May, which turned out to be my birthday. I couldn't think of a better present for myself than a new job, surrounded by books. On my first day, Mike shook my hand, pointed to my desk, and said, "We have an essay that needs work right away."

Becky was much better at the formalities. She introduced me to my colleagues, showed me how to turn on the computer, and walked me through the process of putting out an issue of the *Review*. I was a little rusty in my recall of Atex, the editing and typesetting system they used, but by the end of the day, most of it had come back to me. I left work that day with a small mountain of galleys to preview for the Thursday meeting—some novels, a couple of academic books on arcane subjects, a biography or two, and some current events. When Bob came home from work that evening with flowers for my birthday, I was already happily ensconced in the front room, reading on the couch and making furious notes.

"Oh, she's in heaven now," Bob said to no one in particular, looking at my distracted expression. What could I say? I was.

Chapter 11

I had seen him in the neighborhood before, roaming the streets and avenues in rough-dried clothes, crouching in doorways, his eyes sunken. He hung out with men I realized later were his brothers, and though I saw them selling drugs and making their connections, I never saw him selling. He seemed always in a huddle with his friends, laughing occasionally, his hands waving as he made his points. But in the first three years Bob and I lived in the house, he never spoke.

One warm night in spring, as I climbed the stairs to my front door, I heard a voice behind me. "Excuse me, ma'am," he said. It was clear from his quick appearance that he had been waiting for me to get home. I was tired, but intrigued. No one of his group had ever said a word to me.

"I hear you're the president of the block," he said.

"I'm president of the block association," I told him.

"Well, I was wondering if you could help me get a job."

I already knew I couldn't. We were a civic group that wanted to get the garbage picked up and people like him out of the doorways on our street. Besides, in a number of ways, he was the enemy. But it was hard to see the face of the enemy in a young man who had broken an unwritten rule just by speaking to me. I knew it cost him something to approach me. He'd probably hear about it for days afterward. Besides, I was just as nosy about my neighbors as they were about me. His willingness to talk was my big chance.

"I need to put my stuff down," I told him. "Can you wait a minute, and I'll be back out?"

He said that was fine, he'd wait. I opened the front door long enough to deposit my purse and briefcase and change my shoes. Then I came back outside and sat down on the stoop.

"We don't get people jobs at the block association," I told him. "That's not what we do. But maybe I can help you think of something. What do you know how to do?"

His answer was just what I expected: a little bit of everything, not much of anything. Once there were places in the world for people like him, men who could join a construction site as a helper, load furniture at a warehouse, clean building lobbies or drive trucks. In fact, he did a little cleaning up from time to time, in the notorious apartment buildings across the street. But it wasn't enough to make a living, and he had no permanent place to stay.

When I asked him where he lived, he told me he was staying with a girlfriend. He also told me he had three children, who were staying with their mother and grandmother. When I asked him the last time he'd seen them, he told me not for a while.

"I can't go over there to see them when I don't have nothing for them," he told me. The kids' grandmother, it seemed, subjected him to a tirade of abuse whenever he showed up. Frankly, I saw her point, but there was something about the way he looked when he talked about his children that got to me. And there was enough little girl left in me to remember what it felt like to want your daddy, even if he wasn't perfect. His kids, in fact, were the big reason he wanted a job, he told me—so he could get his kids out of Newark, away from their grandmother who was always bad-mouthing him, and away from their mother, who was, in his words a "dope fiend."

"So you can't get me no job, then?"

"No," I said. "I can't."

"What you all do, then, if you ain't got no jobs?" he asked me.

I told him about trying to get abandoned buildings secured from drug dealers. I told him we wanted the dealers off the block. At this he looked wary. "That's what I heard. You should be careful. People don't be playing about their money."

"I'm not playing about folks selling dope in front of my house, either," I said. I realized I could send a message through this young man. "There are a lot of old people on this block scared to come out of their houses. People over here shooting at each other—hell, I got caught in a shoot-out once. I'm not bothering anybody over here, but I don't intend to let anybody bother me."

"You mess with the wrong people, you're liable to get hurt," he said, looking at me as though I had lost my mind.

"If I did get hurt, whoever did it wouldn't last out here a day," I said. "The precinct would track them to the ends of the earth and put them up under the jail."

I made this arrogant pronouncement with a confidence I felt only partially. Who's to say, after all, whether the people who might hurt me would ever be found? But I could imagine the media crusade conducted by my husband and my peers, and figured that someone would end up doing time. The only problem was, I didn't want to die.

"Are you selling drugs too?" I asked.

"I'm not messing with that stuff," he said. "My brothers keep trying to get me to work for them, but I don't want to do that. I just want me some kind of job. You don't know anybody with no job?" I shook my head; he sucked his teeth and sighed.

"Damn, man. I got to do something out here. I ain't even had no food today."

It had never occurred to me, as I looked at him and his friends hanging out together, that he might not know each day where his next meal was coming from. Where I came from, someone was always willing to feed you. But I came from a world of women, a world separated by at least two decades from the world on this block. I realized the rules had changed; it was men and drugs that had changed them.

"I can get you something to eat," I said to him. "Let me look in my kitchen and see what I have."

Bob found me in the kitchen, crying and making ham sandwiches. He was less impressed than I was, and told me so. I responded that I didn't care, even if the man on the step was taking me for a fool.

"The man looked me right in the face and told me he hadn't had any food today," I told him. "What was I supposed to say—that's too bad?"

I made two sandwiches, found an orange, and went looking for a bag to put them in. When I went back outside, I handed him the bag and told him what was inside. "Thank you, ma'am, I appreciate it."

I asked him not to call me ma'am. "It makes me feel ninety years old. My name is Rosemary."

"Thank you, Miss Rosemary," he said, lapsing into the honorific I remember from childhood. That made me feel old, too, but I wasn't going to argue the point. When I asked his name, he said people on the street called him Bobo.

"Well, I'm not calling you Bobo," I told him. "You're a grown man. What's your real name?"

"Royce," he said (names have been changed to protect privacy).

"Well, it's nice to meet you, Royce."

In a matter of days, I had come to expect him, his nightly knock on my front door whenever he saw the lights on in our front room. The first few times, when I asked who it was, he would say, "Bobo—I mean Royce." Gradually he started calling himself by his given name, at least around me. He almost always came by when he was hungry. Most of the time, I had something he could eat; if I didn't have sandwiches or leftovers, I gave him money to do what Bob and I did so often—have takeout Chinese food. He would take the few dollars I gave him and go round the block to buy a Styrofoam container with a mound of greasy fried rice and several fried chicken wings—not exactly Empire Szechuan. Some nights he would even knock on the door to show me what he'd gotten. "I wanted you to see I really was getting something to eat," he would say.

One night in early summer, he knocked and asked me if I was busy. I said no, and asked what I could do for him. "I just hadn't seen you in a little while," Royce said. "And seems like every time I knock on your door, I be asking you for something."

I laughed. "You do be asking me for something," I teased him.

"Now see, that's just why I came over here tonight. I knew you be thinking that. I just wanted to talk to you. But that's all right if you're busy."

I wasn't busy, and it came to me that Royce was lonely. So I picked up the iced tea I was drinking and came outside with my keys in case the door slammed. Bob wasn't home yet, but he could hardly miss seeing me here. It was a clear, pretty night, and folks were out—including the dealers, some of whom were kin to Royce. It seemed a pretty good time to make a point of sitting out on the stoop with him.

"How come you sitting out on your stoop, but you don't let nobody else sit here?" he asked me as I lowered myself to the stairs.

"Because it's my house. Anyway, I know I won't leave chicken bones out here to break my neck on," I told him. "I'm not going to work all day and then come home and clean up after strangers. Let them throw chicken bones around at their own house."

Royce laughed at this; our laughter caught the attention of the brothers in the doorway. "You know, my brothers are pretty mad at you."

"What for?" I asked him.

"For having the police over here every time they turn around," he said. "Y'all in that block association be reporting everything you see."

In truth, our members didn't report a tenth of what they saw. Half of us were too frightened, and all of us were too busy to spend that much time on the telephone. But we did have good relationships with the precinct, and our community patrol officer was an especially good, vigilant guy. He looked like the stereotype of a hateful patrol officer—very big, very white, a kind of cowboy; one of our members called him "that big, corn-fed–looking white boy." But his hostility was reserved for people who were disrupting life on our street. He walked the block and spoke to everyone, showed up at our Christmas party, and was all over dealers like ugly on an ape. As much as anyone, except the precinct commander himself, this cop was the reason for Royce's brothers' unhappiness.

Royce and I went round and round about the drug dealers. He reminded me that people had to make a living some kind of way, even the wrong way. I told him that what drug dealers did made life hard for other black people and was hurting them.

"Yeah, but people going to take drugs anyway, whether I sell them or somebody else sell them. So you not stopping anything," he said.

"No, but I'm slowing them down. Besides, if there's nothing wrong with selling drugs, why aren't you out there with your brothers?"

He gave me his sly laugh again. "Well, you know, you do have a point."

"See, you know you know better," I told him.

He asked me if I had the morning paper. "I know y'all read the *Times;* I see it tied up in the garbage." I went inside to get it for him. When I came back, he turned to the sports page, to look up the scores of a tennis match. It seemed he was tracking Jim Courier, and had plenty to say about his recent performance. I gaped at him in frank amazement. What the hell did he know about tennis, after all? It turned out that he knew a great deal—certainly more than I did, since I liked only baseball. What little familiarity I had with tennis came primarily from an interest on the part of Bob's mother, who was an avid fan and a seeded senior player in her own right. But Royce knew the players and their styles, had predictions on the forthcoming U.S. Open. I listened without a word for a while, then interrupted him.

"Excuse me—what else do you know?"

"See, you think just because I'm out here on the street that I'm stupid. I was good in school. I used to be interested in a lot of stuff. I used to read the paper every day. I ain't no dummy," he told me.

"I never thought you were a dummy, but I never thought about you being a tennis authority either. Where did you learn this stuff?"

"From watching. I been watching tennis since I was young, in the group homes."

He had grown up on the block. His father was killed when Royce was eleven or twelve—shot in an argument of some kind. Royce went to school regularly, was good at it, too, in spite of the teasing of kids who said he thought he was better than everybody else. But the death of his father, the growing torments from his classmates, the general miseries of adolescence—from the story he told me on my front steps, they all seemed to happen at once. He started skipping school, became "hard to handle"—at least that's what he said his mother told him when she sent him to the first of several group homes to straighten him out. Evidently they did not help him—he eventually dropped out of school.

I sat and listened, trying not to judge his mother, a woman raising three angry sons all alone without a skill in the world except the ability to monitor traffic in a numbers hole. But it was hard not to judge after watching her come and go for months, long before I knew she was Royce's mother. I had seen her lack of affect, recognized the cool, dead eyes I remember in only a handful of women from my own childhood. She was one of the last holdouts, a charter member of the "they don't belong here" club: men and women who'd decided Bob and I had no right to live on "their" street.

I began to pay more attention to her on the rare occasions when we saw each other. She never spoke to me directly, though I heard she did speak about me. Royce was no saint, but he might just as well have been some stray animal that she noticed on a whim. The word on the street was that she believed I had "adopted" Royce; she meant co-opted him. He was now suspect by speaking regularly to me. I worried that our growing public friendship had gone too far, was a risk both to him and to myself. But Royce told me in one of our evening talks that the opposite was true.

"I don't let nobody say nothing bad about you. I told them, 'That lady is all right. She looks out for me.' I told them not to bother you. I don't want to have to hurt somebody." Royce looked as though he meant it.

As I was coming to know Royce, I was also getting a taste of local political strife. The overriding issue was a kind of turf war: on one side were the residents and homeowners who, like me, had fantasies of a restored central Harlem community; on the other were social service agencies, politicians, and state government, with their own competing and contradictory agendas. At the center of the debate sat an issue of genuine need: long-term housing for AIDS patients in upper Manhattan.

Our members never saw it coming. It was an item in the *Daily News* that alerted us to the agreement—reached between the Archdiocese of New York, Mount Sinai Hospital, and the Harlem

Urban Development Corporation—on a site for long-term care and outpatient treatment facilities for patients with AIDS. Two such facilities, originally set to be built at the heart of the 110th Street corridor, would be built instead directly across the street from our house.

One of the association's newer, more hotheaded members brought the story to my attention during the annual Christmas party. "What are you doing about this?" she demanded of me. "I don't want those people over here!" I was not in the mood to hear this woman talking about "those people." One of "those people," our friend Allan, was at Cabrini Medical Center dying of AIDS even as she spoke. I knew the facilities themselves were necessary. Allan, and so many people like him, should have had a better, less clinical place to live out the remainder of his life.

But I couldn't ignore the other things I knew about what this facility would mean. The archdiocese, the hospital, and the state were preparing to build a massive, 325-bed facility (complete with outpatient care for additional patients) around the corner from a 60-unit jail, a half block from 32 units of transitional housing for homeless families that had just been completed the previous year, and a half block from a 300-bed shelter for homeless single men agreed to by the New York City Board of Estimate in one of their middle-of-the-night deals. These projects, each worthy of support individually, combined to dump more than seven hundred units of institutional housing within two square blocks. And we hadn't counted the drug and alcohol rehabilitation facilities that were ubiquitous in the neighborhood. We were a community without a grocery store or a pharmacy, without a produce market or a movie rental store. The ordinary amenities that most communities take for granted didn't exist in central Harlem, and so long as bureaucrats regarded us as a dumping ground, they never would.

The old saying about being trapped between a rock and a hard place began to take on a more personal meaning. If I didn't speak up about this project, my neighbors would be rightfully angry that I didn't represent their opposition—and my own—to the continuing relocation of social services to a residential neighborhood. But if I did act to oppose the facility, I risked becoming the citizen of my nightmares: a whiny, self-interested creature who agreed with the need for all kinds of services for all kinds of New Yorkers—so long as they didn't operate near me.

I put it to the members in an informal way, calling them up evenings after work, or running into them on the street. All of them shared my opposition to the project, and the opposition was compounded by anger that no one had said a mumbling word to our association—even the Harlem Urban Development Corporation, a state agency that ostensibly had the interests of Harlem residents uppermost in mind. More than one person mentioned their discomfort with the sheer size of the project—325 beds was an awfully big site. A couple of members added a bit of block history for my information: several years earlier, the association had asked that the site be turned into a small center for battered women, in keeping with a request made by a women's group. That request had been denied, though no one knew why, and so the building and its adjacent lots sat in increasing disrepair.

Several people were more concerned about the outpatient treatment component than about the long-term care component. Patients being admitted for long-term care of AIDS were too sick to do harm to anyone in the neighborhood. But outpatient treatment meant an influx of people who were sick enough to be treated—but well enough to be mobile. Even if this component were smaller, how could we be sure that the center would be run in a way that didn't further jeopardize the tenuous balance of the neighborhood? Most AIDS patients in neighborhoods like ours were current or former intravenous drug users. Every one of us knew that the park several blocks away from the site was a popular hangout for IV users to have sex—so popular, in fact, that the historic fire tower in Mount Morris Park was not safe to visit even in broad daylight.

A consensus was beginning to emerge. We all resented not being consulted; we worried that the combined facilities were too big and not easily managed; we were convinced the neighborhood had too many facilities already. I decided it was time to contact the major players. I scoured up the names of the relevant people and groups who were serious parties to this decision. All of them got the same four-paragraph letter decrying their oversight of our group and inviting them to our next meeting to talk. I sent the letters by registered mail, so I'd have the signature of everyone who got one—thereby avoiding the common wide-eyed stare of bureaucrats everywhere who tell you that they "never got your letter."

The archdiocese answered first, followed by Mount Sinai, the mayor's office, and the borough president's office. It was a staff member of the latter office, in fact, who let me know that a public hearing on the facility, sponsored by the New York State Department of Health, was being held at the Harlem state office building on the same night as our block association meeting. She was concerned that the people I most wanted to see at our meeting would attend the other meeting instead. I notified our members that our meeting would convene at the hearings. The borough president's office suggested that I ask to speak at the hearing, something I arranged at once.

I wasn't sure how many people from the block would come out on a frigid January night, but I needn't have worried. Nearly every member came, and all sat as a block in the audience as they listened to speaker after speaker. The second-floor room was packed; the president of the hospital was there, along with representatives from the archdiocese, the mayor's office, HUDC, our city councilwoman, even a representative from Congressman Charles Rangel's office. From the tenor of most of the speakers' remarks, it seemed that this project was a foregone conclusion.

Remarks from the state health department were especially unsettling; it seemed that the department was just waiting to sign off on construction of this gigantic facility without thinking about the effect it might have.

The only exception to the business-as-usual tone were the heated remarks made by a group of Harlem residents who'd won their activist stripes on the battlegrounds of the late 1960s. When I heard one woman threaten to dismantle the project brick by brick, I saw a dismissive smile on the faces of the hospital's representatives, and I sighed with displeasure. She had made a threat she couldn't back up and the hospital knew it. What's more, her empty rhetoric reinforced the contemptuous attitude of an institution like Mount Sinai. It encouraged officials to think they could get away with dumping another facility in a neighborhood that was knee-deep in them already. I hoped I might be able to persuade them otherwise.

I stood when my name was called, and walked to the podium with my written speech in hand. I asked for a moratorium on this and every other social service facility set to be built in central Harlem. I outlined for the listeners precisely what facilities already existed within a two-block radius of the proposed AIDS facility and suggested that, as citizens of New York, central Harlem residents had already done more than our share during the current social crisis. As I spoke, I waved the sheaf of green registered-mail cards I had received and remarked at how appalling it was that not ONE community group had answered my letter, even though I knew they'd received it. I spoke about the forty-year history of our association and how outrageous it was that not one institution had said a single word to us throughout the months of negotiation that had preceded this decision. And I reminded the archdiocese and the hospital of the appeal process available to our block association—which I promised to use.

I ended by admitting that they might all be successful in building this facility, but I added that I would do my best to make sure that it cost them twice as much time and money as they'd originally planned to spend. That last defiant statement brought some listeners to their feet. But more gratifying than the cheers of my neighbors was the look of total shock on the faces of some of the hospital and archdiocese representatives. I knew that look; I saw it all the time, usually on the faces of white people who had already made up their minds about who I was, about what I would say or do. It was a welcome acknowledgment that I had changed the rules of this game, at least for the moment.

By the end of the meeting, I'd traded business cards with nearly a dozen people who wanted to be in touch with me about the next meeting. The next day at work, my phone rang off the hook with calls from people wanting to arrange a super-meeting among all the groups with a vested interest in the fate of the facility. I agreed to attend, and found myself enrolled in a six-month intensive course on the horrors of doing your civic duty.

Back on the block, I continued to see Royce hanging around, and he continued to worry me. I knew he drank; I could smell the liquor on him some nights when we sat talking. I suspected he used drugs. I didn't like either activity, but I'd hit a wall about my ability, or willingness, to interfere in those parts of his life. Because he never acted in an obnoxious way, I let it alone. But I never liked giving him money. Food was one thing, even subway tokens to get to the shelter. But when he asked for money, I cringed and most often said no. I thought of my angry father and his hustles, and remembered that these streets were different from my father's; even from my own.

It wasn't as though Royce never worked. His was the employment of the underskilled and dysfunctional young man he was. Sometimes he cleaned up around the neighborhood or traveled to a sporadic part-time job as a caterer's helper on Long Island.

But mostly he hung around in the doorways on our block, waiting for me to come home from work—to talk, to ask for food and tokens.

Bob didn't like my increasing involvement in Royce's life. He was not afraid that something would happen to me; he was angry that I was being used. Many times, I felt used, too—times when I did not want to see him move out of the shadows in search of whatever was in my kitchen. I wanted him to change, of course. I wanted him to exercise the bright, inventive mind I saw at work whenever we sat and talked. I wanted him to visit his children, to regain custody of them and raise them. I wanted him to be someone he had no idea of how to become.

It took a long time for me to understand this about him, a long time to understand this as the source of my anger, which, though I worked desperately to hide it, found expression in other ways. I would not make time to talk the way I used to. When I gave him food, I was just polite, almost perfunctory. When he asked me for money I said no without discussion, disappearing into my house. Bob was satisfied that I had found a way to curtail this fledgling relationship, to put it in its rightful place. But I felt dreadful, betrayed by myself, trapped. Royce began to come by less often. He was no fool; he sensed that I was fed up and asked for food only when he had gone without eating for days.

I realized that I didn't like the way I was acting. I didn't like the way my behavior made me feel. I was doing to him what the world did, and I knew better. Still, I needed to figure out a better sense of boundaries between us than we'd had before. The next time I saw him, I made time to sit on the stoop. He was surprised; I hadn't really talked to him in weeks.

"You been pretty busy," he said to me. "I haven't talked to you in a long time. I don't know, I miss you, I guess."

His head was bowed in the dim evening, so that I couldn't see his face. I could smell him, though, in distinct detail: the sour aroma of old beer, the rotting insoles of the one pair of sneakers he had worn for months, the sweat and salt of living without running hot water and making do with washing up in a cold-water sink. I'd known a girl on Berkeley Avenue who smelled like that, not the beer, but the smell of being poor, of giving up that could claim anyone if he or she let it. I remembered that smell as I sat next to Royce, and sorrow filled me. I could not lie and say I missed him too—that hadn't happened yet. What I did miss, though, was the way I thought about myself as a woman who cared.

"I've been thinking about you," I told him. "I been wondering what you're planning to do with yourself."

"Ain't nothing to do," he said. "No jobs, no place to stay. I can't even get a room. Them shelters are horrible, man, you don't know. My brothers are asking me to help them out, you know. I don't want to go that way, you know, but I can't keep living like this."

He looked up and over at me. I could feel a question in him, and wondered whether it was about something I could do.

"You really need somebody to clean up around here," he said, nonchalantly. He peered into the area beyond the gate downstairs. It was littered with cigarette butts, pungent with the aroma of urine. We were cursed with a high brick wall that kept people away from the basement door, true enough, but provided them, too, with ample cover for its use as a toilet.

"Bob washes it down every week," I told him.

"You know how people are around here," Royce said. "Why don't you hire me to do it?"

"Clean up outside?"

"Yeah. Bob works almost as much as you do, man. I got to make some money some kind of way."

"But it's not a real job, Royce. I can't pay you enough money for it to be a real job."

"Miss Rosemary, I have got to make some kind of money. And I don't want to be coming to you for everything. I got to figure out how to live for myself. But this would let me make a little money so I don't always have to be begging you."

"How about twenty dollars a week?" I asked him. It was a glorified allowance, so far as I could see; I thought he would say no. But he didn't.

"Can I start tonight?" he asked. "It's nasty down there."

After that, the knock on the door meant Royce had come to work. Usually, he wanted a bucket of hot soapy water and the push broom we kept downstairs on our side of the entryway. I paid him on the same night I got paid—Thursday. As the weather got colder, we talked less and less. On the rare occasion that it snowed, he shoveled rather than swept. For the most part, I still saw him in doorways, but he never lingered much after I got home.

Bob, having made peace with the idea that Royce would tend to the outside of the house, now stopped to say hello as he came in from work. One evening, as I watched television in the front room, I could hear the familiar rumble of Bob's voice, but not his footsteps on our granite steps. I waited for Bob to greet me, but heard only the low sounds of talk, punctuated by laughter. I got up and looked out the front window, and saw Bob leaning on the handrail, talking to Royce. They were discussing the American banking system, and what Royce had decided was its imminent collapse. Bob was explaining why the collapse was not so imminent, and Royce listened attentively, even while he swept. The conversation seemed destined to be lengthy, so I returned to my seat on the couch.

Bob came in a little while later, with a thoughtful expression. I knew exactly what had put that expression on his face, but I waited for him to say something. "You know, Royce's not as dumb as he looks."

"He don't look all *that* dumb," I said in answer. "How did you reach this conclusion?"

"I was just talking to him a minute ago," Bob said. "We were talking about bank takeovers. He really keeps up with the news."

"True, but he can't keep up with himself, that's the problem," I said.

As the months went by, a subtle change came over a few of our more marginal neighbors. These were the men and women who were mostly old, and mostly silent about anything that wasn't directly their business. They were people who had never been rude to me, but never went out of their way to acknowledge my existence, either. Now, these same people nodded to me, even said hello. We would talk about the weather, or the Mets, or their getting old. It seemed that Royce was as good as his word. He would tell anyone who would listen that "those people in the corner house" were all right. Some of our less friendly neighbors, it seemed, had taken him at his word.

Meanwhile, my crash course in neighborhood politics was in full swing. At the first meeting sponsored by the Harlem Urban Development Corporation, there must have been twenty people there; community relations people from the hospital and the archdiocese; the two local district leaders; representatives from the Community Assistance Unit of the mayor's office; staff members from the borough president's office, the city council president's office, the office of our councilwoman; even a representative from our congressman.

Mount Sinai seemed open to negotiations on several levels, and certainly appeared to want to work with members of the community to find some common ground. The Archdiocese of New York, however, was another matter. As far as its representatives were concerned, the archdiocese owned the land, and they didn't need anyone's permission to build on it; since the site was once a hospital, they needed no zoning variance; they were willing to relocate their site if HUDC found an appropriate buyer for their land at an appropriate price. I could understand their attitude; I'm not sure I would have felt differently if I'd been in their shoes. The real sticking point, however, was their attitude about providing health education to those people using the facility. The archdiocese made it clear that it was unwilling to discuss the use of condoms as a way to reduce the spread of AIDS. Its representatives had a host of difficulties with the health education components that were mandatory if they expected to receive public funding.

We'd managed to persuade the state to reduce the facility's size to its bare minimum, 280 beds. We'd also gotten the parties to consider using part of it to create a special unit for parents and children afflicted with AIDS. In addition, Mount Sinai made a verbal commitment to seek out neighborhood residents for employment at the facility, and to establish a satellite health care facility for the community.

The only other site large enough to provide the requisite number of beds, adequate parking, and reasonable transportation for employees was a parcel of land on Eighth Avenue near 117th Street. It had in its favor the fact that there were no other social services within several blocks of the site, so oversaturation would not be an issue.

As soon as the hospital and the archdiocese said they would be willing to talk about that site, I asked about block associations and tenants groups in the adjoining areas. "I don't think you should wait as long as you waited with our group," I said at one meeting. "We need to have a meeting with representatives as soon as possible." There was grudging agreement to that, and the district leaders, along with a representative of the city council president's office, said they would take care of it.

And so they did—but not in the way I'd hoped. Instead, things fell apart piece by piece. The planned presentation by the hazardous waste disposal specialists was probably the worst idea ever. Once neighborhood people had an understanding of how important it was that the biomedical waste be handled correctly, they jumped to a completely justifiable conclusion: when it comes to black communities, folks often get careless about very important things. How could they be sure, someone asked, whether these folks weren't just going to dump all that poison in some vacant lot where their children might get at it? Experience told them the answer: they didn't know.

The voices got louder and louder that night, as speaker after speaker tried to discuss possible scenarios for the site. Finally, one member of the audience asked the district leaders and the city council president's representatives whether they had known about this plan before. I stood at the front of the room in utter astonishment, as each and every one of them said they'd had no idea that HUDC or Mount Sinai or anyone else was thinking about placing this dangerous facility in their midst.

Dunce that I was, I'd finally gotten the point. In spite of weeks of planning, night after night of phone calls and letter writing, after my many questions about why the representatives of tenant groups and other neighborhood organizations had yet to come to a single meeting, I realized that none of the people in charge had told any community leader about anything we'd been doing. The people in that room had been blindsided, just as I'd been blindsided by these same smooth operators a few months earlier. And with perfectly straight faces, the government representative stood up and lied about everything. I looked one of the district leaders dead in the eye; he shook his head and held up a hand to me to wait a bit. By now, people were storming out of the room in a fury. I felt as though I'd been hit by a car.

The meeting essentially dissolved, and so did I. At least one member of the mayor's staff said that I shouldn't take it so hard. "This stuff happens at meetings like this all the time," she said. "You're really good at this; don't get discouraged." I didn't feel good at this, I felt stupid, and used by nearly everyone in the process.

In the end, Mount Sinai and the archdiocese abandoned the project entirely. The state health department, in its revised projections for AIDS cases in upper Manhattan, found that the number was half of that originally projected. And community opposition to the facility was now districtwide, and thus the project was not worth the trouble of pursuing. I was burned out in my first true exposure to local government, and realized it was no fluke that I was a writer, not a politician. I was too thin-skinned, too easily upset, to ever be comfortable again in the company of the wheeler-dealers. Books and ideas, I decided, made much better, more peaceful, companions.

Chapter 12

I had been at the *Book Review* for three years, and I'd had a wonderful time. Mike Levitas, the man who originally hired me, had moved on to become editor of the Op-Ed page. We all hated to see him go, but it was a good move for him, and for the paper. His deputy, Becky Sinkler, had succeeded him—a historic moment, since no woman had ever run the section. I was delighted, both professionally and personally. Becky and I had always understood and liked each other. We had a shared affinity for feminist theology, a similar habit of plainspokenness, and the same slightly raucous sense of humor.

I had grown used to the vast difference between outside perceptions of the *Book Review*—before I arrived, I'd even shared some of them—and the reality of working there. There was a certain amount of awe, and enormous speculation, about who we all were and what we did, and a lot of comment about how well we did it. It wasn't hard to conjure up this vision of a dour group of intellectuals who acted as cultural and literary gatekeepers, selecting only the most worthy tomes for consideration, settling personal scores and stoking grudges by choosing some writers and slighting others. It also wasn't hard to imagine that same solemn group sitting down all day reading, reading, reading, with the occasional opening and closing of book covers to break the monotonous silence.

People on the outside tended to forget that we worked for a newspaper—but we never did. We couldn't, because the nature of the job meant we were always working. At any given time, two issues of the *Review* were always being worked on, because closing came in midweek. Our days were spent at our desks, on the phones, at the computer terminals—editing reviews, cajoling authors to review, chasing authors to get the reviews they hadn't yet finished. There was no time left in the day to actually read and evaluate books. That's what we all did with the rest of our lives.

I read on the way to work and on the way home. I read at the dinner table and in the bathtub. And I always, always read in bed—our bedroom, always adorned with whatever Bob and I were reading, began to take on the character of a research library, with piles of books decorated with "pink slips," the formal notes and recommendations that every previewer made for each galley he or she read.

My colleagues were anything but dour; nearly all of them had wicked senses of humor. Some were academics and scholars by training; others, like myself, were journalists throughout our careers, a few of us were both. We were rare, I think, because we really liked each other, we respected each other's judgment and expertise, and we all loved what we did 90 percent of the time. We were also rare because we were far enough away from the nerve center of the newspaper to be left alone—no small achievement at *The New York Times.*

Of all the work I'd ever done, it was this job that came closest to my ideal life—a place in which all my many interests and identities and passions came together. There is hardly a black person in America who has not felt what W.E.B. Du Bois so eloquently described in *The Souls of Black Folk:*

> It is a peculiar sensation, this double-consciousness, this sense of always looking at one's self through the eyes of others, of measuring one's soul by the tape of a world that looks on in amused contempt and pity. One ever feels his twoness—an American, a Negro; two souls, two thoughts, two unreconciled strivings; two warring ideals in one dark body.

For me, there was the added sense of femaleness and the perspective it brought. And yet none of those parts of myself were at issue in my work. Indeed, they were assets, depending on the book I was reading, the discussion I was having with colleagues, the assignment I was making. I was not the only black person there, and not the only woman, so I never felt the pressure to be representative. The piles of books I was responsible for each week were numerous, but varied. If five black people had new books coming, I might get one of them, or three of them, or none of them, depending on the subject matter. I also could get public policy tomes, books on Russian family life, a history of pioneer women or a gruesome true-crime story. It was a delicate balance, the difference between acknowledging an editor's love and expertise and pigeonholing her with one topic or subject area forever. But especially with Mike and Becky, it was a balance that largely worked.

There was only one thing I really missed: the chance to write regularly. When I wrote, it was typically rewriting a review to reflect what a reviewer actually wanted to say but hadn't. I managed to write for other sections of the paper, but I couldn't weigh in on the books I was handing over to someone else to evaluate. It was frustrating when a writer we chose wrote a review that missed the mark, but there was nothing I could do about it. It was a rare frustration in an otherwise happy working life.

When rumors began to float through the building about a reorganization of the daily book section, I realized that becoming a daily book reviewer could be the solution for my restlessness. A chance to write was the only thing that could make me consider leaving the friendly confines of the eighth floor for what one former colleague called, with perfect seriousness, "The Snake Pit." But putting my name into play meant speaking to Becky about the idea of moving on, at least in theory. I wandered into Becky's office late one afternoon while she was signing letters, and told her what I'd been thinking about. She was just as supportive as I'd thought she'd be, though my departure would leave her shorthanded.

"I think you'd be wonderful for the job," she told me, confirming that she'd heard the rumors too. "If there's anything you think I could do to help you, I'd be glad to; of course, I'll put in a good word for you." I couldn't ask for more than that. I prepared a packet of recent work I'd done, along with a brief note to the editor on the third floor who was in charge of the rumored reorganization.

I heard only silence from the third floor for some weeks, but that didn't worry me. In any news organization, the wheels of hierarchy take some time to turn; at the *Times,* their motion was positively glacial. Besides, I would hardly be the only person interested in the job. One afternoon some months later, Becky and I were talking in her office when she told me that the planned reorganization was not likely to happen after all. I was disappointed, but not shattered. Plans to reorganize varying sections of the paper routinely rose and fell and rose again. After a couple of fantasies about what life might have been like as a daily book reviewer, I pushed the whole idea aside.

Another month had passed by the time I got a call from the editor's secretary asking if I was free to come downstairs to talk about the packet I'd sent down so long ago. I told her I'd be glad to come whenever her boss was free. I was frankly curious, and wondered whether some change had occurred that hadn't yet reached the grapevine. The editor was just completing a phone call in the newsroom as I arrived, and his secretary showed me into his private office to wait. When he did enter, I noticed he was holding a sheaf of papers—the clips I'd sent him earlier. He perched himself on the arm of a chair as I took a seat across from him.

He said he regretted that he hadn't gotten back to me earlier about the daily book reviewing job. "I looked at your clips," he said, "and they're fine, as far as they go. But I don't see that you're ready for a job like daily book reviewing. Besides, most of these clips are all about black people—not that that isn't a specialty of its own. But I'd like to see you expand your work."

As he spoke, the heat began to creep into my face, then spread down and out through the rest of my body. I had forgotten that I was capable of the kind of rage that was growing with every word he uttered. I was so furious I frightened myself. I managed to remark that one of the lovely things about being an editor was that whenever I did write, I had the luxury of choosing to write about my passions. "You must know," I added, "that my years in the *Book Review* as a preview editor have required a wide range of knowledge, and interest in all kinds of subjects." At that point, I was still thinking that, though I wouldn't necessarily be considered for the job this round, he might add me to the list of rotating substitutes—reviewers who filled in for the standard columnists whenever they traveled or went on vacation.

Instead, he told me that he was sure that I would eventually "end up" as an editor in the paper's cultural sections. I knew my leaving his office was the most important thing I could do at that moment. I remember that I stood up to go without waiting to hear whatever he was about to say next; I recall hearing my mother's voice in my head, reminding me about how my temper was going to get me in trouble one day if I didn't learn how to control it. Suddenly, that seemed like a vital piece of advice. I was replaying her voice in my head to get me off the third floor and back upstairs, and it was tough to do, because the fury that filled me made its own noise—like buzzing, or static on a badly tuned radio. It was fury that would have to go somewhere, so I took it back upstairs, and I managed to get to Becky's office before bursting into tears.

I told her what happened, apologizing through my tears for throwing a fit in her office. Becky waved away my efforts at propriety, and got a bit angry at the episode herself.

"What does he think you do up here?" she asked, warming to the idea that her judgment had been insulted as well as my own. "Does he think I can afford to have an editor who only knows one subject? Has he ever read your other pieces for the paper? I don't believe this!"

Her outraged sincerity was more comfort than she knew. I wiped my eyes, commiserated a little more, and calmed down enough, I thought, to return to work. But I found I couldn't go back to my usual tasks. Every galley I touched, every manuscript I leafed through, reminded me of the conversation I'd just had, the inherent condescension of it—and fury grew in me again. I thought crying should have purged some of it, but it was only a safety valve of sorts.

Over and over, I replayed the tape of that afternoon in my mind. Over and over, I kept trying to find an explanation for what was essentially unexplainable. I had been told no before, and though I didn't like hearing it, I could live with it. But being dismissed, being told that something I valued was of no import—that was galling. It was doubly galling when I considered again how very wrong that editor was. I had chosen to focus my writing on issues of race and culture and gender at a time when all these areas were undergoing intense reevaluation. The cultural debate was hot and heavy, and not only was I being told that I couldn't weigh in (it was his absolute prerogative, as the editor, to tell me that), but I was being told that there was nothing to weigh in about.

His was a response that went against everything I believed in, everything I'd come to know and respect about reading and writing, about communicating and living in the world. I didn't need to love a book to assign it for review. In fact, I would often come to our Thursday morning meetings with a book I found foolish, even reprehensible by my own political or ethical standards. But I believed in the power of knowledge, of fully informed choice. I believed that readers needed to know that those books were there, that we as a review of books (and of opinion, indirectly) needed to comment on the widest possible range of topics. I also believed that what some viewed as the dismantling of America was, in fact, an act of American restoration. The profusion of voices from people of color, from people of different sexualities—these voices were filling in the blanks about America that so many people had tacitly agreed to ignore. Because of this new energy, America was becoming less static and myth-bound. We were becoming the real, vibrant, sometimes dissonant country we were meant to be; our music, our movies, our books were beginning to reflect that. But in more places than I first realized, these new developments were not a cause for joy, or even for acknowledgment. For some, the response was a declaration of war against declining "standards"—their code for the status quo. For others—and many at the *Times* were among them—war was hardly necessary. They simply exercised their power of the press: it isn't real, because we haven't said it's real.

As the days passed, the rejection festered. I asked a friend why this feeling of terrific rage wouldn't leave me.

"You hate to be thwarted," she told me, laughing. "This guy is in your way."

He was in my way—in more ways than one. Yes, he'd failed to understand the work I wanted to do, but he would hardly be the first editor with a subjective opinion that differed from a writer's vision of the world. What had me stuck was that he had gotten in the way of my own vision of myself. When I first considered the change in jobs, I had seen myself as someone with a lot to offer the paper, someone who wanted an opportunity to stretch myself and grow into something new. What he saw was a narrow writer with parochial and unimportant interests, competent enough as a writer but certainly without the flair necessary to merit a space in the daily culture section. The rage that was my constant companion in the days that followed spoke to the internal struggle that I had stumbled into. I could believe him, or I could believe me.

My father began appearing in my dreams. Not every night, and not very clearly. But all the dreams had in common a feeling of utter normality—we were talking about something, not fighting, or we were on our way somewhere together, or he and Mama were riding in the car. He always said if there were any way to come back to haunt us, he would, but that's not why I was seeing him in my dreams. I had summoned him, I think, out of the loneliness of my rage. Daddy would have been able to put his finger on the throbbing heart of my anger. He would have had more than one story to tell me about a thwarted dream. No matter that Daddy had played his own part in attempting to thwart any dream of mine he didn't understand; he would have *known* this feeling by heart.

Daddy had been so sure than an education would keep me safe from his disappointments, and in many ways he had been right. I thought of what my life might have been like if I had lived even thirty years earlier, if I'd worked in a factory, or in the fields, or in some other woman's kitchen. I was no longer poor, no longer ashamed. I had earned a chance at a life my parents could only imagine.

But I was still black in a country that would have preferred that I not be, or at least not bring it up. Daddy could never have foreseen the blanket insistence on cultural amnesia that would follow my generation of African Americans into the workplace. A white man who devoted his spare time to the study and appreciation of Russian life and culture would be considered a specialist. A black woman who devoted her spare time to the study and appreciation of African-American life and culture was provincial and unprepared for serious literary work. Some things simply did not change. It shouldn't have hurt me, but it did.

Each evening after work, I would settle into a chair or the bed or the bathtub, reading and analyzing and thinking of possible reviewers for the stacks of books that were never far from me. Some of the books were so poorly written, so badly conceived, that we wondered aloud in meetings how they could ever see the light of day. Some books were so brilliant and elegant that they ended much too soon. Most books were some combination of success and failure, and those were a particular pleasure for me. They seemed to me most revealing of what the work of a writer really is, the first half of a transaction that is complete only when another's eyes meet the page. Part of the joy of reading is the hope of deciphering a writer's secret, rooting for his or her success.

What little peace I had during these weeks and months, I found at those moments. I was reminded anew that long before I learned to be an editor, writing itself had been my great love. Now I was on the sidelines—wonderful, even luxurious sidelines, but the sidelines all the same.

Why not get off the sidelines? The thought came to me unbidden, but once it had arrived, it began to grow. I had a thousand projects I'd always wanted to work on, but never had the time: essays on feminism and race, a historical novel, poetry rooted in my Harlem life. All over the house, notebooks with scribbles and first paragraphs bore witness to my dabbling. Always, I had put them aside, waiting for a better, more sensible time. I thought of my dead father; I thought about those long dreamy talks with Bob when I was hardly more than a teenager.

If I wasn't careful, the right time would never come, and I would be left with the same despairing look my father wore to his grave.

I asked Becky for a leave of absence. It was important for me to get away from the cascade of work and into the silence that feeds writing, something I'd never had. I knew if we both planned well, I could leave for a couple of months when the volume of galleys was lowest and return to work for the big rush of fall books. She supported my leave and, after a few weeks of discussion with the powers that be on the third floor, worked out an arrangement for me to take two weeks of vacation time and five weeks of unpaid leave. I would have to freelance a few articles before I left to make up for the salary I'd lose, but I could handle that.

I knew I would have to find somewhere to go, away from New York, from my friends and Bob and the block association and my other commitments. A writer's colony would be ideal; a community of creative people would allow me to work in solitude yet still have companionship when I wanted it. Yet I had missed the deadlines for creative communities like Yaddo and MacDowell. I found information about another small colony, the Blue Mountain Center, in the Adirondack Mountains, and discovered there was still time for me to submit an application. Their notification date was perilously close to the start of my leave, but with any luck, I'd get accepted.

As the weeks passed, I grew more anxious about not being settled. I feared having to work for two months at home, surrounded by the everyday business of life and my civic responsibilities. I didn't want this precious time to be nibbled away by distraction after distraction. I was agonizing about this with two friends at the paper when one of them, Diane, mentioned a house in upstate New York that she and a couple of friends rented each summer. It turned out that one of the women who usually shared the house had made other plans; Diane needed a third person.

The following weekend, Bob and I followed Diane up the Taconic Parkway to Chatham, and across a small bridge to a two-hundred-year-old house that was a writer's fantasy. There was a spacious yard, and a brook nearby. The back windows of the house looked out over the pasture of a neighbor who kept sheep, and every few minutes we could hear the sheep bleating at each other as they munched on grass. Eileen, the owner of the house, was tall and regal, with a great head of silver hair. She'd been a researcher at Time-Life in the days when brilliant and accomplished women had no hope of becoming reporters or writers. We liked each other on sight, and talked for hours after Bob and I had looked at the house and met her son and daughter. By the time we were ready to head back to New York City, Diane, Eileen, and I had worked out a price for the rental and an arrival date that would allow Bob to spend a few vacation days with me before he went back to work.

Bob stayed for four days while I got settled and learned my way around. We drove up and down country roads, filled the house with food, found our way to the stores and gas stations Diane had told me about so that I wouldn't get lost once I was on my own. On my own—for the first time since Bob and I were married, I really would be. I'd been rereading the journals of the poet and novelist May Sarton, whose book *Journal of a Solitude* defined succinctly and beautifully the struggle to shape a creative and meaningful life. I packed several of Sarton's books to take with me, along with other books I loved and books that would help me sort through all the ideas in my head. There was James Washington's anthology of writings; the speeches of Martin Luther King, Jr., *A Testament of Hope;* W.E.B. Du Bois's *The Souls of Black Folk* and his *Prayers for Dark People;* Madeleine L'Engle's journals about Crosswicks, her country house, and her novel *A Wrinkle in Time;* Alice Walker's *In Search of Our Mothers' Gardens;* John Cheever's collected short stories; everything on my shelf by Annie Dillard, and Zora Neale Hurston's *Their Eyes Were*

Watching God. These, and a few reference books, would be my most consistent companions.

These two months were an experiment. Did I know what I wanted to say? Could I find the voice in which to say it? Could I live alone and work alone? Would I be so happy with country living after a few nights here, looking out the bedroom window into a world without sirens or streetlights? More immediate for me: Would I still be steeped in the anger I felt so keenly now?

Bob cautioned me not to sit around worrying about all those questions. A practical man, he urged me in his best husbandly voice to do my best and to see what happened. We kissed goodbye and pledged one another to be careful. I blew him exaggerated kisses as the train pulled away, but this was no tragic occasion. I drove carefully back to Chatham on the winding two-lane roads, pulled into the gravel driveway, and made my way into the wood-paneled kitchen to brew myself some tea. I sat looking out the screen door, listening to crickets and watching fireflies, wondering about tomorrow.

The first thing I promised myself was a chance to discover my natural rhythm. Now that there was no one to please but myself, what would a day look like? I already knew I was a night person. That meant bedtime usually arrived at about three A.M. My day began at ten A.M., as I stumbled into a wash of brilliant sunshine in the kitchen and living rooms. Coffee always came first; since the house didn't have cable, and standard daytime television was inhabited by game shows, I tuned in the classical radio station for music with breakfast. The station, with a transmitter on the New York–Massachusetts border, struck the perfect balance: pastoral music during the day, serious jazz in the evening.

I went into town most mornings to buy the paper or pick up small items like milk or bread. Part of the fun included a daily perusal of the bulletin board by the door. It hadn't taken more than a week for me to think about renting a house in the country year-round. Someone was always posting a notice, and I wondered whether I could convince Bob that our driving the narrow Taconic Parkway every weekend in winter would be good for my spirits. I would drive back home with my purchases, spread the paper out on the huge oak table in the kitchen, and have a second cup of coffee. As I read, I listened to the noon broadcast of National Public Radio, which segued into world news from the BBC. By the time the news report had ended, I was full of coffee, reasonably conscious, and ready to work.

In the beginning, I read and thought and made copious notes for a novel and several essays. Some days, I struggled with writing poetry again, something I'd abandoned in college. Some afternoons I took my books and papers outside into the yard, and lay in the sun reading and napping. These early weeks were restorative. I had given myself room to maneuver, to pursue in a small way a life of the mind; it was far different from my years as a literary midwife, recovering and restructuring the voices of others. It was different, too, from life on the barricades of the block association.

But after three weeks or so, my idyll began to fade. The old ingrained directives to accomplish something began to assert themselves, and for the first time in my life, writing became something to fear. I wondered whether the incident at the *Times* had left me lacking in confidence. I doubted it; the real problem now was my unacknowledged fear and guilt about the kind of public speaking that writing is.

I lay in bed one evening, listening to the night sounds and chiding myself to do better the next day. In the middle of this I could hear another, angrier voice in me. What gives you the right to shut yourself up in this old house, reading and thinking when other people have jobs—or worse, struggle because they have no jobs? it asked. What could you possibly have to say that's so important? Who do you think you are?

My nightly phone calls home were peppered with questions

designed to elicit Bob's approval of what I was doing, his validation that I wasn't being stupid and wasting my time. I bounced wildly between days spent reading beloved writers and deciding that adding my voice was useless, and nights spent coaxing myself to forget the day. Bob's weekend visits were a blessed distraction. Every moment we spent in a museum or a store or an herb garden was a moment in which I did not have to confront my terrors. But always, on Sunday night, he went home, and I returned to my conflicting desires.

On July 1, I opened my morning newspaper to discover the nomination of Clarence Thomas to the Supreme Court. Ever since Thurgood Marshall had announced his forthcoming retirement, there had been rumors that George Bush would take the opportunity to replace him with someone black and conservative. By this time, the trickle of black conservatives I'd first noted in the 1980s had become a steady, obsequious stream. It was no coincidence, either, that their increased visibility had a connection, not to politics, but to fundamentalist and evangelical Christianity.

Evangelical Christianity certainly was a religion that suited conservatives of all stripes; their vision of life seemed colored by a belief in the pervasiveness of sin and the essential unworthiness of everyone. These were Christians whose faith had led them, not to a larger embrace of the world, I thought, but to a profound sense of hopelessness; their great love of God had ruined them for the company of humanity.

Could this be the reason conservatives were always so dismissive of human rights, so bereft of belief in anything except the self rescued by God? What was it about the mercy of God as they had experienced it that made them so merciless toward their fellow human beings? In many ways, black conservatives were no different from other conservatives. They shared the same overweening obsession with anticommunism, the same faith in unbridled capitalism, the same distrust of government. But for black conservatives, other forces were at work. They seemed afflicted with hero worship of white American life, with a corresponding distaste for the black communities from which they had come. It was nothing so bald as the old-style envy of white skin. Instead, it was the sense that being black was a problem only because other black people kept bringing it up. These were men who embraced a mythology that white society believed was the highest compliment a black person could receive: the notion of color blindness. African Americans like myself, who considered color blindness in America both an insult and a lie—we were the real enemy now.

Men like Thomas—and they *were* largely men—seemed determined to co-opt the traditional strengths of the black communities from which they came, to cast those strengths in a more individualistic and conservative mode. Thomas, especially, appeared eager to claim the "bootstrap" theory of personal responsibility for success and achievement. He had done it all himself; there was no one who helped; it was his own strength of will and his own faith in God. The qualities of common struggle, of collective action and mutual dependence that are the legacies of African-American life, that were part of the propulsive energy of the Civil Rights Movement—these were things that did not fit the self-images of black conservatives. This had to be how Thomas, who was the product of the same era as I, could convince himself that affirmative action policies played no part in his arrival at Yale, that, indeed, such policies were an insult to his initiative, rather than a tool to insure that his initiative had not been in vain. This had to be how he could feel comfortable using a family member, his own sister, as the example of a dependent welfare queen, when the truth was she had abandoned her job to care for their ailing aunt. His hunger for disconnection seemed so great, he was willing to scapegoat his own flesh and blood, when he might just as well have held himself to account for his sister's "dependency." After all, where was he when she was becoming a welfare queen? Ingratiating himself with the conservative ascendancy in Washington, leaving the dirty work of family and community behind.

Thomas himself was such a rebuff to Thurgood Marshall and his brilliant, expansive legacy, the Thomas nomination such a shamelessly political act by Bush, that I found myself unable to do anything but obsess on the appointment. As each day's newspapers brought more insight into Thomas's mediocre legal record and his opportunistic politics, I grew angrier and angrier. I found myself with a notebook and pencil, under the trees one afternoon, writing a piece comparing Thomas's formative years and my own. I wanted to suggest that compassion, along with a working memory of his difficult years and the concrete help he received—both public and private—might be more valuable traits to bring to the Court than anything he had learned from his political cohorts.

That piece became an op-ed article for the *Chicago Tribune,* but it did a lot more for me than relieve my frustration at Thomas's nomination and my concerns about the conservative turn of the Supreme Court. It affirmed the answer to the questions I had asked myself since my arrival—who I thought I was, what I thought I was doing. I was a writer, for one thing, no matter what anyone else might say about the subjects I chose or the kinds of writing I did. I was a woman of African descent who felt called to write about the people and the communities and the cultures that formed her. I had the right to speak because I could speak. I had the duty to speak, because at a time when a segment of the African-American community sought to abandon the life and the culture that created them, and at a moment when white Americans sought to declare that the racial divide had been healed, I needed to articulate another voice, a *more* conservative position. What I hoped to conserve was the spirit and commitment to justice I felt was being ridiculed and scorned.

I remembered a week at the Book Review a year or two earlier. I was the preview editor for the historic collection of nineteenth-century black women writers being published by Oxford University Press in conjunction with the Schomburg Center for Research in Black Culture. It was an impressive achievement in reclamation; the editors had brought together the intense and heartfelt work of black women who had labored in the vineyards of public life at one of America's most troubled moments. The reviewer to whom I'd assigned the project shared my enthusiasm, and his review would be on the front page of the Book Review in time for the Fourth of July issue. Though only the editor and deputy editor decide what book is featured in any given week, the timing of this review couldn't have been better if I'd planned it myself.

Part of a previewer's job is to work with the art department and the photo editors to find ways to illustrate reviews. We'd all agreed that the best possible illustrations would be portraits of the women themselves, as many as we could find. Yolanda, our photo editor, was on the phone with the Schomburg Center to arrange the delicate task of copying the archival photographs of women most people did not know ever existed. Meanwhile, the copy editors were working with the multivolume set to match names and titles. It was, in most ways, a very typical closing week for us.

But it was hardly a typical week for me. I'd been reading the volumes for weeks by this time, immersing myself in a history I thought I knew, but didn't. Few people did, because these women—Maria W. Stewart, Fannie Barrier Williams, Frances E. W. Harper, Anna Julia Cooper—had spent their lives crying in the wilderness; making their mark in the nineteenth-century American debates on slavery and abolition, on suffrage and the budding women's movement; articulating the voice and sensibility of black womanhood, only to be silenced by time and the forces of indifference. But more than a hundred years had passed. A new generation of black women and men, armed with the education and opportunity for scholarship won by a modern Civil

Rights Movement, had gone searching for women who weren't supposed to exist, found them, and restored them to a world in need of them.

At some point on a Tuesday afternoon before the close, Yolanda brought me a proof of the cover page of the Review, and asked if I would check to make sure that all the names matched all the faces. I took the proof page and walked over to a desk in the copyediting section, where the ten initial volumes stood. They were small, elegant books, beautifully bound in navy blue, with gold lettering on their covers and spine. The series logo graced every book, a blue-and-gold silhouette of a nineteenth-century black woman in profile, her hair gathered atop her head in the fashion of the time. As I began to check the photos and captions, I felt incredibly proud, and understood something transcendent about the moment. There has always been, in much of the African-American community, a sense that God calls people to do certain work, certain things that are their tasks and no one else's. Some of those tasks are large, so large that they seem unachievable. Some of them are small things, links in a larger chain. This was my moment to be the link in a chain. I was here as a kind of midwife to the rebirth of ideas and sensibilities thought to be forever lost, and their reclamation renewed me in ways I had only begun to understand.

Those women would never be lost again. But their fierce love of black people, their unwavering commitment to the survival and health of their communities—these qualities seemed muted now as black Americans found themselves under siege again. Activism was the heart of black political and social progress, but writing and thinking was its backbone. On those sunny afternoons in the country, I realized that some part of my life's work still waited for me.

Near the end of my stay upstate, Bob and I decided to give a party at the house, so all our friends could have at least one day in the country. Bob had manned the barbecue grill after setting up chairs. I, in turn, did what I do best—organized, ordered things, and talked.

The Thomas nomination, set to be voted on in a matter of weeks, was still a hot topic of conversation; our friends, both black and white, had their reservations about him. So under the hot sun of summer, we drank beer and inhaled smoke from the grill and debated Thomas's laissez-faire legal tendencies and, by extension, his Darwinian politics. Mostly, however, we talked about race, and about cynicism and opportunism on the part of many of our fellow Americans. We were too diverse to agree fully, it's true, but we could always find something to say to each other.

It reminded me of another party, one recounted in a book I'd read that summer, Shelby Steele's *The Content of Our Character.* Steele made readers privy to a small piece of his social life in an attempt to explain what makes race such a volatile issue in America. At the party he writes about, the only other black person at this small gathering has had the bad taste to refer to the issue of race: "Out of nowhere, the engineer announces, with a coloring of accusation in his voice, that it bothers him to send his daughter to a school where she is one of only three black children. 'I didn't realize my ambition to get ahead would pull me into a world where my daughter would lose touch with her blackness,' he says." Steele writes that "this subject, race, sinks us into one of those shaming silences where eye contact terrorizes. . . . Two women stare into the black sky as if to locate the Big Dipper and point it out to us." He ends the story with these words: "An autopsy of this party might read: death induced by an abrupt and lethal injection of the American race issue."

Only in California, I thought, could a serious discussion ruin a garden party. But the story was enlightening for me, in ways I suspect Steele did not intend. He attributes the difficult silence to a larger problem of guilt or innocence. He seeks to reduce the issue to one of forgiveness between blacks and whites, and spends a great deal of time in his book conflating forgiveness and memory. Forgetting, he seems to suggest, is the only path toward forgiveness. I couldn't have disagreed more. Consciousness is the only path to forgiveness and reconciliation.

I looked around at the dozen or so people camped out under the trees around the house, chasing children, shooing flies from the potato salad, eating in shifts. We were black and white and Hispanic people, Jews and Catholics and Unitarian Universalists and Presbyterians, women and children and men, married and single and committed, straight and gay and lesbian. Some primal part of us would never, ever, forget our histories. How could we, when they had shaped and defined us in a thousand ways, for good and for ill? But we needed our memories intact in order for our being there to have its fullest meaning.

It was just a party, of course, but it was more than that. It was tangible proof that a new and conscious community was possible—a community built not on amnesia and evasion, but on truth and courage and hope. It was a world I had glimpsed before—in high school, in college, during the course of my working life. We were eating chicken, drinking beer, building our part of the beloved community that was Dr. King's true legacy. I didn't have to forgo my life, my history, my experience to do that: these were part of the tools of the new creation.

It was hard in such a moment not to remember my father, a man filled with a rage he had every right to feel, but which destroyed him just the same. It was Daddy who had warned me, many years earlier, how impossible it would be to have this life. It was just another fear to add to all the others he'd created for me. For all his formidable courage, Daddy had found being black a hateful, shameful, fearful thing. It had come to represent every closed door and missed opportunity in his life. He feared his blackness the way I feared his ceaseless nighttime rages. It was why, I suspect, he was always telling me to stay away from white people and from "nigger shit."

But I had decided long ago that I would ignore Daddy when it came to this; he was wrong about this dream of mine. I would stay away from no one except those people whose lives were ruled by fear, especially the fear of memory. It was important for me to think and to remember, to envision the world to come, to create that new world wherever I could, to live in it every chance I got. I owed it to myself, I owed it to the children I would have. And I owed it to the man whose bitter life taught me both to appreciate my freedom and to insist upon it.

Epilogue

As I enter the cheerful low-rise building, I can hear the squeals of preschool children at work—painting, computing, pretending. This school is also a laboratory for the training of early-childhood educators, so the room is equipped with a two-way mirror for observation of a child's behavior. I love the big window because it gives me a glimpse of the preschool world and, for me, its most important citizen.

He is tall for a three-year-old, more wiry than thin, and as enthusiastic as he is strong. He is hurling himself around the room right now, racing toward the hat rack for an astronaut helmet, emitting an exuberant zooming noise as he runs. His eyes are sparkling; he is delighted with the idea of going to the moon with his best friend of the moment, a red-haired boy named Jacob. It feels mean to break up this imaginative moment, but I think he'll forgive me.

As I enter, his back is to me, but one of the teachers alerts him. "Allen, guess who's here?" His head swivels with enough energy, it seems, to give him whiplash, and he lets out a delighted shout and races away from Jacob and the coveted helmet.

"Mommy!" he yells, running toward me and my very pregnant belly. I catch him just in time to swing him in the air (at considerable risk to my lower back) and kiss him on his stomach.

"How's my boy?"

"Fine," he says, finally at rest, perched on my left hip and surveying the classroom. I know that look. He is deciding whether he wants to play more, or go home. He slides down my leg and heads toward his cubby for his coat. Today, he wants home. I turn my attention to Allison, one of the two teachers in his classroom.

"How was his day?" I ask.

"Fine. Ate all his lunch, took a good nap."

"Mommy! I paint a picture to you," he says, emerging from the alcove with a lunch box and a recycled piece of paper covered with scribbles and destined to be taped to my refrigerator. As he hands it to me, he eyes my stomach again.

"Is my brother finished yet?"

"No, not yet," I tell him. "But you can say hi while you're waiting."

He places his hand on my stomach with a giggle. "Hi, brother! Come out!" The formalities over, he takes off toward the door, then turns to look at me.

"Come on, Mommy. I want to go!"

I waddle behind him, a prisoner of love, amusement, and exhaustion.

In a few hours, he is asleep for the night, after wrestling with his father in the Finger Debate (a private joke too lengthy to explain) and splashing in the tub, after dinner and a few more cookies than we should have given him, after a story and five renditions of what he calls "the cloud song."

The song he means is "Look for the Silver Lining," a foolishly hopeful popular song that is Jerome Kern's version of an old spiritual's ageless wisdom, and my mother's mantra: "Trouble don't last always." I listened to a lot of Jerome Kern while I was pregnant and learned the song's words while Allen was in utero. It is a song filled with images of sunshine; I learned it as a talisman to protect him against my fears of his childhood—and of my own. I wanted to program him in some way, long before we could speak and understand each other, that would safeguard him against despair. I would have liked something a little more complex, a little more nuanced. But I decided I had the rest of my life to teach him the fine points of life's twists and turns. Above all, I wanted him to believe with all his heart that fundamentally life is good, in spite of everything we know to the contrary. And I didn't want it to take him nearly forty years to figure it out, which is what it took me.

But there have been so many days, lately, when I have felt like a hypocrite, when I have wondered whether I am lying to my son in ways that will do him permanent damage. There is nothing like the presence of a child to make you examine the state of the world; nothing like the expectation of another child to make you reassess everything in your life. In the short term, of course, life for Allen and his little brother, Daniel, will be as good, as safe, as happy as his middle-class, college-educated, suburban buppie parents can make it.

After a career move to Detroit—ended abruptly by a newspaper strike—we moved back east to Montclair, New Jersey. Otherwise known as the Upper West Side of suburbia, it was the only suburb Bob and I could have tolerated. Montclair is more like a small town than a bucolic enclave. One third of its residents are African-American; its schools are integrated, its politics largely progressive. The place is filled with writers and journalists (many of whom are friends of ours), overrun with children, and serious about education, recycling, the political process in general, and local politics in particular. It is the kind of town I would have loved to grow up in, and so I am doing the next best thing—letting my kids grow up here.

But it has been a hard year for political principles, even in

Montclair. Nothing was harder, in fact, than observing helplessly while Congress and the President of the United States obliterated the country's obligation to its poorest citizens. It didn't seem to matter how many calls to the White House I made; how many faxes to Health and Human Services, how many appeals to my representatives. The debate about welfare—about the lives and futures of poor women and children—had been placed in the hands of people who were neither poor nor, with few exceptions, women. The momentum was on the side of punishment and blame, disrespect and contempt, racism and a hatred of women, and, above all, a profound unease with dependency, even the dependency that is in the very nature of childhood and motherhood.

The myth of rugged individualism and self-sufficiency ran wild in the 1996 election season. As I listened to speeches by white and black men in suits about empowering the poor, I thought back to my own life, and to my own childhood. How would these men have empowered me at age five, or at ten, thirteen, or seventeen? What would they have done to help me, to shield me from a world I was not prepared to live in? How would they have prepared me for the world I have since come to inhabit?

Had it been in place thirty years earlier, the new welfare bill would have taken my mother out of our home each day. Mama would have been required to attend a training program, in the hope that two years of training to work in food services or day care would serve as an adequate educational supplement to the third-grade education she had gotten a generation earlier. The four of us children, on the other hand, would have been left to fend for ourselves after school, in one of the worst neighborhoods in the United States. There would have been no one to be with us after school, no one to protect me from the viciousness of my classmates, no one to intervene between me and my father's endless rages. And my mother's absence from home would have fueled my father's persistent jealousy. A man who could not tolerate his wife's grocery shopping would have been hard-pressed to accept her going to school eight hours a day with strangers. No, this plan for self-sufficiency would have meant the disintegration of my already fragile family life.

It is no accident that the movement (however involuntary) of poor women out of the home and into the workforce mimics precisely what has occurred voluntarily or reluctantly in homes all over the United States. Women in America have found they must work so their families can survive—even women who don't want to. How convenient for less progressive forces in our midst to tap into the unspoken rage of working-class women, struggling in low-wage jobs, missing their own children left home alone. Who better to blame for their predicament than the only women in more dire circumstances than themselves? Add to this potent mixture the poison pill of race—complete with images of big black women churning out babies while on the dole—and you have all the ingredients for the betrayal of women and children in America.

The welfare bill and its passage was most assuredly a betrayal of our interests as women in general. It was most particularly a betrayal of those of us who are mothers. In its own way, it was equivalent to the passage, beginning in 1976, of the Hyde amendments, which banned federal abortion funding for poor women. Many women who were not poor were silent during the fight against Hyde, since, after all, the restrictions didn't have anything to do with them. If this position conflicted with their other feelings—that the poor should stop having all those babies anyway—they kept that to themselves. But these same women were outraged when they discovered that the forces out to ban abortions for the poor were working their way up the economic ladder, headed toward them. Ever since Hyde, it has been a piecemeal battle to protect the right of women to choose when and how to bear children. The forces at work to control and regulate the behavior of women have always begun their work with the poor, and the welfare reform bill, otherwise known as the Personal Responsibility and Work Opportunity Reconciliation Act of 1996, is no exception.

It is clear by now what makes this bill so odious. For the first time in more than sixty years, we have removed the federal guarantee of assistance to poor women and children. States are charged to care for the poor, but except for New York, whose constitution mandates such care, no state has the legal obligation to do so. By July 1997, each state submitted to the government its own welfare program, to be funded by block grants from the federal government. Formerly, states had to match federal money with a portion of their own funds; that requirement is eliminated. The devolution of responsibility to the states means fifty widely different assistance programs for poor women and children, and what some critics have called "the race to the bottom" has already begun. The governor of Mississippi, for example, has already said that the only assistance he plans to provide for poor women is an alarm clock, presumably to wake them up in time for the workfare jobs that have been agonizingly slow to materialize.

There are other insidious provisions of the new bill. The amount of federal money is limited by law to $16.4 billion for all fifty states each year for the next six years. This sounds like lots of money, until the need for job creation and training is factored in, along with inflation. When these areas are considered, states will be receiving less money as time passes, not more, to provide benefits, create jobs, and train poor women for work. There is a five-year lifetime cap on welfare benefits: once you've received five years of benefits, you're forever ineligible for further help; states are entitled to an exception of 20 percent of their caseloads.

The consequences that organizations such as the Urban Institute have calculated are nothing short of disastrous. Assuming the economy stays out of recession, assuming that 67 percent of long-term welfare recipients are able to find work, assuming that states don't siphon off their own contributions to the support of the poor, 2.6 million people will join the ranks of the American poor as a direct result of this bill. Of this number, 1.2 million will be children.

The welfare bill was not so much about welfare as it was about work, about access to work, and about access to the larger world—more specifically, about who would have that access and who would not. A woman who has only two years to train for a job as a day-care worker will rarely gain the education and skill it takes to start her own day-care center. A woman preoccupied with a five-year lifetime cap on welfare benefits will have little support to continue her education so that she may become self-sufficient, not at subsistence level, but at a level that would allow her to improve her life and the life of her family.

Those improvements take a lot longer than two years, or five years. Sometimes, as in the case of my mother, they are a generation away. In spite of all the lies generated by opponents of welfare concerning the culture of dependency it creates, I am living proof of the 78 percent of African-American women who are raised on welfare but never return to the system. (For whites, the figure is only slightly lower—76 percent.) The remaining women are usually teenagers who become pregnant before finishing high school, thus stunting their chances for education and workplace advancement.

Had the opponents of welfare targeted their reforms to help women who were at greatest risk in the system—pregnant teenagers—these draconian measures might have been less difficult to accept. But the so-called reformers ignored the most pertinent information about these young women and their situation. To have noted their circumstances would have demanded a change in policy and a focus away from the moralistic control of women that has characterized the debate for some time.

Roughly 60 percent of these teenage expectant mothers are pregnant, not by teenage boys, but by grown men, a fact that at the very least should encourage the strengthening of statutory rape laws and their enforcement across the United States. Moreover, with regard to girls pregnant by adult men, as many as half of those sexual relationships were coercive in nature—involving rape, sometimes incest. Was there more than a token voice of protest or outrage raised on behalf of those women in any debate by the House or the Senate? There was not.

Instead, there was vigorous debate on the similarity between welfare mothers and wolves. Congressman E. Clay Shaw of Florida regaled the House of Representatives with his comparisons between welfare mothers and alligators. There were countless references to welfare mothers as leeches, as an offense to the working people of the United States, as a symptom of the failed and libertine policies of the Great Society. So I waited for an outcry from people other than myself. I particularly waited for the President of the United States, who has called for civility in political life from one end of America to another, to challenge the members of both parties. I waited for him to remind people that poor women and children were human beings, not animals. I waited in vain. Instead, I was treated to the spectacle of William Jefferson Clinton throwing a party on the White House lawn as he signed a welfare reform bill that, had it existed thirty years ago, would have guaranteed my family's dissolution. By the time I was ten years old, my mother's eligibility for welfare—as well as her children's—would have been at an end. She would have had to withdraw from us to focus on her race against time; she would have had to choose between saving us physically by earning money through workfare, and saving us psychologically, by being present and attentive in the midst of our difficult lives.

These are the issues that make me wonder what right I have to tell my son what a wonderful world it is. How do I tell him that the wonder of this world depends in part on how free you are to notice it? How do I explain that thousands of little boys and girls whose lives were only marginal are now in genuine jeopardy? How do I tell him about people who don't mind allowing children to live in fear and in squalor if it means a chance to punish the parents of those children? How do I explain that some little kids never have a chance to feel delighted, or happy, or safe?

I was not a wolf, or an alligator, or a mistake, or an affront. Neither were my brothers and sister, or my mother. No, not even my father was any of those things. What all of us were was vulnerable; what we needed most was a chance. For the most part, we children got that chance. We are all productive working people now, with children of our own. Two of us are writers; one of us works in customer service at a worldwide delivery service; one of us drives trucks. However divergent our ultimate careers, we would not have become such people without the help of a welfare system that, however imperfect, had at its core a promise that needy people would not go without the basics in the richest country in the world.

That promise was rooted in other promises that America has made, and that we have always been at war with ourselves about keeping. For more than two hundred years, we have struggled with what it means when we speak of inalienable rights, or the general welfare, or the blessings of liberty. We have never agreed on whom we mean, or what those phrases mean, or how exactly we can make those promises real. There have always been those who claimed that the promises, such as they are, go too far, extend a "radical egalitarianism" to the rabble, instead of judiciously assigning power and authority to the worthy. That is what is most frightening about the passage of the Personal Responsibility Act and its insidious doublespeak. The welfare bill substitutes social Darwinism for democratic and religious values that are at the core of our nation's identity—values of compassion, concern, and the protection of the vulnerable. It is legislation that invites us to abandon the collective responsibility we all have for one another, and instead places a crushing burden on those least able to sustain it. It is a burden that ultimately will shift to us again, only with more dire consequences than we now see. The children stunted by this great experiment will share the world with my children—our children. The fragile hope I knew as a child, the possibility of change taken for granted by my children—it may not make its way to these children. When I think of the moment when these worlds collide, my heart breaks.

Allen is a fearless child. He will run anywhere, climb anything, explore whatever is out there. I am most touched, however, by his love for the dark. Even as a toddler, he loved to walk to the window and point outside, calling out "Dark!" in a tone of glee. He is still willing to go to the window at night, inspect what he sees, then turn to us and announce, "It's very dark out there." It is a dark that he refuses to interrupt with night-lights or other paraphernalia. To Allen, the moon and the stars are his friends; the dark is a safe place in which to rest.

I know it cannot last; I know he will eventually fall prey to the developmental moment in early childhood when it occurs to him that there are things in life to be afraid of, including the dark. But I love the idea that I have given life to a child who laughs in the face of what I once feared so desperately. No writer, no parent, can resist the metaphor inherent in his faithful trust of me, of his father, his assurance that night is followed by morning.

In the end, it is his pure and childlike trust that makes it impossible to believe that the world is permanently flawed, that our country and its people are disintegrating before our eyes in a morass of hatred and greed. It's not that I never think such things. It isn't even that I don't think them often. Turning on the news, opening a newspaper, is another opportunity to gather testimony about our failures as a nation and as a people. But it is not all we are. For all the sweeping xenophobia, the reinvigorated racism, the deepening scorn for women and women's work—including and especially mothering—I see and know and live amid pockets of resistance.

Allen is not afraid of the dark, and I am learning not to be. I am learning to love being a black woman in a world that often fears and resents my presence, and using that identity as a passport to my citizenship in the world. I am learning to accept those shadowed moments in which my nation cyclically rests; we are most assuredly in one now. I am learning to continue in the face of failure, as caring women and men have done before me for generations. Like Allen, I can announce, "It's very dark out there." For the sake of my precious sons, and for the precious children not my own, I can stay unafraid of the dark, and work my way toward morning.

Acknowledgments

To the God of many names and one Spirit, for everything.

To my father, who made writing necessary, and to my mother, who made it possible.

To my brothers and sister, who washed a lot of dishes during my apprenticeship.

To Geri Thoma, agent and friend, who had faith in me long before I did.

To my editor, Kate Medina, for her insight, good humor, and Job-like patience.

To the staff of the Miller Institute, especially Dr. Emil Pascarelli and physical therapist James Wang, for healing my hands.

To Edward A. Schwartz, whose clarity, discernment, and support made him my "good luck in a dirty time."

To Angela, Yanick, Lena, Diane, Shawn, Felicia, Renee, and other members of the Style Posse, both official and unofficial: you all know why I put you here!

To Eileen Dickenson, for her kindness, and for the house of a writer's dream.

To the women of Epoch Child Care in Detroit, especially Nancy, Linda, and Sue; to the women and men of Montclair State University Childcare Center, especially Susan, Pat, Dana, Allison, and Janey; and to Judy, LaVaughn, Camille, and Simone—your work and love for my sons made my work easier.

To the Monday Night Group.

To the memories of Allan B. Williams, Wyatt Paul Davis, and Carl Brown; how I miss you. . . .

To Richard E. Nicholls, whose friendship and support has been tireless; I owe you a case of fax paper!

To Mary Sams, with love and thanks for the tools.

To my beloved husband, Bob McNatt, with gratitude for his constant love, our beautiful babies, and endless cups of tea.

ABOUT THE AUTHOR

ROSEMARY L. BRAY, a former editor of *The New York Times Book Review,* is a writer whose work has appeared in a variety of magazines and newspapers including *The New York Times, Ms., Glamour, Essence,* and *The Village Voice.* A weekly commentator on MSNBC, the cable news channel, she is also the author of two children's books, *Martin Luther King* and the forthcoming *Freedom: The Story of Nelson Mandela.* She lives with her husband, Robert McNatt, and their two sons in New Jersey.

ABOUT THE TYPE

This book was set in Galliard, a typeface designed by Matthew Carter for the Merganthaler Linotype Company in 1978. Galliard is based on the sixteenth-century typefaces of Robert Granjon.